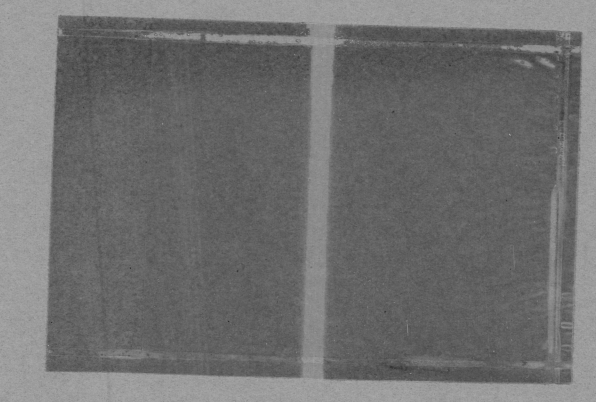

PLATE 1. WILD TURKEY IN PINE WOODS
(Greatly reduced)

A Guide to the Winter Birds of the North Carolina Sandhills

By

MILTON P. SKINNER

with chapters by

DR. JOHN WARREN ACHORN

Illustrated in color by EDMUND J. SAWYER

ALBANY, N. Y.
1928

THE SCIENCE PRESS PRINTING COMPANY
LANCASTER, PA.

DEDICATION

To the memory of one who loved wild
Nature deeply—the grace and songs of birds,
the beauty of his native river, pinewoods,
and the sea; whose restless soul yearned ever
to bring these happily into the lives of all;
kindest of critics, who strove to draw us
unaware up to our higher selves; trusting,
faithful, fearless, strong; who loved his
neighbor as himself; who gave to each in
need his very heart, with joy, and counted
not the cost,—our gentle Woodser

JOHN WARREN ACHORN

this book, the echo of his happy dream, is
affectionately dedicated by his friends.

FOREWORD

This book is the outcome of a keen interest in birds long cherished by Doctor John Warren Achorn, a retired Boston physician, who for many years had spent his winters in the Sandhills of North Carolina, and who was from the first identified with the popularity of that region as a winter health and recreation center.

The Doctor was a man of unique personality, great enthusiasms, and active mind. Through his sympathetic interest in the people around him he found his greatest pleasure in working with them for the common good. His solicitude for birds and for people's happiness in the appreciation of outdoor nature, led him to secure the establishment of the Sandhills Bird Reservation at Pine Bluff, his winter home; and also to organize a local club for the study of birds. In connection with his active leadership of this club he invented, most appropriately in this wonderful winter golf region, the game of "bird golf." He had long been impressed with the lack of a field guide-book for winter birds of the region, as indicated by his article reprinted in this volume. The present book is an attempt to fulfill his earnest desire to meet the needs of bird watchers in the Sandhills, especially the thousands of winter visitors, an increasing number of whom delight in following the trails,—whether in the open fields, or the oak and pine woods, or by canoe on the historic Lumbee River.

Doctor Achorn discussed his hopes for a winter bird book, in May, 1925, with Professor Alvin G. Whitney, who thereupon presented the idea to Doctor Charles C. Adams, then Director of the Roosevelt Wild Life Experiment Station of the State College of Forestry at Syracuse, New York. A plan was soon agreed upon for a special study of the birds of the Sandhills, to be the first step in a comprehensive investigation of the wild life resources of that region, and field work was commenced the following winter. Upon the death of Doctor Achorn the next summer, this larger plan had to be abandoned; and later, with the departure of Doctor Adams and Professor Whitney from the Roosevelt Wild Life Station for other fields of activity, a release of the project was secured by them from the College of Forestry, and the completion of the work has

v

subsequently rested in the hands of the present Memorial Committee. Under its supervision the complete study has been made, and the book prepared, in accordance with the wishes of Doctor Achorn.

The original plans were matured in December, 1925, and Mr. Milton P. Skinner, a leading field ornithologist, was selected to make the survey and write the Guide. Mr. Edmund J. Sawyer, ornithologist and talented bird artist, at the time Park Naturalist of Yellowstone National Park, was chosen to make the necessary life studies in the field and prepare the colored plates. The field work was conducted through two winters, 1925–6 and 1926–7.

While a "guide" to the birds of the region could have been compiled from existing books and museum specimens, such a book would have been of little interest and value compared with one based on fresh and painstaking observations carried through two seasons, during which local habits and details of winter plumage could be carefully studied. The Committee feels that this original field study has been amply justified in the present volume, on which no effort has been spared to make it a useful and worthy Memorial; and trusts that it will stimulate intelligent and enthusiastic appreciation of our winter birds. The sad feature of the whole undertaking has been the loss of Doctor Achorn, August 5, 1926, and of his close friend and generous donor to the project, Mr. Alexander P. Holbrook, who died in December, 1925, during the inception of the plans; but it is our hope that this modest volume will continue for many years to keep alive the fine public spirit of these leaders.

We are grateful to Mr. H. H. Brimley, Curator of the State Museum, Raleigh, North Carolina, for the loan of bird skins needed by the artist and also to Mr. E. J. Stein of the New York State Museum, Albany, for assistance on the illustrations.

There remains the pleasant duty of expressing, on the part of the Committee, their sincere gratitude to the many friends and donors for their contributions of funds and kindly cooperation, and for their efforts in various ways in bringing to a satisfactory conclusion this memorial tribute to Doctor John Warren Achorn.

Mrs. John Warren Achorn

Charles C. Adams   Alvin G. Whitney

Andrew I. Creamer

Millard H. Turner

Memorial Committee

Pine Bluff, North Carolina,
November 1, 1928

CONTENTS

vii

ILLUSTRATIONS

COLORED PLATES

FROM DRAWINGS BY EDMUND J. SAWYER

ix

Illustrations

x

xi

PREFACE

There are many books about birds in summer, but only a few scattered articles describing winter birds, and no book relating directly to the Sandhills. Yet winter is the season when most bird-lovers visit the Sandhills region, so they need a winter handbook descriptive of the colors and haunts and habits of the birds at that season. The late Dr. John Warren Achorn of Pine Bluff early recognized the need, and this little book is the direct result of his early observations afield, and of his foresight, energy, and resourcefulness. In deference to Dr. Achorn's love of *living* birds, these studies were gladly made, and this book written, without the collecting of a single "specimen." Where it was necessary to make measurements, and verify plumage characters, this was done by the use of museum specimens already collected and preserved for scientific studies.

That part of the book included under "Field Identifications" and "Descriptions" of birds is new, and has all been gathered in the field during two winter seasons, especially for this guide. All of the statements made throughout the book (unless the text states otherwise) refer to *winter* birds in the Sandhills, and therefore both the color descriptions and the "habits" sections often differ markedly from corresponding material referring to other seasons and other regions. Although this study was restricted to a comparatively small area, it is believed that this book will be found useful throughout that part of North Carolina, South Carolina and Georgia lying between the piedmont and the lowland strip along the seacoast.

The usual "keys" have been omitted, and in their stead there are first given a number of characteristic field identification marks followed by a more detailed description of each species. All other identification material is to be found under the heading of "Habits."

This book has been written primarily for people who are, or who may wish to become, interested in birds, rather than for scientists. For this reason, technical terms have been avoided so far as possible, but extreme care has been taken to make every statement accurate and exact. It is designed for field use rather than for the identification of dead birds and museum specimens.

The bird student may become so interested in the birds of the Sandhills or elsewhere that he, or she, will desire to pursue this study further. I have therefore listed at the end of the general chapters lists of books helpful for the study of birds in spring and summer as well as giving much additional information.

In the delightful work of preparing this little volume for your use, I have had the constant help and encouragement of Dr. Charles C. Adams, now Director of the New York State Museum, and of Prof. Alvin G. Whitney, now of the School of Forestry and Conservation at the University of Michigan. The colored plates that embellish it are the work of Mr. Edmund J. Sawyer, naturalist and artist. To all three of these men my thanks are due.

In carrying out the field work I have been deeply indebted to the late Dr. John Warren Achorn for valuable advice and careful notes on birds, and to Mrs. Achorn for numerous courtesies; to Messrs. A. I. Creamer and M. H. Turner for advice and for accommodations at the Holly Inn, Pinehurst; to Mr. and Mrs. Levi Packard for notes on birds and for the open-handed hospitality of their home in Pine Bluff; to Mr. Arthur T. Wayne of Mt. Pleasant, South Carolina, for revision of my list of birds; to Mr. H. H. Brimley, Curator of the North Carolina State Museum at Raleigh, for valuable suggestions; to Mr. C. J. Pennock for notes on previous work done at Pinehurst[1]; to Dr. H. C. Oberholser of the U. S. Biological Survey for various items of interest; to Mr. Bion H. Butler of Southern Pines for valuable notes on North Carolina farm crops; and to numerous other persons for miscellaneous help and encouragement.

M. P. Skinner

44 Broadhead Ave.,
Jamestown, New York,
February 16, 1928

[1] "Bird Notes from Pinehurst, North Carolina." (*Wilson Bulletin*, Vol. 23, pp. 34-42, 1911.)

THE WINTER BIRDS OF THE SANDHILLS OF NORTH CAROLINA

By Milton P. Skinner

THE STUDY OF WINTER BIRDS

Everywhere we turn we find some new interest in birds, some new pleasure in watching them. By their beauty of plumage and the music of their song they appeal to our artistic appreciation; in their traits and reactions they interest us because of their very human likeableness. They take us away from our troubles; they provide us with fresh interests in life; they teach us the wonder of Nature; they help us to renew our health by taking us out into the fields and forests to our very evident advantage. Instead of remaining shut indoors all winter, we should get out and study the birds, winter being a peculiarly good time for several reasons. True, it is colder, but on the other hand there are no flies and mosquitoes as in summer. Of course every season is good for bird study because we learn different things about them at different seasons. For instance: the Robins that are friendly dooryard birds in summer, are generally wild and suspicious in their winter homes, and live in large flocks in the depths of inaccessible swamps. But winter has other advantages peculiarly its own. I can remember when I thought it a waste of time to go into the fields and forests in wintertime, but I have changed my views radically since then, for some of my most delightful hours with birds have been in winter. It is a true starting place in point of time, for all bird activities, other than those connected with food and protection, are dormant, and bird-life is reduced to its simplest terms. It is best to study bird-life first when it is simplest, and to progress from the simplest to the more complex life later in the year. Winter is the resting period before the cycle of northward migration, mating, nesting, care of the young, molting and the return migration begins.

Of course I know it is the time of year when colds and influenza are prevalent, but these troubles are born in overheated and ill-ventilated rooms where we follow a more or less sedentary life. So if the birds induce us to go out and fill our lungs with good fresh air, they are doing us an inestimable service. And while they are

1

doing this they furnish us with many a charming scene to arouse our interest and add to our pleasure. Let us, then, cease to imitate the hibernating woodchuck, and visit the fields and woods in winter to see what Nature has in store for us.

Dr. Chapman has well said that "Birds occupy a fourfold relation to man: an economic, esthetic, what may be termed a mythological or symbolic, and a scientific relation."[1] In some ways, wintertime gives us a better idea of the economic value of birds, for we see more of their activities then; and, because we note day by day the lessening quantity of seeds, we realize better how many are destroyed. It has truly been said that man could cultivate no crops without the assistance of the birds in destroying the seeds of the vast numbers of weeds that spring up everywhere. The destruction of weed seeds by birds is important throughout the year, but in winter the proportion of seeds eaten is greatly increased. Perhaps winter destruction of insects and insect eggs is not so great, but it is just as important as it is in summer, because the hardy insects eaten in winter would give birth so much earlier to prolific descendants. Eating, as they do, tons of weed seeds and hardy insects, the winter birds of North Carolina are valuable protectors of the gardens and fields even before those gardens and fields are planted. And this great economic help is brought home to us still more forcibly when we are not distracted by the multitudinous sights and sounds and perfumes of summer.

We react in another way to the steady food-search of winter, for it is then that we realize how much we can help the birds by furnishing additional food. Our generosity in this respect brings its own reward, for the birds are quick to respond by showing themselves familiarly about our gardens and homes. Although they may first be drawn to human habitations by artificial feeding, they remain to devour many seeds and insects that might have escaped but for them. This drawing of the birds closer to man is a marked feature of winter and one in which we can all take delight. It is more appreciated because the silence and solitude of winter days make the companionship of birds all the more welcome to us. And, having enjoyed this companionship about our homes, we are induced to take long walks to other bird haunts afield. Here we find the

[1] Chapman, Frank M. Handbook of Birds of Eastern North America. D. Appleton & Co., New York and London. 1914. P. 1.

same avian welcome more evident in winter than at other times; and we feel exalted by the confidence shown by our feathered friends.

This friendly attitude of birds is usually so much more evident that we begin to wonder if these can be the same birds we see in summer. Before long we notice that the number and variety change with changing weather conditions, and we wonder why. Then we become conscious that the whole bird population changes, especially at the beginning and the end of winter. In many ways winter in the Sandhills has its advantages for a study of the problems of migration. Here there are marked changes in the bird population to differentiate one season from another and to fairly force the fact upon us that the birds of winter are not those of summer. It is evident that the local abundance of birds at various times throughout the winter is due to weather conditions to some extent and still more to the relative abundance of food. When we see these local movements in winter (and they are not so easily observed in summer) we are impressed with the fact that birds are mobile creatures and we wonder if these temporary movements are not incipient migrations. Because we actually see these movements and recognize the reasons for them, we are better able to comprehend the larger migration movements when they come later.

In the Sandhills we see one set of birds leaving in November and another set arriving; and because this second lot is manifestly made up of birds that like colder days we appreciate better that they have probably come down from the north. Then, when March arrives, we see the hardy birds leaving and the set that left in November returning from the south. Particularly interesting in this connection are the Robins. The wild, swamp-loving Robins that winter in the Sandhills disappear in late February, but seem to be replaced by Robins that are tamer and that come familiarly about our homes and dooryards. Because it is unlikely that a species of bird would change its ways so completely in any one region, we conclude that the wild Robins have gone and the tame dooryard Robins have come back for the summer to home areas familiar to them.

Migration is also impressed upon Sandhills observers by the fact that winter is the only time when certain strange birds may appear. And because they come during the coldest weather and during the infrequent snowstorms, it is easy to suppose that they have been driven down from the north by the inclement weather.

Because the Sandhills are south of the usual winter range of a large number of species, these temporary movements are more marked. It is in winter that we can observe such weather movements to the best advantage because in spring the birds are all pressing north and not apt to oscillate with the weather; in summer they are bound to the vicinity of their nests by home ties; in autumn the general movement is directed southward, and while a warm spell may halt the movement temporarily it is not apt to cause a retrogression.

In other ways, weather is an all-important factor in the winter study of birds. Daylight being the normal feeding time for most birds, the short days of winter shorten the feeding hours and concentrate them in the middle of the day. That winter food is scarcer and harder to get causes the birds to search for it continuously. And both conditions combined cause winter birds to feed all day long, and especially in the middle of the day, a much more convenient time for most of us to study them than the early morning and late afternoon hours of summer.

This constant feeding of winter birds, and their tendency to congregate where food is abundant, means that in winter we usually find more birds of a kind than we do in summer; a condition that is further heightened by the gathering of birds into flocks. We may therefore compare the ways and habits of one individual with another and keep ourselves from falling into false generalizations, as we might if we saw only a few members of a species. Seeing a larger number of individuals makes us familiar with a species and we can assemble a larger fund of facts regarding that species and readily note variations from the usual. Our ability to see more birds in winter is very much increased by the absence of leaves from so many of the bushes and trees. Indeed, in winter we can feel assured of seeing most of the birds, for it is strange how small a leaf can effectually hide quite a large bird. And the ground-loving birds are even more readily seen when they do not have the high grass and heavy herbage of summer to literally swallow them. I would even venture to say that in winter we see two out of every three birds present, whereas in summer we scarcely see one out of three.

This ready visibility in winter goes far toward making up for the fewer species then about, for a lesser number of species is also characteristic of wintertime. But a smaller number of species is really an advantage, for it enables us to identify each one with certainty before others appear and confuse us by the multiplicity of our riches. Because winter has only a few species it is a peculiarly advantageous time to begin the study of birds before we are overwhelmed by the army of migrants that come with spring. Should we begin our bird study when species are numerous, we either slight the work of identification by hurrying on to the next species to be seen, or we become confused and give up the seemingly hopeless and endless task. Now of course it is very gratifying to us all to see a large number of birds of many different kinds, but such a gathering is not the best when we want to *know* the birds. Many of the daily studies that went to make up this book were made with only one or two birds in sight at a time. But I must confess this proved disadvantageous when, just as I was about to make an interesting discovery, some one came along and scared my subject. But here again winter proved better than summer, for many people are not so apt to be wandering about as during the warmer season.

For additional information on this subject see:

CHAPMAN, FRANK M. *Our Winter Birds.* D. Appleton & Co., New York. 1919. Pp. 1–180. Price, $2.00.

JOB, HERBERT K. *How to Study Birds.* The Macmillan Co., New York. 1910. Pp. 1–272. Price, $1.50.

MATHEWS, F. SCHUYLER. *The Book of Birds.* G. P. Putnam's Sons, New York and London. 1925. Pp. 1–323. Price, $3.00.

THE SANDHILLS AND THEIR BIRDS

The Sandhills of North Carolina form a peculiar part of the south central section of the state, comprising most of Moore and Richmond Counties and the adjoining parts of Lee, Harnett, Hoke, Scotland and Montgomery Counties. They are situated between the coastal plain and the piedmont sections. While resembling the piedmont in some respects, the Sandhills seem more closely allied to the coastal plain. As the name indicates, the region is hilly, but it varies from nearly level to gently undulating and hilly. The soil is composed of sand and sandy loam and is warm and underlaid at the depth of a few feet with clay. Originally all the uplands were covered by open forests of long-leaf pine (*Pinus palustris*) (Figs. 1, 4, 15), and in places with loblolly-pine (*Pinus tæda*); but now these forests have all been cut off. Since their removal, shrub oaks (*Quercus catesbæi* and *Q. marylandica*) (Figs. 2, 5, 16) have occupied a great deal of the upland, but are everywhere mixed with second growth long-leaf and loblolly pines. Along the streams and bottoms there is a dense growth of deciduous trees of which the most predominant are the various gums (Figs. 3, 11, 23), mixed with swamp magnolias, hollies, and luxuriant underbrush and vines.

Although these conditions seem simple they all combine to make bird study particularly pleasant. The rolling character of the country makes drainage quick and sure. The sandy soil helps this rapid drainage so much that the surface is dry and good for walking within a very short time after even quite a severe storm. Even along the streams and the edges of artificial ponds and marshes the ground is dry and not at all wet or boggy. This means that it is a pleasure to be out walking almost every day in winter. In addition, such a dry rolling area covered by pine forests is a notably healthful one for human beings.

The forests are open and one can easily walk anywhere through them and readily see the birds (Figs. 5, 16). Only at the crossings of the streams do we have any difficulties. These streams are all small (except the Lumbee and Little Rivers) and are locally called "branches." They are overgrown by dense thickets, made all the more impenetrable by blackberry thorns and cat-briars that can not

Figure 1. Long-leaf pine saplings, Sandhills region, near Jackson Springs, Feb. 2, 1926.

Figure 2. Shrub-oak and pine-sapling forest, west of Pinehurst, Feb. 2, 1926.

be forced aside with impunity (Fig. 11). Almost always a path or a route through can be found within a short distance. Aside from this slight inconvenience, these thickets are really a help, for they afford to the birds valuable food and protection from storms and pursuing enemies. It is along such thickets that most of the birds of the Sandhills are found (Figs. 13, 14, 22). By way of contrast the dry upland forests are usually devoid of all but a very few species of birds that prefer such a habitat.

Most of the vegetation along the streams has great food possibilities for the birds and is directly dependent on moisture and temperature. The rainfall is light and evenly distributed throughout the winter. Normally the weather is cold enough for a light frost each night, but the bright sun soon warms up the air to a point delightful for walking and not too cold to permit of the long waiting that bird study often entails. The elevation of this region, being only about six hundred to eight hundred feet above sea-level, is not great enough to reduce the temperature below that of the surrounding country. On the other hand, possibly because of well-drained sandy soil and a high percentage of slopes facing south and southwest, this area is notably warmer than the rest of the state. In fact, its vegetation, birds and mammals are all more closely related to South Carolina than they are to the rest of North Carolina. Light snows occur at long intervals, perhaps an average of one or two each winter. But this snowfall quickly melts and probably does not injure bird-life at all. The only really dangerous weather conditions, with regard to birds, are the sleet storms that occur at long intervals, and cover all food supplies with an icy coating that is too hard for the weaker bird bills to break through. No doubt this favorable climate, abundance of good food, and rarity of severe storms are what make birds so much more numerous in winter in the Sandhills than they are at the same time in more northern regions. Favorable climate combined with secure retreats from the all too numerous foes are responsible for the Sandhills containing many unusual birds, such as Wild Turkeys, Red-cockaded Woodpeckers, Pileated Woodpeckers and Bachman Sparrows.

Owing to the sandy soil and good drainage, natural ponds and swamps are not common. A great many dams have been built across small streams, resulting in artificial ponds (Figs. 10, 15) sometimes of considerable extent and usually with a swamp or low flooded area at their upper ends. This flooding has often resulted in the killing of a considerable number of trees where holes in the dead limbs and trunks afford valuable roosts and retreats in time of storm. Some of the trees on unflooded areas also have hollows in them, although not to the same extent in live trees as in dead ones.

With the increase of cultivation in the Sandhills, the conditions favorable to birds are changing. For the wild, shy lovers of the forest lands, it is a change for the worse; but for the open field birds, and birds that like human alterations, it is a change for the better. Many birds are actually benefited by the establishment of towns; especially if there be a good deal of shrubbery and berry-bearing bushes planted (Figs. 24 and 26).

WHY BIRD STUDY APPEALS

Although we frequently stress the economic value of birds, it is actually their beauty and their esthetic appeal that attract us most often. For we all love a beautiful and graceful sight, especially if it is a living, moving creature. Here in the Sandhills we are favored often with the sight of a brilliant Cardinal flaming in striking contrast across the deep green of the heavy evergreens, pleasing us both by its harmonious color and its dainty grace in the dark and somber trees. Just as pleasing in a different way is the beautiful blue of the Jay, the yellow flash of the Myrtle Warbler and the quieter reddish brown of the Thrasher. We are also sometimes favored in winter in this southern climate with appealing songs that are the more charming because they seem out of season. Another attraction that often draws bird-lovers in the Sandhills is the graceful and majestic flight of the Turkey Buzzards and Vultures. Soaring as they do, high against the blue sky, weaving in and out in intricate patterns of interlacing circles, without visible motions of the wings, they are the very personification of grace and power in motion. They arouse our wonder and our love of the beautiful and the mysterious, as few other flying birds do. Although these birds are perhaps the most graceful and powerful of the Sandhills birds, others charm us with this same wonderful mastery of the air.

In many ways the gift of song is one of the greatest of the birds' attractions. Others of Nature's children have beauty of form and color, but song is peculiarly an avian charm, although some mammals and even insects have pleasing calls and short songs to delight our ears. True, there is music in water-falls, in the beat of the ocean's surf, and in the sighing of the winds through the trees. But these sounds, musical as they are, do not depend upon the mood of the water or the wind: whereas singing birds express their joy and happiness and impart some of their mood to us. We feel closer to these small musicians voicing so much that is akin to our own feelings. Neither does it require a trained ear to learn bird songs, nor even a knowledge of birds to appreciate their music.

Although the hearing of an attractive bird song has often started a bird student on his, or her, delightful quest of birds, it is more often a dainty nest, a beautiful bird, or even a book with col-

11

ored plates that first arouses interest. Sometimes this interest comes to us all at once and sometimes its first growth is more gradual. Sometimes a single song or a single bird will arouse the desire within us, and sometimes we acquire slowly the inclination to know more about the enticing song we hear every morning, or the flashing bird that we catch a glimpse of, morning after morning. After such interest is aroused we appreciate bird music and color so much more when we have some knowledge of, or acquaintance with, the bird itself. Our enthusiasm increases still more when we find we are discovering things for ourselves. To be sure, most of our early "discoveries" about our commonest birds are well known to others. But soon, almost before we realize it, we are making real discoveries and seeing interesting things that are truly our own. For bird study requires no elaborate preliminary training and equipment. Naturally, a trained observer will see *more* that is interesting, but the latest beginner, the veriest tyro, often observes something entirely new. It is not likely that any unknown American species remain to be discovered, but individuality is everywhere manifested by birds and leads to many interesting sights and experiences.

Fortunately one's pleasure in birds does not depend upon discovering something "new to science." Actually, we take more pleasure in making *our own* little discoveries even if others already know them. It is a pleasure to read about birds, but it is a far greater pleasure to find a bird and learn about it all by ourselves. When we find a bird and study it, it ceases to be a mere figure in a book, or a colored drawing, and becomes ours, a part of our own possessions. This interest in living creatures other than ourselves is good for us. It gives us a new field for our faculties; it takes us out into the clean forests and the sparkling fields; it lures us on with the hope that just around the next corner we may see a bird new to us; it renews our spirits by showing us other creatures blithesome and happy in the new day, joyfully going on, no matter how dark and gloomy yesterday may have been. "The uplifting influence that birds may thus exert upon the lives of men constitutes their greatest value and charm. A growing appreciation of the esthetic and educational value of birds has sent many cultured folk to the woods, fields and shores. People are turning toward nature study, and the observation of birds in the field is one of the most popular manifestations of an increased and abiding interest in animate Nature."[2]

As soon as we learn something about birds we hope for closer acquaintance and would like to bring them about our homes. We want to make them a part of our daily lives, but we realize we do not know enough about them yet, and that we must study them further. And when we do at last succeed in attracting birds to our yards we are charmed by their very confidence in us and in our ability to protect them from their many enemies. Such a group of birds is a continuous source of interest and pleasure; and it is one that is apt to be repeated year after year; for the same birds, or similar ones, will return again and again to renew their acquaintance with us. Here again we see the great simplicity of bird study, for these dooryard birds come to us and we can watch them at our convenience, for only a few minutes at a time on busy days, or a few hours at a stretch when we have more time. When the winter is ended and they leave, we experience a pang at parting as if dear friends had left us. These birds are indeed friends, for they will come back again another year to answer the same call that drew them the first time. They are truly old friends—always the same, yet ever changing in their endless ways and habits. In this respect, birds are more enduring than human friends. Human friends may come and go, but once we have learned to know a certain kind of bird we will always be able to find it and renew our pleasure in knowing it. Our friendship is with the whole group of birds that make up a species, not with individuals; and although individual birds may die, other members of the same species will take their places.

We are so constituted that the mere search, pursuit and discovery of living birds are delights to us. Probably this pleasure is a remnant of the old days when we sought our food in the wilderness, and when the hunt was the most important of our activities. Even now, game birds afford sport and pleasure to many men. But the study of even these same game birds is much more fascinating than shooting them, and affords us much the same kind of thrills. More important still, bird study gives us new viewpoints, and stimulates our bodies and minds. For bird study is a healthful occupation

[2] Forbush, Edward H. The Utility of Birds. Dept. Bulletin No. 9, second edition, revised. Massachusetts Dept. of Agriculture, Boston, Mass. 1922. P. 82.

whose steady activity causes the blood to flow faster through our veins, and replaces old worn-out tissue with fresh new material. When we come back from a bird tramp, we tackle our everyday problems anew and with fresh energy. We have been given a new angle on life and have even added to our culture and education, for we now understand better some of our finest literature. Many exquisite poems that thrilled us before, now mean much more to us because of a better understanding of the frequent allusions to birds.

With such an educational feature as this, it is but natural that bird study should become a valuable school study. Unlike many subjects that children have to be forced to study, bird study has a great natural attraction for them. It satisfies some of the child's taste for, and curiosity about, the world that surrounds it. Most of them are born with a love for Nature, and birds are easy to find and easy to observe. Hence they form an ideal starting point for the study of natural sciences. Even where the boy or girl has no inclination, or opportunity, to dig more deeply into the subject, a little bird study is of great value because it starts a love for the finer and more beautiful things of this world. "A teacher once had in his school a group of boys who sometimes amused themselves by firing stones at birds. This form of sportsmanship had several good points to recommend it, in the eyes of a boy. It requires and develops marksmanship; it is, like any other kind of hunting, exciting; and without actually causing any serious mortality among birds, it gratifies one's natural, inherited instinct to kill prey. As regards the individual boy, the practice could hardly be called immoral. Nevertheless it is contrary to the interests of the community; if not immoral, it is unsocial. Moreover the development of sympathy for lower, weaker, and dependent animals probably strengthens the general principle of sympathy in one's nature. And therefore the teacher wished to cure these boys of the undesirable habit of stoning birds. He did not, however, call them before him for a lecture on the iniquity of throwing stones. Instead he devised a little piece of nature study that he thought might be corrective. There was a **Robin's** nest nearby to which he took the group for a little observation and study, with note books, of the habits and development of birds. The boys watched from day to day for the eggs to hatch, examined closely the curious blind gaping naked young, saw the parents hard at work supplying food for the

Figure 3.   Gum trees and swamps, north of Pinehurst, Feb. 4, 1926.

Figure 4.   A road through the long-leaf pine woods near Southern Pines, Feb. 20, 1926.

infant prodigies, weighed the little birds from day to day on postal scales to discover their astonishing powers of assimilation and growth, noted the curious mode of feathering out, were delighted with the progress of the young in brightness and bird-savoir-faire, thoroughly enjoyed the whole experience and, perhaps needless to say, lost most of their former primitive attitude toward birds. This may probably be called a *moral* result.

"The very interesting business of feeding, watering, and housing birds, especially in times of stress, with the sense that one is helping to keep useful creatures alive, is a species of training in good citizenship; and it certainly also helps to develop sympathy. Evidence of this truth is accumulating. The remark is often made by parents and teachers that the attitude of boys toward birds and animals has greatly improved during the past few years."[3]

Bird-protection taught in the schools is the surest way of building up a body of friends for the birds. Boys and girls should learn the value of birds and should be encouraged in all their efforts to increase and protect them. As it is now, birds have so many natural enemies, in addition to cats and thoughtless boys and men, that they need all the safeguards and help that can be given them. Furthermore, bird study is an important method of training in careful observation; an experience that is valuable in all paths of life.

For additional information on this subject see:

CHAPMAN, FRANK M. *Our Winter Birds.* D. Appleton & Co., New York. 1919. Pp. 1–180. Price, $2.00.

JOB, HERBERT K. *How to Study Birds.* The Macmillan Co., New York. 1910. Pp. 1–272. Price, $1.50.

CHAPMAN, FRANK M. *Handbook of Birds of Eastern North America.* D. Appleton & Co., New York. 1914. Pp. 1–530. Price, $4.00.

TRAFTON, GILBERT H. *Methods of Attracting Birds.* Houghton Mifflin Co., Boston and New York. 1922. Pp. 1–171. Price, $1.75.

MOSELEY, EDWIN LINCOLN. *Tree, Stars and Birds.* World Book Co., Yonkers-on-Hudson, New York. 1925. Pp. 1–404. Price, $1.80.

HENDERSON, JUNIUS. *The Practical Value of Birds.* The Macmillan Co., New York. 1927. Pp. 1–342. Price, $3.50.

[3] Leavitt, Robert G. Bird Study in Elementary Schools. Bulletin No. 4. National Association of Audubon Societies, New York. 1920. Pp. 112–113.

HOW TO ATTRACT BIRDS ABOUT OUR HOMES

No matter where the bird-lover lives in the Sandhills, whether in town or in the country, it is always possible to increase the number of birds by improving the neighborhood for them. First, they must be reasonably safe. In fact, much can be done to attract birds by merely protecting them, for they soon find out where they are safe from foes, and, other things being equal, they will go to the protected areas and remain there. A particularly good instance of this is the reservoir near the Mid Pines Club where the ducks are carefully protected from enemies. Happening to pass this artificial pond one day I was delighted to find its surface dotted with ducks of three different species—Scaup Duck, Mallard and Black Duck; especially as this proved to be the only place in the whole Sandhills region where I found ducks at all common. Furthermore these ducks, while on this pond, were much tamer and could be studied to good advantage; but they became as wild as usual whenever they left this protected area. This desirable result (and I noticed the club members and golfers playing on the shore of this pond were very much interested in the ducks) was obtained solely by preventing the shooting or molesting of the birds while they were on, or about, this pond.

Such an idea as this can be extended and applied to other kinds of grounds for other kinds of birds. The area does not need to be big, even a single dooryard can be made a refuge for birds. So important does our Government deem this question of refuges that it will assist whoever wishes to establish a "bird refuge" by giving it official sanction, by supplying interesting pamphlets about how to do it, and by providing more severe penalties for trespassers. An important work for bird clubs to work toward is to have cemeteries, parks and other public lands declared bird refuges and sanctuaries. Farmers and rural bird-lovers can form neighborhood associations and have larger blocks of land made into such protected areas. That all such work has direct, beneficial results in bringing birds to destroy injurious weeds and insects and to please us by their songs and bright colors, has been proven again and again in all sections of our country.

Although making a regular "refuge" or "sanctuary" is the ideal way, we can greatly help the birds even if we are unable to go that far. Much can be accomplished by banishing cats where we wish to attract birds. The home pussy is bad enough, but the homeless cats of the cities and especially the semi-wild cats that have taken to the fields and forest are worse. Even in such a small area as the Sandhills there are probably more than 15,000 cats, virtually every one a bird destroyer. The yearly death list of our beautiful birds in the Sandhills alone is at least 750,000 from this one cause.

We can not very well increase the birds about our homes unless we protect them. In various countries of Europe, large private estates have been the salvation, not only of birds, but of other creatures as well. But this practice of reserving great tracts of wild lands, especially to preserve and protect the birds and animals for the pleasure of a few persons has not been popular anywhere. Shorn of its private ownership feature, such a plan has its good points and I am glad to see we are adopting the good features in America in the State Parks and National Parks where the protection and increase of wild life for the pleasure and enjoyment of the whole people is a basic idea.

After we have made sure that the region, whether a city lot or a huge wilderness, that we want birds on, is protected and reasonably safe for birds, we are ready to take further measures. Chief of these is food and water, especially food in winter and water in summer. Here again we can practice several degrees of help— *anything* we do is good, but *everything* we can do is better. Since we can readily replenish the food supply, an important item in cold and stormy weather, and control the immediate surroundings more feeding stations are the best answer to the food problem.

These artificial stations are of many kinds, varying from the simplest, a clear place on the ground where crumbs are scattered, to the more elaborate structures of wood or concrete usually elevated above the ground. The simpler stations can be established anywhere, but to secure the greatest benefit, especially in the case of the more elaborate affairs, we should first study carefully the surroundings, the kind of birds we are likely to attract and also the kind of birds we want to attract. Most important of all in the maintenance of feeding stations is the *regular* replenishment of food supplies—attention one day and neglect on another is sure to lead to failure. Some of these stations may be simply pieces of suet tied, wired or nailed to a tree, limb or post. The roof of a piazza or the floor of a little balcony may be utilized to spread food over; the latter having the advantage of being covered whereas the former would have to be swept after the infrequent snows of the Sandhills. This would be the case with any uncovered device because birds are always ravenous at snowy times, and small particles of food will sink out of sight in the soft snow just when they are needed the most.

To escape this labor and also to keep the small pieces of food from being scattered over the floor, the food is sometimes placed in baskets made of netting and hung from porch rafters. If preferred, the baskets can be hung from the limb of a tree in a sheltered place. In doing this it would be well to note that although birds like shelter, they are sometimes timid about venturing under artificial cover. But when they become used to it, they will readily fly under any roof or other covering.

A further improvement in stations is to nail some lath around the edge of a short board in such a way as to make a small tray with a low rail about it. This can then be nailed in a tree, on a post or to a porch railing and food offerings spread over it. Such a station as this affords no shelter and for that reason a box with its back toward the prevailing wind may be nailed up in place of the "tray" and the food placed inside. Naturally we would like to see our bird friends as close as possible, so the board tray is often nailed to a window sill. The desirability of this latter arrangement has led to another improvement wherein a box built of glass is placed in a half-opened window in such a way that the one open side of the box is open to the outdoors. The window then shuts down on the top of the transparent box that projects into the room and has the bird food within it. This has the advantages that the birds seem to be brought into the room and they can be seen while feeding from any part of the room; that the birds are sheltered and protected; and that fresh food can be dropped through the movable top of the box without opening the window each time. But birds are not accustomed to finding food in such a location, so they have to be taught to come to a window box. This is easily effected by establishing a movable feeding station first at some distance, and, after the birds become accustomed to it, moving it each day a little nearer to the window until the birds find the food at the window. This is best effected by stretching a wire, or rope, from the window to a distant point, and hanging from a trolley on it a broad, shallow, open basket or tray holding the food. Aside from its use to teach the birds to come to the window, a moving station so arranged has other advantages. By its use, one can place food on it at the window and then draw the station to a more distant position without going out of doors. When necessary the station on its trolley can be hauled back to the window for replenishment or cleaning.

All of these stations are more or less artificial and birds really prefer a more natural feeding perch than a flat board floor. To obviate this, it is suggested that a small evergreen tree, or a suitable branch, be hung with packages of food after the manner of a Christmas tree and set up where the birds can get to it. Another method is to mix a good quantity of seeds, dried bread crumbs, dried berries and chopped nut-meats with twice their weight of melted suet and pour the hot mixture over the twigs and limbs of a similar food tree. Of course a valuable living tree should not be treated so for the hot mixture would undoubtedly injure it.

Another method of offering this suet mixture is to pour it while hot into a shallow wooden mould and allow it to harden into a "food cake" or "food stone." Then nail the mould with the "food cake" still in it to a tree limb, post or window sill as preferred. If the English sparrows partake too freely of the "food cake" the mould can be fastened upside down to a limb or overhead support. These sparrows do not appear able to reach it there, although our native American birds have no difficulty in clinging and eating in an inverted position. The inverted position has the added advantage that it prevents rain and snow from falling on the "food cake."

Although snowstorms are rare in the Sandhills, they are a good deal of a bother to those who maintain feeding stations, especially as the birds need the food much more at such times. To protect the food from snow, feeding stations of more elaborate design than those already mentioned have been built. These may be constructed of rustic design or of dressed lumber, and may be open above, or closed over and open below. Usually in the latter case the food is placed on two platforms—one close up under the protection of the roof with the other one far enough below so that birds can reach it readily. The idea is that the birds will then more readily progress from it to the upper platform. If the builder desires, the upper platform may be more or less enclosed by glass although this may interfere somewhat with the free passage of the birds.

At most feeding stations there is some food scattered by the birds and wasted. Usually it occurs when a bird darts away with a sudden sweep of its wings. Personally, I have always considered this an advantage because it scatters the food over the ground where sparrows and other ground-feeding birds find it, and are led to the feeding platforms themselves. But for those who object to this scattering, a "food bell" has been devised, especially by Baron Hans von Berlepsch, of Germany. This consists essentially of a large hopper to hold the food supply, and a small vertical tube dipping into a shallow tray below. The food is placed in the hopper, flows through the tube into tray, and there becomes available to birds perched on, or near, its edge. The tray may be large or small according to the number of birds to be accommodated at one time. The hopper may be made large to hold a supply of food and thereby making replenishment less frequent. But this arrangement has the disadvantage that only grain or similar small, heavy particles will fall properly through the supply tube.

The best foods to use for birds are suet (although bones, either cracked so the birds can get at the marrow, or with adhering gristle and particles of meat, are almost as good), bread-crumbs, doughnut crumbs, all kinds of nuts (especially cocoanuts and raw unsalted peanuts), sunflower seeds, hemp seed, broken dog-biscuits, Japanese millet, mixed "chick-feed," such raw cereals as rolled oats or grits, and raisins. But you can also use all sorts of table scraps chopped up fine, raw pork and raw pork rinds, all kinds of grain especially if broken up or crushed, maple seeds and seeds from ash and birch and box elder, ragweed seeds, pumpkin seeds, squash seeds, melon seeds, timothy seed, sweepings from hay mows and barns, dried thistle heads, canary seed, Kaffir corn, rice, cheese crumbs and rinds, boiled eggs (crumbled or chopped up), dried elderberries, dried blueberries, dried currants, dried raspberries, figs, and even cones from coniferous trees if they still contain seeds. Salt and salted foods should not be used.

Another way to feed the birds is to plant flowers, bushes and trees that grow acceptable seeds and fruits. Of these I have just mentioned sunflowers, maples, ashes, birches, elderberries, blue-

Figure 5.   Open pine forest, not enough cover for most birds, but liked by Flickers, Doves and Red-headed Woodpeckers. East of Pinehurst, Feb. 1, 1926.

Figure 6.   A cotton field, showing lack of bird food.   Taken from state road at Montevideo Park; Highland Pines Inn on hill in distance.   Feb. 8, 1926,

berries, raspberries, and cone-bearing trees. In every case it is preferable to plant the wild varieties, for most birds prefer them to the domesticated kinds. In the case of pumpkins, squashes and melons, it is better to dry the seeds and crack them for use on the feeding stations. Probably the best shrubs and trees to plant in the Sandhills for winter attraction are privet bushes (allowing them to grow untrimmed so that they will bear berries), sumach, elderberries, frost grapes, dogwoods, persimmons, cherry trees, mulberry trees and cedars.

Although artificial feeding is largely a winter practice, birds will come to feeding stations at all seasons of the year if proper food is offered them. This is particularly true in late spring and early summer when the growing nestlings make extraordinary demands on food supplies. Some bird-lovers advise the discontinuance of feeding stations with the coming of warm weather because they say it unfits the birds for finding their natural foods. This argument does not seem just right to me for I believe all birds in spite of abundant artificial offerings will search out their natural food at all seasons if they can find enough of it. Nor do I believe that artificial feeding lessens the attack of the birds on injurious insects in our gardens and fields. For birds prefer these insects to our offerings. I believe feeding stations really increase the consumption of insects, because they attract many additional birds to the vicinity, and actually save many birds during periods of stress that recover and later consume injurious insects. Still, artificial feeding is manifestly more successful in cold weather than in warm.

This is reversed with drinking fountains and bird baths. While birds like places to drink and bathe during all seasons of the year, they use such facilities more during warm weather. Generally birds want water most when it is most difficult to get and they always want it fresh. So it is better to replenish it two or three times a day. Drinking fountains may be put any place, that is not too near brush and cover that might conceal a lurking enemy, but we should see to it that the birds have a non-slippery perch while drinking. Since they usually alight on the edge or rim, the rim should not be too high above the water. If a drinking perch can not be arranged any other way, a flat stone that will partly project above the surface may be placed in the water. Bathing places are even more attractive than drinking fountains, and like them, should be kept filled with fresh clean water. Almost any size or shape vessel will do, but the water should not be over an inch or two deep. The bottom should be of some other material than tin or enameled ware because both are very slippery and disconcerting. But if such a vessel is the only one you have, put enough clean pebbles and sand in the bottom to cover it at all times. Stones or gravel have the added advantage that they usually afford different depths of water to suit the tastes of different birds. Varying depth of water can also be secured by either a sloping bottom or by tilting the vessel until the bottom is sloping. Furthermore, inability to provide a simple one. Varying depth of water can also be secured by either a sloping bottom or by tilting the vessel until the bottom is sloping. Furthermore, inability to provide a large elaborate bath should not deter you from providing a simple one. After you have established a bird fountain or bird bath, it may surprise you to see in what cold weather birds will come to it. At such times most birds will appreciate water in baths and fountains at a temperature of 60 to 70 degrees F. after you have allowed for the cooling effect of the cold receptacle.

Next in importance after food and drink comes shelter and protection—shelter from storms and protection from their many natural enemies. Both of these are provided by thick evergreens such as magnolias, hollies, pines and red cedars (Figs. 17, 21, 24, 26). Not so much shelter, but even more protection from enemies, is furnished by thick thorny bushes like roses and blackberries into which a pursued bird can quickly dart. And of course many of the shrubs and trees already recommended for bird food will also serve for shelter and protection if their branches be thick. Piles of brush, although very unsightly from a landscape gardener's point of view, are dearly beloved by birds. In rural sections it is of benefit to the birds to allow the thick brush and cat-briar thickets to remain over springs and streams. Because these thickets, together with the hedges of weeds and blackberries that spring up between fields and in fence corners, are the finest of natural growths for bird retreats and also the safest places for birds to nest. The great majority of birds still prefer to nest on natural sites just as they have always done. By far the larger proportion of these will pick out the natural thickets, hedges and fence corners, and many more will utilize the crotches and limbs of trees above. On many farms and in many communities it is customary to cut out all the dead limbs and dead trees. This seems a mistake where their removal can be delayed or prevented, for these are the only nesting places for many birds.

For some of the birds that formerly nested in hollow trees or limbs we can provide artificial substitutes and this fact gives us another chance to draw birds about our homes. While bird boxes and nesting sites do not relate directly to winter birds, the subject is of interest to us because many of the birds that nest in early summer frequent the same neighborhood during the following winter. This is particularly true of such birds as Carolina Wrens, Bluebirds and woodpeckers. Suitable box nests are not hard to provide, especially as birds care little whether their boxes are simple or elaborate, if we will only take care to meet their needs in a few respects. Unless the grounds are large, you will be able to attract only one pair, or at most two pairs of a kind, to your home grounds. Purple martins, however, prefer to nest together and will peacefully occupy a community house of several rooms. But you can get a pair of every box-nesting species in your locality to nest with you by providing the right kind of boxes and helping the birds when help is needed. So, before beginning operations, you should check up the opportunities and decide on just what birds and how many you can attract. Bird houses may be constructed of several materials but perhaps the best are hollow limbs, slab boards, or weathered dressed boards. Although boards may be dressed outside it is best to have the inside always rough so that the young birds may clamber about. The hollow should be big enough for the birds to turn around in conveniently, and it should be comparatively deep. The opening should be only just big enough for the intended bird to enter, and it should be located near the top of the box and with *no perch near*. The roof should slope down from the rear toward the front; the top should be hung on hinges at the rear so that the house can be easily cleaned out; the roof should project three inches over all sides of the box and if it seems to extend down and shelter the opening, so much the better. Houses can be made of tin, metal or clay but in such an event still more care should be taken to place them in the shade or they will be too hot inside. It is well to have one or more small openings besides the entrance—in the upper part of the box for ventilation purposes and in the bottom for draining off any water that might enter. The earlier these boxes are erected the better. They should be fastened securely, so they will not rattle, to trees, posts, grape arbors or even to the sides of a building. The entrance should face away from the prevailing storms and the house should be shaded from the hot afternoon sun. If placed on a pole, a metal or barbed wire cat-guard can be put around the lower part of the pole to protect the bird family. Bird houses should be cleaned out as soon as the birds leave and a dusting with insect powder will do no harm. Martins will nest either in community houses or in small clusters of dry empty gourds, but nests for Martins should be placed on a pole fifteen or twenty feet from the nearest houses or trees. Martins like to nest about twenty feet above the ground. In the case of Martin houses, the entrances should be placed lower in the house, and it is well to put shelves or perches on the outside at least an inch below the openings but not on a level with the entrances. Many birds, even those that refuse to use artificial nest boxes, will avail themselves of nesting material left in convenient places for them. Usually this will be strings, threads, rags, bits of paper, flax, unravelled rope, cotton batting, horsehair, sheeps' wool and even feathers and wood shavings. But it is also well to remember that birds, notably Robins, Barn Swallows and Eaves Swallows, use mud in their nests and must often find it difficult to get enough for their use.

While inducing birds to occupy nest boxes there are two enemies to be guarded against. Of these the worse is the cat. Fortunately English Sparrows are not yet very abundant in the Sandhills, but whenever they appear they must be driven away, otherwise they will monopolize the feeding stations and bird baths as well as the nest boxes. They may not actively fight the native birds (although the chances are that they will) but our native birds will soon cease to come where these aliens are. To drive these sparrows out, they must be fought steadily whenever they appear. Nest boxes should be closed as soon as the rightful owners leave and not reopened until just before they are expected to return. All nests of the English Sparrows should be torn out and destroyed and the birds prevented from breeding if possible. Finally the birds themselves should be killed. There are three ways of accomplishing this— poison, shooting and trapping. Since there are so many native species present, poison is not suited to the Sandhills conditions.

Figure 7. Peach orchards require too much cultivation to allow grass seeds and bushes to grow for the birds. Taken near Manice, Moore County, Feb. 2, 1926.

Figure 8.   A stream through cypress-gum swamp.   Lumbee River at State Road No. 50, between Pine Bluff and Hoffman.
Feb. 12, 1926.

But these sparrows can easily be shot with a rifle using small-shot cartridges, or they can be trapped in box traps. European Starlings are beginning to establish themselves in the Sandhills and will soon be competing with Bluebirds, Flickers and woodpeckers for nest sites. To discourage them, they will have to be treated as advised for the English Sparrows. These are some of the ways we can help birds that would nest with us, and to have them succeed and furnish the pleasure they can, we should be ever ready to go to their assistance.

In fact a readiness to go to protect the birds can be made an important factor in attracting them about us. I have known of several instances where Robins would fly down and utter sharp cries of alarm or distress until someone went to help them. I remember once in my own yard I found a Mockingbird scolding over an intruding cat but, as soon as I drove the cat away, the Mockingbird began to sing. Mrs. Miller tells of a pair "of Wood Thrushes which nested last summer in the yard of her house in the city of Orange, N. J. The birds soon found out that some of the family would come to drive away strange cats which came in. After they learned that, when a cat appeared they would give a peculiar cry, unlike any other heard from them. On hearing this, one of the family always hurried out and drove the enemy away. If the birds could not get any response from a call at the kitchen door, they would fly to the front of the house, perch on the piazza rail, and call till some one came out. All through nesting time they thus called on their friends for protection, and the delight the family had over the nest and the friendly birds amply repaid them for their trouble."[4]

For additional information on this subject see:

CHAPMAN, FRANK M. *Our Winter Birds*. D. Appleton & Co., New York. 1919. Pp. 1–180. Price, $2.00.

CHAPMAN, FRANK M. *Handbook of Birds of Eastern North America*. D. Appleton & Co., New York. 1914. Pp. 1–530. Price, $4.00.

MILLER, OLIVE THORNE. *The First Book of Birds*. Hough-ton Mifflin and Co., Boston and New York. 1899. Pp. 1–149. Price, $2.00.

[4] Miller, Olive Thorne. The First Book of Birds. Houghton Mifflin and Co., Boston and New York. 1899. P. 133.

LANGE, D. *Our Native Birds.* The MacMillan Co., New York and London. 1899. Pp. 1–162. Price, $1.75.

PEARSON, T. GILBERT. *Stories of Bird Life.* World Book Co., New York and Chicago. 1925. Pp. 1–236. Price, $1.00.

BAYNES, ERNEST HAROLD. *Wild Bird Guests.* E. P. Dutton & Co., New York. 1915. Pp. 1–326. Price, $2.00.

MERRIAM, FLORENCE A. *Birds of Village and Field.* Houghton Mifflin and Co., Boston and New York. 1900. Pp. 1–406. Price, $2.25.

TRAFTON, GILBERT H. *Methods of Attracting Birds.* Houghton Mifflin and Co., Boston and New York. 1910. Pp. 1–171. Price, $1.75.

EATON, ELON HOWARD. *Birds of New York.* New York State Museum, Memoir No. 12. Albany, N. Y. 1914. Vol. 2, Pp. 1–719. Price, $6.00 for set two volumes, plus postage. Mailing weight 15 pounds.

TAVERNER, P. A. *Bird Houses and Their Occupants.* Canadian National Parks Branch, Dept. of the Interior. Ottawa, Canada. 1920. Pp. 1–15. Free.

DEARBORN, NED. *Bird Houses and How to Build Them.* Farmers' Bulletin 609. U. S. Dept. of Agriculture. Government Printing Office, Washington, D. C. March, 1915. Pp. 1–19.

KUSER, JOHN DRYDEN. *The Way to Study Birds.* G. P. Putnam's Sons, New York and London. 1917. Pp. 1–85. Price, $1.25.

MOSELEY, EDWIN LINCOLN. *Trees, Stars and Birds.* World Book Co., Yonkers-on-Hudson, New York. 1925. Pp. 1–404. Price, $1.80.

HOW AND WHEN TO FIND FIELD AND FOREST BIRDS

While attracting birds about our homes is fascinating work and has many advantages for close intimate studies of the life of individual birds, there are many species that never come near our homes. To see these, we must hunt them up where they prefer to live. One method of studying birds we can practice either in our yards or in wilder areas, and that is to call them about us. We can do this by imitating the birds' own calls if we wish. But a simpler way, much used by ornithologists, is to sound low notes by kissing the back of their own hands. At times this is very effective and I have known cases where no birds at all were to be seen, and yet after these sounds were made the nearby bushes would be alive with various birds all keenly curious about the strange sounds.

Birds have keen ears to hear such sounds, and readily respond to them. But when we try to hunt the birds up we find that this good hearing is a disadvantage, for they can hear us long before we find them. So that if we would be successful we must practice all the patience at our command and walk just as carefully as possible. This is especially necessary in order to see birds acting in a natural way. Although the noises we make may not start them into active flight and alarm, birds are shy and they will not act naturally if they know we are about and think we are watching them. Because two persons make twice as many unavoidable noises as one, it is always best to go "birding" either alone or in the very smallest parties possible.

Although birds' hearing is so very acute, their eyesight is even more remarkably keen. For instance: I have seen a Shrike perched on a telephone wire fly a hundred feet and capture a small insect that it showed every evidence of having seen before it left its perch! A bird's eyesight is further aided by the fact that its eyes are on the side of its head and their bulging surface permits the bird to see in all directions. Remember this, and you will see why it is impossible to sneak up on a bird unless you are as quiet and patient as an Indian. Never run after birds, for all you can then accomplish is a second view of an alarmed bird that is very much frightened and acting unnaturally.

The birds' good hearing and sharp eyesight may increase the fun of getting the best of them, but they are responsible for two methods of studying them. If you are anxious to find and see as *many* birds as possible, you should be prepared to cover a great deal of country and to walk all day if necessary. Be sure to investigate every strange call and song that you hear. But if you want to study each kind of bird *as much* as possible, a better plan is to go to some place the birds frequent, sit down there, keep your arms still, and wait patiently until they come about you. If you are quiet and inconspicuous and do not move, you will be surprised and delighted with many intimate scenes of avian home life. This second method requires much patience, but it gives greater rewards. If you have a blind, such as described later on, be sure to take it and use it. Birds will come near where you are seated quietly on a log or stool, but the more you are concealed the better the results, always. There is no easy way to bird study, but if you will use ordinary good sense, go slowly, use patience, keep your eyes and ears alert, avoid conspicuous dress and loud talking, and persevere, you will soon be overjoyed at the rewards you will get. You should keep the sun in back of you, if practicable, so as to see the birds in the best light possible. Above all, you must avoid sudden motions, especially of your hands and arms.

You can study birds all day long in winter because the days are short and the birds must keep constantly active to find enough food. But even then, morning is the best. As the weather gets warmer and the days longer, birds are active only in the morning and late in the afternoon. To get the best results then, it is necessary to be out *early* in the morning. Birds can be found in all kinds of weather. You can find them on windy days or on still days, on dull days or on bright days, and in clear weather or in storms. So do not think there are no birds to study just because it is cold or raining. On the other hand the very best times in winter in the Sandhills are still, bright mornings immediately following a rain or snowstorm.

As already explained many birds can be attracted about our homes even where the yards are small and there seems little room for birds. If we apply the same rules to larger areas the rewards are even greater, for then we have a greater diversity of conditions to offer. This is particularly so in the larger parks and public lands of our towns and cities. Not only are the birds in such places fed and protected from enemies, but there is usually a greater variety of trees and shrubs to furnish bird food and safe retreats. Better yet, there are apt to be water and both drinking and bathing places for the birds. Such areas are usually the best within a short distance of many homes and an hour can profitably be spent there when we can not take longer time. Another advantage is that park birds are usually tame and permit us to observe them closely. But it is always better to visit wilder woods and fields when possible because birds there are less influenced by artificial conditions.

As a rule birds will not be found in bare fields or in very dense woods, for such places have few attractions for them. Some birds, such as Horned Larks, Killdeers and Pipits, will be found only in fields, but even so, these fields will be covered by grass or herbaceous plants of some kind; and such birds as hawks and vultures will be seen flying over both fields and forests. Dense forests may have an occasional bird in them, but these same kinds of birds will be much more numerous in more open forests and about the edges. Forests of mixed trees are better than the oak-and-pine forest so common in the Sandhills. Peach orchards and cotton fields are not good bird haunts because the constant cultivation of the ground there destroys most of the attractive bird food. On the other hand birds are often attracted to such areas *when plowing or cultivating is actually going on*: and birds of several kinds may often be on the *edges* of orchards and cotton fields especially where bordered by thickets or other good cover.

The best country for birds is a varied one with rolling ground (Figs. 2, 13, 14, 18, 19, 20, 22, 27), groves of different kinds of trees, hedges of brush, some cultivated fields, a few streams and maybe a pond or two. Such an area is bound to have on it several kinds of foods suited to all kinds of birds. And where one bird is attracted, others are most apt to follow. The best places of all are along the edges of weedy cornfields where ditches or streams encourage the growth of thickets of blackberry shoots, eat-briars, wild grapes, sumach, dogwoods, wild cherries, and other food plants. Such places will be especially attractive if they are protected from winds but exposed to the morning sun. A small patch of broom-sedge nearby will attract a few more birds. For water and swamp birds an undisturbed stream or a protected pond edged by marsh plants should be visited. Water always has its attractions for many other birds as well. In fall and early winter wild fruit trees such as gums, wild cherry trees, persimmons and dogwoods are magnets that may draw large flocks of birds during the fruiting time. Cedars and junipers are also very attractive to birds, and if the crop of cedar or juniper berries be large they may attract birds all winter. It is a good plan to visit all trees of this kind as long as any food remains on them. Old neglected orchards may have a host of birds feeding on the waste fruit or on insect pests flourishing on the neglected trees. Patches of tangled weeds, even if low, may shelter many sparrows and their companions.

Some birds, such as owls and Woodcock, prefer dark places in swamps and thickets to pass the day (Fig. 11). A few birds like damp thickets, although there may be no actual water exposed there. However, this feature is not so marked in winter when the rate of evaporation from a bird's body is less. In winter, when they have no nests to hold them to one vicinity, birds wander more and are frequently found in unusual places. Birds that prefer certain heights from the ground in summer foliage may be at all heights in winter. Should you hear a flock of Crows or Blue Jays making a noisy tumult, better go carefully and see what is going on. You may find them tormenting hawks or owls that you might not otherwise find.

For additional information on this subject see:

CHAPMAN, FRANK M. *Handbook of Birds of Eastern North America.* D. Appleton & Co., New York. 1914. Pp. 1–530. Price, $4.00.

MERRIAM, FLORENCE A. *Birds of Village and Field.* Houghton, Mifflin and Co., Boston and New York. 1900. Pp. 1–406. Price, $2.25.

SILLOWAY, P. M. *Guide to the Summer Birds of the Bear Mountain and Harriman Park Sections of the Palisades Interstate Park.* Bull. No. 11, The New York State College of Forestry, Syracuse. 1920. Pp. 1–105.

Figure 9.   Cotton field, west of Pinehurst, too much cultivated to be attractive to birds.   Birds will not haunt the most attractive of places if food is absent.   Feb. 2, 1926.

Figure 10.   A dam forming an artificial pond, haunts of Grebes, Ducks, Hooded Mergansers and Kingfishers.   Near Pine Bluff.
Photo by A. G. Whitney.

EQUIPMENT NEEDED TO STUDY BIRDS

With a pair of good ears, good eyesight, a supply of good sense and unlimited patience and carefulness, a bird-lover can accomplish much, see many interesting sights and thoroughly enjoy himself, or herself. But there is additional equipment that would add to the pleasures or make the securing of them easier. As one nature enthusiast has said, bird study has no fashions or conventions along the line of clothes. Nevertheless, the birds are less alarmed when we go after them in quiet, dull-colored cloths that blend with the background as inconspicuously as possible. Old clothes can be used if desired, but everything should be of wool, especially in winter, for wool is warm. Even if you get an unexpected ducking in a pond, or a pond, or encounter a sudden shower, wet woolen clothes are far warmer than any other *wet* clothes. That they permit the gradual escape of perspiration is important because you will often walk hard until perspiration starts and may then want to stop and watch for birds. Such a state of affairs in anything but woolen clothes will chill you and may bring worse troubles. Be sure to be warmly clad if you adopt the practice of waiting anywhere for birds. No matter how comfortable the temperature is while walking it may be too low for a long motionless wait under shady trees unless you are prepared for it. Finally, woolen clothes are noiseless. Hats should be small and inconspicuous. While most of the walking in the Sandhills is dry underfoot, you ought to have rubber boots if you want to explore gum swamps or cypress swamps. A dull-colored rubber coat or oilskin is a good thing to have in stormy weather, but is noisy at all times.

Glasses are needed for all but the tamest of birds. But do not think you need an expensive pair with which to start. To be sure you can do more work, and do it more easily, with a good glass of adequate power; but after all, the prime factor of success is the user. Good work can be done with even such a glass as an opera glass. If you can afford them, the best glasses are binoculars, because they are powerful and light and more convenient to handle than other types of the same power. These binoculars are made in 3-power, 5-power, 6-power, 8-power and 12-power and have different size lenses. A 6-power is the best for the average person, and

39

it should have as large lenses as your purse will permit, for large lenses permit you to see your bird distinctly in much duller light than the smaller lenses do.

As necessary as a glass, and perhaps even more important, is a good reference book. At the end of each subject treated here is a list of good current books. At the end of the section devoted to bird descriptions will be found a list of the more important books on birds. In addition, you should have the best local list, the best current State list of the State in which you are working (for North Carolina: Pearson and Brimley's "The Birds of North Carolina"), and a book covering either the whole United States or the eastern section thereof. Having procured these books for yourself, or found a library where you can borrow them, or refer to them, you can add others as you become more interested.

Should questions arise to perplex you, you will find that every ornithologist is willing to help you and answer your letters. I know that I, for one, will be glad to answer any questions. As a general rule, the ornithologist working nearest to your field of study is the one best qualified to help you. Or you might consult the officers of the bird club nearest you. Better yet, join your local bird club. There should be one in every locality and nearly every high school and college has at least a junior bird club, or an Audubon Society. By joining one of these local bird clubs you will have the advantage of exchanging interesting bits of bird lore with fellow enthusiasts and you are helping whatever bird work they are doing. After you become further interested you should join one of the larger clubs covering the country where you are working. These are:

AMERICAN ORNITHOLOGISTS' UNION. Founded 1884. This is the leading as well as the largest scientific ornithological organization in the country. Official organ, "The Auk," free to all members. Address, American Ornithologists' Union, care of the American Museum of Natural History, New York, N. Y.

COOPER ORNITHOLOGICAL CLUB. Founded in 1893. Organ, "The Condor." Address, care of the University of California, Berkeley, Calif.

NATIONAL ASSOCIATION OF AUDUBON SOCIETIES. Founded 1902. Organ, "Bird-Lore." Issues also educational leaflets for teachers and literature relating to bird conservation. Address, 1974 Broadway, New York, N. Y.

Wilson Ornithological Club. Founded 1888. Organ, "Wilson Bulletin." Address, care of Oberlin College, Oberlin, Ohio.

As you will note, one of the great advantages of joining one of these larger associations is that you will then receive the printed "organ" of the one you select. These periodicals often contain the finest descriptions of birds and bird-life, and they will give you the latest news about birds in your own territory. By the time you have become so far interested in bird work, you will no doubt find that you would like to do something a little more serious and permanent than satisfy the curiosity and pleasure of the moment. This is particularly the case if you become interested in bird migration. For this purpose, and as a basis for all permanent work, you will need a note-book. There are many forms advertised, but after all it does not greatly matter what kind of a note-book you use provided you make accurate notes of exactly what you see.

If you can draw or sketch, you will find sketching materials a wonderful help to record and fix some interesting scene you have noted. Indeed, making even a rough sketch of a strange bird is one of the surest ways to fix that bird indelibly in your memory. But if you do not get all you want by sketching, a camera is a big help in bird work and serves even better to record details of bird haunts and the condition of the vegetation. As with glasses, do not be dismayed at the cost of the expensive cameras. Of course it is nice to have the best outfit possible, but very good work can be done with the simplest camera. When it comes to serious studies of birds and especially work with sketch-book or camera, a movable hiding place becomes advantageous. Of course one can work without such a hiding place or "blind," but not so easily, successfully, or comfortably. The simplest of all blinds is a small tent, just big enough to sit in, that can be erected within a few feet of a bird's haunts. Another simple blind is made with a large umbrella. The walls of this blind is a single sheet of cloth with a draw string at the top that can be tied over the top of the umbrella so that it hangs down on all sides and hides the observer. The handle of the umbrella is lengthened by a short pipe, whose other end is thrust into the ground. Naturally there must be a slit or "window" through which the birds can be watched and their photographs taken. Many other forms will suggest themselves, but whatever is used should be of as inconspicuous a color as possible.

For additional information on this subject, see:

BAYNES, ERNEST HAROLD. *Wild Bird Guests*, E. P. Dutton & Co., New York, 1915. Pp. 1–32. Price, $2.00.

MILLER, OLIVE THORNE. *The First Book of Birds*. Houghton Mifflin Co., Boston and New York. 1899. Pp. 1–149. Price, $2.00.

CHAPMAN, FRANK M. *Handbook of Birds of Eastern North America*. D. Appleton & Co., New York. 1914. Pp. 1–530. Price, $4.00.

FORBUSH, EDWARD H. *Outdoor Bird Study*. Dept. Pub. No. 115 (reprint 1925). Mass. Dept. of Agriculture, Boston, Mass. Pp. 1–32.

KUSER, JOHN DRYDEN. *The Way to Study Birds*. G. P. Putnam's Sons, New York and London. 1917. Pp. 1–85. Price, $1.25.

PLATE 2. WATER BIRDS ALONG RIVERS AND RESERVOIRS

1: Mallard (female).
2: Mallard (male).
3: Pied-billed Grebe.
4: Belted Kingfisher (male).

5: Belted Kingfisher
      (female).
6: American Woodcock.
7: Black Duck.

(All figures about ⅛ life size)

FOOD OF BIRDS

No doubt many of the changes from one place to another is due to more, or better, food, from the birds' standpoint, to be found in different places at different times. The activity of birds is so great, and their process of digestion so rapid, that they require large amounts of food at quite regular intervals. As birds seldom store up food supplies, a large share of their time is spent searching for food. Indeed, it is thought that food, raising families, and protection from enemies, are the three great influences on bird ways and movements. Abundance of food will cause a great number of birds to gather: on the other hand, birds will not occupy the most attractive place if all food is absent. The abundance, or scarcity, of a favorite food may account for the comparative abundance of certain birds one winter, and their absence the next. Scarcity of food in one area may drive birds to unusual places in search of it. On the contrary, an abundance of one food may lead birds to abandon foods of other kinds to partake of that which is plentiful.

Aside from these changes due to local abundance or scarcity, there is a close relation between habitat and food, for birds spend most of their time in search of food. As there are birds to suit every habitat, just so surely are there birds to consume every kind of food. Not only insects that we see on the ground or amongst the grass, but also such insects as grubs and ants that live in the ground; insects that live on bushes, on grain, and on the leaves of herbs; insects that live on the bark of trees; insects that bore into the wood of trees or under the bark; insects that live on the foliage of bushes and trees; insects that fly through the air; and even insects that live on, in, or under, the water surface. All are the prey of certain birds. Apparently all insects, no matter how securely they may seem to be hidden, are sought for and found by at least some kinds of birds. Since the great majority of insects eat vegetable food that is easily obtained and abundant, they are apt to be voracious eaters and increase with wonderful rapidity. Hence, they must be kept in check, or they would devastate the world. Now I do not mean to say that birds are the only enemies of insects, but I am sure they are very powerful and important ones.

Just as important as checks on mice and other rodents are those birds like the hawks, owls, crows and shrikes that feed on these small animals. Perhaps we are not so conscious of mouse destruction by birds as we are of insect hunting, probably because we see so little of it.

A few of the winter Sandhills birds, such as the grebes, the kingfishers and some of the ducks, eat fish, but they generally take small and unimportant fishes, from our point of view. As we approach the sea-coast, we discover more and more birds eating fish. Most of the birds feeding on fish have special adaptations for holding their slippery prey. The fish ducks or mergansers, have toothed or sawlike bills; and the Fish Hawks, or Ospreys, have very rough undersurfaces to their feet. Most of the fish-eating birds will also devour snails, frogs, tadpoles and crawfish. Some of the hawks will take small snakes at times.

Many birds prefer living prey, and some will eat only food of their own catching; but others will eat dead animals, or carrion, as well. Still, when one speaks of carrion birds, he usually means such birds as Turkey Buzzards and Black Vultures that depend on finding dead animals. These birds are probably the most universally recognized useful members of the bird world. No doubt because we all see the evidence of their work. Certain it is, that there are no other birds accorded such full protection.

Insects and animal food are perhaps the most important bird foods in summer. But in wintertime, most birds that remain in North Carolina turn largely, or wholly, to eating seeds and fruits. At this work of destroying seeds, these birds join the regular seed-eaters whose food at all seasons is chiefly seeds. All kinds are eaten, but mainly those from the most common weeds. Some of the seed-eaters will also eat grain, but they cause very little damage because the grain they eat in winter is what has fallen to the ground, or has been wasted in other ways. In summer, when crops are being raised, these birds turn to insects as a staple food and do not usually eat seeds and grain again until after the crops have been harvested.

Many of the birds feeding on other kinds of food normally, turn to wild fruits in winter. A few of them do so for the sake of the seeds inside the berries and other wild fruit, whereas other birds will eat the pulp and reject the seeds. This is particularly

Figure 11.　Cat-briar tangle over a small stream, well-known as a Woodcock thicket.　Near Pinehurst, Feb. 4, 1926.

Figure 12. Golf links, frequented by Killdeer, at Pinehurst, Feb. 22, 1926.

true of cedar berries and the sour gum berries. On the other hand, almost all birds that eat persimmons and wild cherries, eat the pulp and leave the seeds and pits behind. But sumach berries are eaten entire by nearly all the birds that eat them at all. The fruits most frequently eaten in winter in the Sandhills are the sour gum (*Nyssa silvatica*) berries, dogwood berries, sumach berries, wild grapes, frost grapes, persimmons, wild cherries, choke cherries, blackberries and cedar berries. The fruit-eating birds include the better known ones, such as Robins, Cedar Waxwings, Mockingbirds, Catbirds, Brown Thrashers, Bluebirds, Purple Finches, woodpeckers and sapsuckers.

The buds and fresh leaves of trees are attractive to some birds, and so are various nuts; the Blue Jays, Tufted Titmice, and some of the woodpeckers, being very fond of acorns. In fact, any vegetable food that is tender and easily obtainable, is sure to be eaten by some bird or other, especially in winter.

For additional information on this subject see:

TRAFTON, GILBERT H. *Methods of Attracting Birds.* Houghton Mifflin Co., Boston and New York. 1910. Pp. 1–171. Price, $1.75.

PEARSON, T. GILBERT. *Stories of Bird Life.* World Book Co., New York and Chicago. 1925. Pp. 1–236. Price, $1.00.

MERRIAM, FLORENCE A. *Birds of Village and Field.* Houghton Mifflin Co., Boston and New York. 1900. Pp. 1–406. Price, $2.25.

CHAPMAN, FRANK M. *Handbook of Birds of Eastern North America.* D. Appleton & Co., New York and London. 1914. Pp. 1–530. Price, $4.00.

MILLER, OLIVE THORNE. *The First Book of Birds.* Houghton Mifflin Co., Boston and New York. 1899. Pp. 1–149. Price, $2.00.

BAILEY, HAROLD H. *The Birds of Virginia.* J. P. Bell Company, Inc., Lynchburg, Va. 1913. Pp. 1–362. Price, $5.00.

INGERSOLL, ERNEST. *Primer of Bird Study.* Published by the author, New York. 1916. For sale at The National Association of Audubon Societies, 1974 Broadway, New York. Pp. 1–24. Price, 18c.

HENDERSON, JUNIUS. *The Practical Value of Birds.* The Macmillan Co., New York. 1927. Pp. 1–342. Price, $3.50.

Some of the bird foods are to be had only in certain places even during the season when that food is most abundant. So that even the birds that are with us then are forced to move often to considerable distances to find the food they want, often the foods they actually must have. Often, different species of birds are so closely adapted to certain foods that they can not do well on other foods. The Martins, for instance, are especially adapted to catching certain insects that fly high in air, and without them are forced to go elsewhere or die of starvation. With the change of the seasons, particularly in the autumn, some of these foods are unavailable, especially insects. But there are still insects of the right kinds to be had farther south; so it is very natural that these birds should move thither.

This movement, being temporary and irregular, would hardly be known as migration. But it might easily develop into migration; for true migration is a similar movement regularly directed in a generally southerly and northerly direction at the proper seasons of the year. No doubt it started in some such way, and possibly food is the most important factor now controlling migration; but there are many other factors that also add their influence. Almost all insectivorous birds go south in winter, but some like the kinglets remain even farther north than the Sandhills. And again, if food was the only controlling force, birds would never leave to go north in spring, just when the insects were getting really numerous here.

In many ways, the Sandhills region is well situated for the study of migration, and winter is a favorable time. Some of the Sandhills birds are resident, like the Bob-whites; that is, they remain in a comparatively small area at all times, but most of the Sandhills birds are migratory. As early as the middle of August, and even as early as the middle of July in some years, migration movements begin with the arrival of a few transient birds. Transients are temporary visitors that come down from the north, stay a few weeks, and then fly on to more southern homes for the winter; or they come in spring for a few days, and then fly on to the north to their summer homes. Possibly, the first bird to come down from the north, and stay in the Sandhills all winter, is the Marsh Hawk that arrives as early as the first of September. Other species come regularly every autumn for a few days, and others that stay all winter make their appearance after the Marsh Hawks. All through September, October and November, first one and then another of the summer birds leave. Should a record be kept of these arrivals and departures, it would be found that the dates vary only slightly in different years. Soon, it would be noticed that these variations were more or less closely related to variations in the weather. The regular migration movements start inconspicuously, but gradually gather force and become more and more apparent, with species arriving and departing daily, at the height of the autumn movement in late October or early November.

By the first of December, most of the autumn movement has ceased, although there may be a few stragglers, especially if the early winter be warmer than usual. Should a sudden cold snap come in December, after a warm spell, there is a sudden inflow of visitors and it then becomes apparent that the movement is closely connected with temperature. Of course, cold weather may operate directly, or indirectly by destroying the birds' food, or at least by making food more difficult to secure. While it is probable that the warm feathers that cover birds prevent them from feeling the cold acutely, it seems evident that movements are often caused directly by changes in the temperature. On the contrary, many birds stay as far north in winter as they can find either their accustomed food, or a satisfactory substitute. Perhaps the worst effects of cold weather is the likelihood that the snow or ice brought by it may cover the food otherwise available. All through the winter we see sudden movements of the winter birds caused by changes of weather. These movements are spasmodic and temporary, and while not in themselves of a migratory nature, they help us to understand migration. In the Sandhills, we readily observe how these sudden changes change the supply of bird food.

When spring is approaching, the birds get more and more restless, the migratory ones particularly. Soon their numbers commence to decrease. Finally, on the first warm days, we suddenly note that one of the species that passed through in the autumn has come back again. Knowing that there is a warmer climate south of us and a colder climate north of us, it is easy to realize that the great changes in bird life of a region, in autumn and spring, are due to birds going south and later returning north. Furthermore, we can often see such birds as ducks, hawks, blackbirds and swallows actually going south, or north, at the proper time, for these birds migrate by day.

But the great majority of our birds come and go during the night, and we see little proof of their travels except their sudden abundance after a night's flight to the Sandhills, and their absence some bright morning after they have departed on their journey. Sometimes the birds passing over at night are seen through astronomical telescopes; and quite often we can hear the calls as they pass overhead on a still night. Some birds fly low, and even close to the ground, or water; but others are higher. Contrary to the old beliefs, it is now thought that the majority of migrating birds fly comparatively low, and not many over four thousand feet above the earth. In spite of another former belief, birds do not fly fast on migration and many do not go far each day. Unless the flight is across an expanse of water, migrating birds are more apt to fly a hundred miles or less at one flight, and then wait from one to several days before making another flight. But all the general customs of migration have some striking exceptions.

Possibly, when we learn more about migration, we may be able to make rules to cover all cases. But as yet, we know so comparatively little that migration is still "the great mystery" of bird life. Even such fundamental facts as why, when and where migration started are still the subjects of constant discussion and difference of opinion. Migration is connected with climate, but just what are the biggest factors are still unknown. But the more we learn, the more we are amazed at the wonderful urge that causes these frail creatures to make such long and extended trips each year. We wonder how they find their way and what remarkable calendars they must have to leave at the same time each year, travel thousands of miles, and yet arrive back at their starting-points at approximately the same dates.

To our further wonder and amazement, we learn that the migrants follow definite routes year after year. While these routes generally follow some well-marked feature like a sea-coast, or a river valley, they do not always do so. Some bird routes strike out directly from the shore, crossing from island to island, or making a saving cut on the longer route along shore. Many routes cross rivers and valleys instead of following them, and some even cross important mountain ranges. Although the routes in autumn and spring are likely to be the same, or at least nearly so, there are some species whose going and returning routes differ widely. Some species follow a route through North Carolina in the fall but not in the spring, and some go through in spring but not in the fall.

Possibly, the most wonderful of the bird migrations is that of the Arctic Terns, a far northern species, of which Prof. W. W. Cooke has said: "It deserves its title of 'Arctic' for it nests as far North as land has been discovered; that is, as far North as the bird can find anything stable on which to construct its nests. Indeed, so arctic are the conditions under which it breeds that the first nest found by many in this region, only seven and one-half degrees from the pole, contained a downy chick surrounded by a wall of newly fallen snow that had been scooped out of the nest by the parent. When the young are full grown the entire family leaves the Arctic, and several months later they are found skirting the edge of the Antarctic continent.

"What their track is over that eleven thousand miles of intervening space no one knows. A few scattered individuals have been noted along the United States coast south to Long Island, but the great flocks of thousands and thousands of these Terns which range from pole to pole have never been noted by ornithologists competent to indicate their preferred route and their time schedule. The Arctic Terns arrive in the Far North about June fifteenth and leave about August twenty-fifth, thus staying fourteen weeks at the nesting site. They probably spend a few weeks longer in the winter than in the summer home, and this would leave them scarcely twenty weeks for the round trip of twenty-two thousand miles. Not less than one hundred and fifty miles in a straight line must be their daily task, and this is undoubtedly multiplied several times by their zigzag twistings and turnings in pursuit of food.

"The Arctic Tern has more hours of daylight and sunlight than any other animal on the globe. At the most northern nesting site the midnight sun has already appeared before the birds' arrival, and it never sets during their entire stay at the breeding grounds. During two months of their sojourn in the Antarctic the birds do not see a sunset, and for the rest of the time the sun dips only a little way below the horizon and broad daylight is continuous. The birds, therefore, have twenty-four hours of daylight for at least eight months in the year, and during the other four months have considerably more daylight than darkness."[5]

For additional information on this subject see:

CHAPMAN, FRANK M. *What Bird is That?* D. Appleton & Co., New York and London. 1923. Pp. 1–144. Price, $1.50.

WETMORE, ALEXANDER. *The Migrations of Birds.* Harvard University Press, Cambridge. 1926. Pp. 1–217. Price, $2.50.

MOSELEY, EDWIN LINTON. *Trees, Stars and Birds.* World Book Co., Yonkers-on-Hudson, New York. 1925. Pp. 1–404. Price, $1.80.

MATHEWS, F. SCHUYLER. *The Book of Birds.* G. P. Putnam's Sons, New York. 1925. Pp. 1–323. Price, $3.00.

5 Cooke, Wells W. Bird Migration. U. S. Dept. of Agriculture, Bulletin No. 185. Government Printing Office, Washington, D. C. 1915. Pp. 9–11.

THE PROTECTION OF BIRDS

It would seem as if the need for the protection of birds was self-evident, and yet it is one of the greatest problems connected with them. Probably more money and time and effort are expended on how to protect birds than upon any other activity connected with them. The problem is chiefly one of education, and countless pamphlets and magazine articles are written every year concerning some phase of the problem. Although most people agree on the general proposition that most birds should be protected, individual persons will reserve to themselves the right to decide about any particular bird. It is the old question over again, of the giving up a few individual ideas and prejudices for the good of the whole community.

In primitive days, birds existed as a part of Nature and they did not need "protection" because there was a delicate "balance of Nature," wherein insect, plant, fish, reptile, bird and mammal had its place. Sometimes, through a change of climate, or some fundamental change affecting wild life, this balance was changed and readjusted. But generally speaking, it was more or less stable. Birds had many natural enemies, but they were not greater than the birds could cope with by themselves. But when men, especially white men, entered upon the scene, they speedily upset the balance of Nature, either directly by killing the birds and introducing new enemies, or by making the living conditions too difficult for birds. The flesh of birds is good to eat and therefore man killed them, sometimes with such unreasoning thoroughness that certain kinds, such as the Great Auk, the Dodo, and the wonderful Passenger Pigeon, were exterminated. The eggs of birds being good to eat, this has led man to greatly decrease those species of sea birds that nest in great colonies. That their feathers are beautiful and desired by man has led to the serious diminution of egrets, herons, terns and gulls, and to the practical extermination of birds of paradise.

But there are other ways in which man decimates birds besides actually shooting and trapping them. The clearing of farms destroys the nesting places of forest birds. The annual burning of grassy fields kills many, and deprives the remaining birds of

53

food by destroying insects. The destruction of brush and trees by cutting and burning eliminates the places where some birds prefer to nest, or if they nest in spite of this, their nests are out in the open and easily found and destroyed by natural enemies. Many swamps are being drained and the swamp-loving birds are driven out and deprived of their homes. Very often swamp birds, even more than others, are unable to adjust themselves to new conditions and nest elsewhere than in the swamps. The mowing machine annually kills many, and exposes the nests of additional ones that later die by heat, or by enemies that more easily find them. The spraying of fruit trees kills many birds that feed on the poisoned insects. All of these operations are connected with modern civilization, and this unintentional destruction of bird life is one of the prices we pay for being civilized.

But civilization has brought about many new enemies, and among the worst of these is the domestic cat. The pets that are kept about houses kill some birds, for all cats, no matter how well fed they are, are inveterate hunters, because of the inborn instinct that impels them. The bird hunting of a cat goes on even when it is well fed. They can not be taught to stop hunting birds, and the only way to cope with this bird hunting by pet cats is to keep them shut up where they can not reach birds. Pet cats are bad enough, but stray cats and cats that run wild are infinitely worse for hunger and the necessity of getting food redoubles their efforts, and they become even more skillful through this constant practice. Particularly careless of the birds are those people who keep cats during the winter, only to leave them behind when they shut up their houses and go away. It is estimated that the average cat kills a bird a week (in early summer when the nestlings are growing, and just after they leave the nest, the rate is much higher) throughout the year, or over fifty birds a year. It is also estimated that there are twenty-five million cats in the United States, and that they kill more than a billion wild birds per year!

Probably the first attempt at bird protection was to preserve the game birds that, through steady hunting, had decreased to an alarming extent. Not only was this the case throughout the United States, but all the older countries have had to meet the same problem. Some of them have done so, more or less effectually. Although the United States was originally blessed with a greater number and variety of game birds than most other countries, we have always had a large hunting population. First, from the necessity of securing food, and after that, because of the pleasure and recreation that sportsmen demand. This led to early efforts to protect our game with some success, in places delayed because of the ever increasing army of hunters, and because of much political jealousy. In this respect, North Carolina has had much the same experience as other communities, although perhaps blessed with more than her share of both game birds and jealous county politicians. When this state was first settled it contained so many game birds that it was the wonder of many less fortunate communities. Up to a few years ago, North Carolinian game, especially Bob-whites, Wild Turkeys, wild ducks and geese, were famous and attracted hunters from far and near. Such an army of sportsmen poured into the state that laws governing shooting soon became necessary. Unfortunately, in North Carolina every county made its own game laws. Unfortunate, because such a multiplicity of laws caused confusion, and because each county was too poor to maintain each its own game protection service. Furthermore, such a variety of different laws enabled the illegal hunter in one county to escape to another before he could be brought to account for his illegal acts. But politics prevented the enactment of a modern state law replacing the various county laws until the spring of 1927. Meanwhile, the game birds have suffered severely, the Woodcock and Turkeys being almost exterminated, and the Bob-whites, ducks, geese and small game birds seriously reduced.

In their efforts to protect their chickens, the farmers of North Carolina have carried on a serious warfare against the hawks and owls. And in this they have been ably assisted by hunters trying to kill all the supposed enemies of the game birds. And both these supposedly legitimate endeavors have been aided by the men and boys who carry guns, and shoot at every large bird for the mere pleasure of seeing it fall. Think of it! Killing birds it has taken Nature thousands of years to develop, for the mere pleasure of seeing them fall! This would be bad enough in any case, but they have picked out valuable birds to destroy! No one doubts the destructiveness of mice, especially on the farms and fruit orchards. Hawks and owls are the direct enemies of the mice, apparently provided especially by Nature to keep the destructive rodents in check.

To be sure some chickens and some game birds are killed by hawks and owls, but we should be sure we kill the *guilty* ones if we really want to protect the chickens and the Bob-whites. The big showy hawks that sail and circle high overhead are not bird eaters, they are hunting rats and mice, frogs and snakes. Yet, because they are easier to shoot and trap, these are the birds that are killed, while the real culprits are the ones that sneak through the forests and the brush. The only hawks that habitually prey on birds in the Sandhills are the Sharp-shinned and Cooper Hawks, and they are both wary, hard to find, and seldom out in the open. But by the policy previously pursued, the big beneficial hawks have almost been exterminated, while the Sharp-shinned and Cooper Hawks have not been decreased at all! The practice of placing traps on poles should be discontinued, because the guilty hawks do not perch in such places. Every hawk caught in a pole-trap in the Sandhills would have caught each year of its life the rats and mice that destroy about twenty dollars worth of grain per year!

The two most abundant owls of the Sandhills are the Screech Owls in winter, and the Barn Owls in summer. At present, they are the most efficient checks on the English Sparrows in Southern Pines and Pinehurst. The Barn Owl also catches mice, and as a mouse-catcher it attracted the attention of one of the Australian governments that recently imported a hundred or more of them to prey on the mice and rats that have been introduced there. I do not believe in introducing strange birds into any country *unless a careful study has been made in advance.* In this case, the study of the habits of the Barn Owls has been made and the Australians have decided that it is the best mouser, with fewest bad habits, that they can find. And yet the Sandhills farmers persecute these owls just because they are owls, inasmuch as a *few of the other owls sometimes kill birds.*

Perhaps the most promising movement of late years in the protection of birds has been that to establish sanctuaries, places where hunting, or any other killing of birds, is not allowed, and where the birds are watched over, protected and fed. A regular sanctuary can be established with the help of state laws giving additional protection, but any one can establish a sanctuary of his own, even if it be only a city lot. Birds are as quick to find out, and appreciate, the areas where they are welcomed as if they had some method of

Sandhills of North Carolina

Figure 13. Broom sedge, a favorite haunt of Bobwhites, Field Sparrows and other birds. Near Southern Pines, Feb. 5, 1926.

Figure 14.   Broom sedge with small oaks and a small pine, just south of Aberdeen, Feb. 20, 1926.   The best kind of country for birds and their enemies, the Sharp-shinned Hawks.

spreading the good news. Where many farms have less than one pair of birds nesting on an average acre, it might be possible to increase the number to about six pairs per acre. A pair of birds is considered to be worth at least fifty cents a year to any farm they choose to inhabit.

The most successful sanctuary that I know of in the Sandhills is the land surrounding the pond near the Mid Pines Golf Club, and watched over by the members of that Club. Because of this protection and the stopping of all shooting, ducks resort to this pond every winter in numbers, and remain there, when only a solitary duck can be found here and there on waters that are constantly open to hunting. Should the Mid Pines Club care to carry the experiment further, there is little doubt but that the planting of suitable native duck foods in their pond and artificial winter feeding of ducks would result in attracting so many birds that the place would be visited by many people just to see them.

For additional information on this subject see:

PEARSON, T. GILBERT, C. S. BRIMLEY and H. H. BRIMLEY. *Birds of North Carolina.* North Carolina Geological and Economic Survey, Raleigh, N. C. 1919. Pp. 1–380.

LANGE, D. *Our Native Birds.* The Macmillan Co., New York and London. 1899. Pp. 1–149. Price, $1.75.

HENDERSON, JUNIUS. *The Practical Value of Birds.* The Macmillan Co., New York. 1927. Pp. 1–342. Price, $3.50.

VALUABLE STUDIES STILL TO BE MADE

Considering all that has been said and written about birds, it might seem as if the work had all been done, and that nothing more could be added. As a matter of fact, comparatively little studying has been done on even the most common species of our birds. Take, for instance, the Mockingbirds: some have yellow eyes and others have brown eyes. Are the brown eyes more prevalent in one sex than in the other? Are yellow eyes a sign of maturity? If so, when does the color change from one color to the other? What determines whether the eyes be yellow or brown?

Perhaps the greatest unsolved avian problems are those connected with migration. Every one can help to unravel these problems by keeping careful lists of migrating birds and noting just when they arrive and depart, and all the particulars of wind and weather associated with these movements. The Biological Survey, U. S. Dept. of Agriculture, Washington, D. C., is very glad to get this information from all over the United States, and is acting as a great clearing house for migration data. This central collecting agency for data is necessary because this work can only be done by combining the observations of many bird-lovers over a wide extent of territory. Even the reports on the most common birds are wanted, and the bird observer who knows only a half dozen birds can report some very interesting data on them.

When a bird observer has advanced far enough to know practically all the birds of a neighborhood, he can become one of the bird-census takers for the Federal Biological Survey. This work is new, extremely important, and like the migration work, can only be accomplished by combining the reports of many observers. This work is being done entirely by volunteers and consists in counting and enumerating all the different birds nesting in a certain area, either by counting the singing male birds, or by counting the actual nests. The benefits to be secured from this work have already been given in a pamphlet by the U. S. Dept. of Agriculture: "Many problems concerning bird life can be solved by no other means than by bird censuses; that some can be solved, in part at least, by this work has already been proved, but many have not yet even been touched upon. How many birds per acre breed in the different

60

parts of the country, in the permanent marshes, and the forested regions of New England, the eastern mountains, and the Rockies? What is the relative abundance of the different species in the country as a whole and in the different life zones, and how are they distributed? Where are the centers of abundance for birds generally and for the several species? Are birds most abundant where they are most needed, about the farm, gardens, and orchards? How do altitude and latitude affect the numerical distribution of birds? What effect upon bird life has the presence of water, as a small stream or a river, a pond or a lake? What fluctuations take place in bird life from year to year, or over longer periods? When protection and encouragement bring about an increase in the number of birds nesting on a given tract, are there actually more birds in the locality, or is the increase due to a concentration of the birds from a larger area for nesting purposes? How do birds respond to changes in such environmental conditions as more intensive cultivation, changes in crops, or the clearing of woodland? How is irrigation affecting the bird life of the arid lands of the West? What changes will occur there in numbers and species, and how rapidly will they take place? How much have birds increased under protection? Are the present Federal and State laws adequate? What changes, if any, are taking place in the numbers and relative abundance of the several species?"[6]

For further information on this interesting work, the intending census taker should write to the Chief, Bureau of Biological Survey, U. S. Dept. of Agriculture, Washington, D. C.

Closely related to the studies anent migration and bird censuses is the making of local lists. To be sure, you may find a list has already been made for your section. In North Carolina very few local lists have been made and the Curator of the State Museum at Raleigh, Mr. H. H. Brimley, recently told me he is very anxious to see such lists from all parts of the state published.

Even if you find some other bird-student has already prepared a list for your locality, you still will have the pleasure of making your own list for your own use and for your friends. And herein lies one of the great attractions of bird study. You will soon find that

[6] Cooke, May Thatcher. Report on Bird Censuses in the United States, 1916–1920. U. S. Dept. of Agriculture. Dept. Bulletin No. 1165. Government Printing Office, Washington, D. C. 1923. Pp. 2–3.

your pleasure and enjoyment is not at all dependent upon discovering new facts unknown to other people. There is just as much satisfaction in watching, *and learning about for yourself*, a bird unfamiliar to you, as if that bird had not already been watched and studied by other people. It is this ever recurring newness of birds that makes them so very interesting to us.

If you have any leaning that way, be sure to write out your notes and experiences with the birds. Your writing will be very interesting to yourself and your friends, and you will be surprised to find how the mere writing out of your observations will serve to fix them in your own mind and how they will then seem to become more truly your own. Then, as your experience increases, you will find your articles more and more in demand by papers, magazines and other publications. With the fast increasing interest in birds, even short interesting letters from eight-year old boys and girls are being printed in increasing numbers.

The economic value of birds is another recent development of bird study, but it is one where an immense amount of information is still needed for the good of our gardens and farms as well as for the birds themselves. Any and every item you can get and make known about the good that birds do is a good accurate shot in the battle to protect and increase our birds. For the same reason we need all the information that can be obtained about birds at artificial feeding stations. The following suggestions have been given to direct these studies along the best lines:

"1. Try a variety of foods and note what kind of food is eaten by each species and what kind each seems to prefer. Does each kind of bird eat both vegetable and animal food, or confine itself to one kind? What bird eats the greatest variety of foods? Which birds will eat suet from a tree trunk?

"2. How do the various birds approach the counter? Do they give any warning of their coming by giving any call notes?

"3. After reaching the counter, note their actions. Do they stay on the trough and eat the food, or do they fly away with it first?

"4. Do the birds all crack seeds in the same manner?

"5. At what time in the morning are the first visits made, and at what time in the afternoon the last?

"6. Which birds seem to visit the counter most frequently during the day? Which least frequently?

"7. Make a list of the birds in accordance with the degree of which they show, placing the tamest first. Which ones will come to the window sill? Do any become so tame as to feed out of the hand?

"8. How early in the season do the birds begin to feed? Which come first? How late in the spring do the birds continue to come? Which remain the longest?

"9. Do any of the migrating birds in the spring come to feed?

"10. Make a list of the birds in the order of fear shown toward other birds, placing first those which are not driven from the trough by the approach of other birds and last those most easily driven away.

"11. Occasionally an individual bird has some peculiar marking by which it may be recognized. If you find any of this kind, make a special study of that individual, noting in what ways he differs from other individuals of the same species.

"12. In what kind of weather do the largest number of birds come to feed?

"13. Toward night, watch the bird houses or shelters that you may have provided and see what birds use them."[7]

We need more study of artificial bird houses so that we may know how to make the best. How can we get rid of the English Sparrows that monopolize the bird houses we put up? Why is one kind of bird house preferred to another? How can we make a house that birds will like better? Where should we put the house to attract birds more surely? Why is one site preferred to another? Is it better to clean out bird houses or let the birds do it? Why? What kinds of houses or nesting sites will bring a new species to nest near us? And countless other questions about this fascinating branch of study.

Finally, there is that most prominent trait of birds, their ability to sing, about which we know relatively so little. How did the first song start? When did it start? Through what stages of development did songs pass? Are bird songs truly musical? Can they be reduced to a score and reproduced by musical instruments? Why does a bird sing? How does he learn to sing? Is it a good thing for the singer, himself, or does his song expose him to new enemies? Do females sing? Why is it generally the male that sings? Why do different species have different songs? Why do different individuals of the same species have different songs? Why does the same individual bird vary his song at different times, or

[7] Trafton, Gilbert H. Methods of Attracting Birds. Houghton Mifflin Co., Boston and New York. 1910. Pp. 149–151.

during different periods of his life? And so we could go on pro-
pounding questions indefinitely, but enough has been said to show
that, much as we know about birds, there is infinitely more about
even the simple doings of common birds that we do not know.

For additional information on this subject see:

Mathews, F. Schuyler. *The Book of Birds.* G. P. Putnam's
Sons, New York and London. 1925. Pp. 1–323. Price, $3.00.

Mathews, F. Schuyler. *Field Book of Wild Birds and Their
Music.* G. P. Putnam's Sons, New York and London. 1921.
Pp. 1–325. Price, $3.50.

Saunders, A. A. *Bird Song.* N. Y. State Museum, Handbook 7. 1929. Price, $.50.

PLATE 3. CUTOVER FORESTS WITH OAKS AND LONG-LEAF PINES

1: Southern Hairy Woodpecker (male).
2: Southern Downy Woodpecker (male).
3: Southern Hairy Woodpecker (female).
4: Southern Downy Woodpecker (female).

5: Sharp-shinned Hawk (male).
6: Blue Jay.
7: Red-bellied Woodpecker (male).
8: Red-bellied Woodpecker (female).

(All figures about ½ life size)

DESCRIPTIONS AND HABITS OF THE WINTER BIRDS OF THE SANDHILLS

Note. First under each "Description" will be given the common name of each bird, followed on the same line by the number, or numbers, of the colored plates in this book showing this bird. The second line will give the Latin name by which the bird is known to the scientific workers, followed by the American Ornithologists' Union's number given to that bird in the List of North American Birds North of Mexico.

PIED-BILLED GREBE. Plate 2, page 42

Podilymbus podiceps (Linn.) A. O. U. No. 6

Field Identification. These are duck-like diving birds one-third the size of Mallards, with much longer necks in proportion. They can be identified by their dull brown color and small, whitish, chicken-like bills; and by their inclination to swim and dive when alarmed, instead of flying.

Description. Upperparts dull brown; throat, breast and belly white; upper breast washed with brownish; undertail conspicuously white; bill unmarked. In summer the upperparts are darker and more glossy; throat has a black patch; a black band across bill. Total length 13½ inches.

Distribution. Rather common throughout the winter; smaller numbers remaining at other seasons. In winter, members of this species go as far south as Chile and Argentina; in summer, they live as far north as New Brunswick, Quebec, Keewatin, Mackenzie and British Columbia.

Habits. In early February these grebes become markedly darker in plumage. A week later their throats begin to show black, but no marks, nor black rings, are seen around the bills until late in the month, but after that time all bills are ringed. They resume normal spring plumage late in February, and after that month they are all in spring plumage, although they continue to get darker and darker until the middle of March. In the Sandhills, these grebes are rather common all winter, there being at least one on every pond and reservoir, on some of the ponds there are two.

Once, I found four on a pond near Jackson Springs on February 26, 1927. All kinds of ponds (Figs. 10 and 15) seem suitable, but those with growths of water weeds, with rushes and cattails lining them, with old stumps sticking up here and there, and those with clear stretches of unbroken water, are preferred. But they like clear water better than muddy water, and still ponds better than streams having currents in them, although not caring much whether the water is shallow or deep. They are more on shallow water in the morning when actively feeding, and later they are out on more open water when they want to preen or sleep, or when they have been alarmed.

Once, I suddenly came upon a grebe in some brush and flooded trees near the shore of Silver Lake. It dived at once and made its way out through the flooded bushes but kept under water except to raise its bill above water for air now and then. On the other hand, another grebe alarmed on the open water, dived and came in near shore. Its swimming was done under water but at times it came up to breathe and peer about with only its bill and eyes above water. Once, it varied this by swimming some distance between dives with only its head above the surface. It is but proper to say that the last bird had deep water to retreat to along shore and it evidently knew that the background of bushes would be effective in hiding its head.

Usually grebes, in diving, spring forward and down in an arc, but at times one sinks without other motion, and so quietly and without ripples that the water seems to rise and swallow the grebe. When not so much alarmed, grebes often swim from one end of a mile-long lake to the other. They seldom leave the water but occasionally one jumps up on a floating log for a moment or two.

So much a matter of course did it seem to see Pied-billed Grebes diving and swimming when going from place to place, that I never thought of their flying, except on migration. So I was greatly interested to see one, with nothing to alarm it, suddenly take wing from the surface and fly to another part of the same lake. Apparently it flew simply because it was easier than swimming or diving. And, to my surprise, its rising and flying did seem easy; certainly its flight was easier, stronger and surer than the flight of a Coot. The grebe rose against the wind, kicking the water behind at each wing-stroke, and was soon eighteen inches or more above the sur-

Figure 15.   An artificial pond, long-leaf pines.   A favorite haunt of winter Kingfishers, near Pine Bluff, Feb. 11, 1926.

face. It only flew fifty feet but the whole proceeding reminded me of a feeding Goldeneye.

Other observers say that Pied-billed Grebes are rather scarce in North Carolina and not often seen, so I was rather surprised to find them comparatively common in the Sandhills. But that was before I noticed a possible reason for the former seeming scarcity. I found these grebes very wild indeed and also expert at hiding. On February 23, 1927, I found one on the upper end of a lake: at first, I did not see it, but soon afterward it was right there in front of me. By coming to the surface in, or near, weeds and other vegetation, it had completely escaped my notice. Again, on February 10, when I arrived at Juniper Lake in the morning, I examined its open part rather carefully without seeing any grebes. Yet, when I returned an hour later, there was a Pied-billed Grebe preening. Soon it disappeared again, although I did not see it go. All this was illustrative of how easily these birds can hide, especially if aided by a few stumps and bunches of weeds to break the open expanse of water. Another watchful Pied-billed Grebe on Juniper Lake hid in a small patch of water-grasses. After I had concealed myself for fifteen minutes it cautiously came out again and began moving about, but in doing so it was still careful to dive under the open spaces and appear above the water only in, or near, other bunches of grass.

Aside from this extreme caution when possible hunters come in sight, grebes are not easily frightened. I found I could park my car beside a lake and often the grebes would swim up as near as if I were not there at all. One grebe that I had previously considered wild, paid no attention to a train that thundered by and even whistled within two hundred yards of it. On the other hand when a fisherman rowed his boat past, a grebe I was watching dived at once and first came up near a stump with whose bark its color blended, then retreated into a flooded forest by diving and swimming under water. During its retreat it came to the surface at intervals for observation, but always came up quietly and remained perfectly motionless except that its head twisted from side to side. When swimming unalarmed on the surface, its head did not move forward and back as a Coots would. I noticed also that where the grebe was out on open water it appeared quite wary and difficult to approach, but in flooded brush it was quite easy to surprise one.

Toward spring I found some of the grebes so tame that they must have been migrants not yet aware of the extreme amount of shooting they would be subjected to in the Sandhills.

Grebes are curious. On March 24, 1927, two of them crossed a good-sized lake and swam up to the far end to investigate when they caught sight of a dog in the bushes on shore. One day when some Wood Ducks appeared, a grebe swam up near them with apparent curiosity and watched them as they swam past. Another time a grebe swam up near a pair of Hooded Mergansers and seemed to want to join them, although finally swimming off without doing so. Although I found from two to four grebes together at times during the winter I did not think their desire for companions was very keen. And as for other birds, the few times I saw grebes with Scaup Ducks, Mallard, Black Ducks and Wood Ducks these were mere chance happenings due to a desire for similar food.

About five weeks after the grebe flight already mentioned, I saw another grebe make a short flight. In this instance there were two grebes together, and one in the course of its feeding got ahead. Then the other grebe rose from the water and flew the hundred and fifty feet in pursuit. Again I was surprised to see how easily this bird got into the air. Like other birds of similar size it rose and flew against the wind.

On only one occasion (February 15, 1927) did I hear the love-call of a Pied-billed Grebe,—"cow, cow," repeated an apparently unlimited number of times. At least, I got tired of it before the grebe did, and that made it seem unlimited to me! Although this bird was "singing" in the middle of February, there was very little seasonal change as yet in the grebes, for it was not until later that the plumage changed. On February 21, 1927, I noted what I considered the first incoming migrant grebe. Otherwise, I found them present when I came to the Sandhills on December first and still present when I left on April first.

Grebes get practically all their food by diving, although once in a while they skim some seeds from the water surface. When they come back from a food dive, they come up with a rush that often carries them above the surface like a cork. Not only do grebes dive in open water and often dive and feed among the deep-water weeds and old, partly submerged stumps, but they are frequently seen diving near shore or along the edge of the weeds that extend from the shore out into the shallow water. Sometimes one grebe is diving and feeding out in the open water at the same time that another on the same pond is feeding in near shore. Sometimes the same grebe will alternate between the open water and the shallow water. Occasionally a grebe coming up from a dive flushes an insect from a tuft of grass, and dashes after it with long neck outstretched. Usually it scoops up the insect from the water's surface after chasing it but a few feet. Occasionally they catch small minnows in shallow water. One was even seen returning from a deep-water dive with a minnow two or three inches long that was swallowed soon after the surface was reached.

Usually after feeding a short time, grebes swim out into deeper water to preen. They preen their necks, wings and back but they seldom turn over on their sides as diving ducks do, or even attempt to dress their under plumage. Only once did I see one preening between dives, and at least once turning far over on its side to get at its underparts. After preening awhile, grebes rest quietly on the surface with their heads held back and their bills resting on their folded lower necks. Thunder and lightning do not alarm them, but during very hard showers they may keep only the tops of their heads and bills above the water.

Pied-billed Grebes were in couples most of the winter, but I am not prepared to say the sexes were actually paired. Soon after acquiring their breeding plumage in late February, they really began to pair.

HOODED MERGANSER

Lophodytes cucullatus (Linn.)　*A. O. U. No. 131*

Field Identification. These are trim, black, white and brown ducks smaller than Mallards. They are notable for the black and white crests of the males and the scraggly crests of the females; and for their small size.

Description. Male has his head, neck and back black; front of his large fan-like crest black, with the remainder white, but bordered by black; breast and belly white; sides cinnamon. Female has her throat, lower breast and belly white; remaining plumage various shades of brown; her head darker brown with a scraggly cinnamon crest. Total length 17½ inches.

Distribution. A few pairs of these pretty little mergansers are present in the Sandhills throughout the winter. In winter, Hooded Mergansers go as far south as Cuba, the Gulf states, Mexico and Lower California; in summer they range north to British Columbia, Great Slave Lake, Keewatin, Ungava and Newfoundland.

Habits. These mergansers are to be found on quiet waters such as reservoirs and artificial ponds (Figs. 10 and 15). Here, the Hooded Mergansers may be out on the open water, or near the shore, or even at the edge of a flooded gum tree forest. They do not appear to like streams and running water as other mergansers do.

They are very handsome and trim little ducks, especially when the crests are erect. Usually the females keep their crests up all the time, but the crests of the drakes are often down. When feeding, the drakes sometimes erect their crests. While in pairs, and especially while courting, the drakes' crests are erect most of the time, at other times they may be flashed up and down in a series of quick motions. Hooded Mergansers are quite tame in the Sandhills in spite of sharing in the persecution to which all the ducks there are subjected at all times. They are socially inclined and apt to be together; but they do not associate with any other species as a rule.

Of two pairs seen on February 9, 1927, one pair swam out across a small lake. When they had reached the far shore, the second pair flew up and across to join them. The start of their flight was somewhat labored, with heavy wing-beats, and a score of kicks at the water surface behind. When finally under way the flight was steady, rapid and direct. When they alighted they slid into the water full speed and plowed up a wake fifty feet long. The food of these Hooded Mergansers was small aquatic forms of animal life that they secured by diving. When they went down, they merely stretched their bills forward and went down in an are with very little effort or splash. As a rule a dive lasted ten to fifteen seconds. Generally when the birds reappeared on the surface, they shot high like a cork, but occasionally they came up very easily with only a bill appearing first, followed soon after by the head and neck and gradually the rest of the body. Once I saw a drake catch a minnow at least four inches long. After swallowing this catch head first, he preened for some time while his mate continued diving. Probably this pair were also feeding on vegetable matter.

In the Sandhills, these mergansers are in pairs all winter. On February 4, 1927, near Jackson Springs, I noted two pairs of Hooded Mergansers that were evidently mated, for they kept close together; if momentarily separated, they soon swam together, especially if the other pair was near. In this jealous display of affection the females were as conspicuous as the males. Five days later I saw these same two couples going through their mating ceremonies. Immediately on getting together the drakes began flashing their crests, and soon kept them up altogether throughout the series of mating motions that followed. These consisted of several short, fast swims in circles with many whirls and sudden turns. At short intervals the performer would rise in the water and stretch head and neck as high as possible, thrusting its bill high up and finishing by lowering the bill and jerking the head back once or twice. As each drake rose he kept his feet kicking the water below, vigorously. Sometimes two or three of these risings followed each other in rapid succession. Toward the end of the performance the head was thrown back from the extreme upper point until the crest rested on the drake's back, with the bill pointing up over the tail at an angle of forty-five degrees. From this extreme position the head gradually returned to normal. During the whole performance, lasting fifteen minutes, the drakes continued to swim here and there, in small circles, but never very far from each other. Both drakes took part, but the females manifested no interest whatever except that their crests were occasionally lowered. The drakes did not approach the females, and did not attack or chase each other, although they were never more than a few feet apart. Finally the females began swimming back toward the former feeding grounds and the drakes followed, although still engaged in their maneuvers even after the females had begun diving. Before and after these maneuvers each pair remained together.

MALLARD.   Pl. 2, page 42

Anas platyrhynchos Linn.   A. O. U. No. 132

Field Identification. Mallards are large ducks of the same size, or perhaps a little smaller, than domesticated mallards. They are easily identified by the green heads of the drakes and the mottled browns of the females; both have purple patches on each wing and both show a conspicuous white V formed in flight by the tail-feathers.

Description. The male has his whole head and throat glossy green; a white collar; breast rich chestnut; upper back dark grayish; four middle tail-feathers recurved above; spot on each wing rich purple, bordered by black and white. The females are yellowish brown, streaked, splashed and spotted with buffy and grayish brown. Total length 23 inches.

Distribution. Frequent on undisturbed waters throughout the winter. At this season they are found from Maryland, Ohio, Indiana, Wisconsin, Nebraska, Wyoming, Montana and Alaska south to Panama, Mexico and the Lesser Antilles. In summer they live from Maryland, Indiana, Missouri, Kansas, northern Mexico and Lower California north to the Pribilof Islands, Alaska, northern Mackenzie, Keewatin and Greenland. They are also inhabitants of Europe and Asia and in winter go south to Africa, India and Burma.

Habits. As a rule Mallards are found along the shores of ponds and small streams both with, and without, marshy shores; still, they sometimes go out on the open water when alarmed. In a section where they are so steadily hunted as they are in the Sandhills, the Mallards are wild and suspicious, even on waters where absolutely protected. Once I was watching a small flock from a blind when they became suspicious and swam out toward some previously unalarmed Scaups on the open lake. Evidently the Mallards were able to communicate their alarm to the other ducks for all of them swam to the far side of the lake before resuming their feeding. But the Mallards, themselves, were not very much alarmed for they soon came swimming back again. They swam one behind another in a line, and less frequently in a compact group.

On all occasions, Mallards are sociable and keep close together both on the water and while flying. But their association with other species of ducks is very slight, at least in the Sandhills. They are occasionally associated with Lesser Scaup Ducks and much more often with Black Ducks.

In the Sandhills at least, the Mallards eat seeds that they glean from grasses, or skim from the surface of the water. Occasionally one chases and catches an insect, but insect food seems to be taken only as chance brings it their way. When feeding in shallow water, the Sandhills Mallards occasionally put their heads under water, but spend most of their time gleaning seeds from the surface, and do none of the tipping so characteristic elsewhere. After feeding they usually swim out to open water, preen a while and then go to sleep a safe distance from shore.

BLACK DUCK. Pl. 2, page 42

Anas rubripes Brewst. A. O. U. No. 133

Field Identification. Same size as a Mallard and closely resembling it in every thing but color. These ducks are black, large in size and with a purple patch on each wing. In flight the black underparts and silvery linings of the wings are distinctive.

Description. Whole plumage so dark it seems black except in strong light. Top of the head rich brownish black; underparts dark blackish brown, the feathers all bordered by ochraceous-buff; back darker; spot on each wing purple, bordered by black and white. Total length 22 inches.

Habits. Black Ducks are found along the shores of ponds and small streams, although they often swim out on the more open water when alarmed. They inhabit waters having high dry shores as well as low marshy ones. If anything, the Black Ducks are more wary and, when suddenly alarmed, they fly promptly, shooting up into the air even more perpendicularly than Mallards do.

Black Ducks are more sociable in nature than others. Not only are they always in flocks during the winter, but they are usually associated with Mallards and Lesser Scaup Ducks whenever they are on the same waters. I have even seen them with a Pied-billed Grebe.

Distribution. Occasional all winter on undisturbed ponds. These are birds of eastern North America only; in winter, they go as far south as Florida, Georgia and the Gulf states; in summer, they live as far north as Keewatin, Ungava and Labrador.

A favorite food is the seeds of the grasses growing along shore, and gleaned by the Black Ducks from the plants or skimmed from the surface of the water. If, while they are feeding, they find insects also, this animal food proves very acceptable and is promptly caught and swallowed. When through feeding, Black Ducks are apt to seek a lee shore, or a hidden cove, where they can preen while sheltered from keen, wintry winds.

GREEN-WINGED TEAL

Nettion carolinense (Gmel.). *A. O. U. No. 139*

Field Identification. This is a small, dark duck only half the size of a Mallard. The male may be known by his chestnut and green head; the female by the green markings, without blue, on her wings.

Description. The male has a chestnut head with the sides of head green; chest vinaceous, with round black spots; back and sides with finely waved black and white lines; lower back grayish brown; a deep black stripe on each wing, and below that a metallic green spot. In the female the upperparts are varying shades of brown, each feather edged with gray or buffy; throat and sides of neck white, with small black spots; breast and sides rusty and spotted with black; wings similar to male's. Total length 14½ inches.

Distribution. These are winter birds only in the Sandhills, arriving early in the autumn and leaving late in the spring. In winter a few go as far south as the West Indies and Honduras but some remain as far north as there is any open fresh water. In summer these Teal live as far north as northwestern Alaska, northern Mackenzie, Keewatin, northern Ungava and Newfoundland.

Habits. Because of the incessant hunting this species is uncommon in the Sandhills except in the most secluded parts of clearwater streams such as Lumbee (Fig. 8) and Little Rivers. I have found Green-winged Teal making merry in shallow places with Mallards and Black Ducks, quacking sociably, swimming and dabbling about in the water. They are noticeably gregarious, huddling close together in small waters. Where entirely undisturbed, these are perhaps the tamest of ducks and the first to lose their fear of man. Elsewhere they are wild and suspicious. When alarmed, these little ducks swim together on the water and then all spring into the air at the same time like a covey of Bob-white. In pairs, the females take alarm and flush first. Their flight is very swift and the comparatively small wings make a whistling sound. They are fond of warm nooks, preening there and taking sun baths.

BLUE-WINGED TEAL

Querquedula discors (Linn.).   A. O. U. No. 140

Field Identification. A brownish duck much smaller than a Mallard. The male can be identified by the white crescent before the eye and the gray blue patch on each wing; the female lacks the white crescent.

Description. The male's head brownish black on top; a white crescent in front of eye; rest of head and throat dark ashy; breast and belly brownish, thickly spotted with black; back brownish black; a large grayish blue spot on each wing. The female's head and neck whitish, finely dotted with blackish; breast and belly lighter than male's; back similar to male's. Total length 16 inches.

Distribution. This species is found all winter in the Sandhills but is not common there. More often seen during migrations in autumn and spring. In winter members of this species are found as far south as the West Indies, Chile and Brazil and as far north as Illinois, Maryland and Delaware. In summer they live in our northern states and Canada as far north as Great Slave Lake, central Ungava and Newfoundland.

Habits. In the Sandhills, these small ducks are occasionally seen on quiet stretches of clear-water rivers (Fig. 8). They do not frequent the ponds because duck-hunting is too steady and incessant. In spite of this wariness and wildness, they are easily tamed where they are protected and encouraged to stay. They are sometimes seen with Mallards but are more apt to be in flocks composed only of their own kind. Food is secured by stretching their heads and necks down to the utmost, and by dabbling in shallow water. In places they skim the seeds off the water surface.

WOOD DUCK

Aix sponsa (Linn.).   A. O. U. No. 144

Field Identification. This is a rather dark duck smaller than a Mallard or Barn-yard Duck. If one gets close enough to see them, the rich and varied colors of the drake and the quieter but pleasing mottled colors of the female are unmistakable. Otherwise one should look for the dark coloration, the wings and other parts outlined by narrow white lines in flight, and the small chicken-like bill.

Description. The male has the crest, cheeks and crown green with purplish iridescence; many white lines on sides of head and a long one at base of the crest; throat white; breast purplish chestnut, with many white spots; sides buffy-ochraceous, thickly barred with fine black lines; back olive-brown; spot on each wing deep blue. The female has the throat and a stripe around her eye and extending backward, white; head brown; breast and sides grayish brown streaked with lighter; back darker brown. Total length 18½ inches.

Distribution. This species is found throughout North Carolina at all times and is probably the only species of duck that nests in the Sandhills. Wood Ducks range as far south in winter as southern Texas, Florida and Cuba; in summer they go north as far as Nova Scotia, New Brunswick, northern Ontario, Saskatchewan and southern British Columbia.

Habits. These ducks are found in two different types of habitat: streams flowing through forests or weedy marshes; and open ponds (Figs. 10 and 15) and lakes, especially where old stumps protrude above the water or where there are water weeds and grasses to conceal the ducks. They are more active than other ducks and are usually moving from place to place, sometimes swimming quite rapidly. At times a Wood Duck perches on a submerged stump or log. Whenever one comes too suddenly upon them, they do not rise so perpendicularly as the Mallards and Black Ducks do, but they get under full headway even quicker if that be possible.

As with so many ducks, the females gave the alarm and darted away first with the drakes following. And yet, when feeding in pairs, it was the drakes that were the more watchful and suspicious. In spite of this, these ducks were usually quite tame, permitting railroad trains to pass within a few hundred feet. Even when an engine whistled within two hundred yards a pair of Wood Ducks remained unmoved. A freight train within two hundred feet of a pair preening on shore caused them no uneasiness at all. They paid no attention to automobiles passing, and not even to my own car when I stopped it within two hundred and fifty feet. But, strange to say, a passing wagon caused more alarm and the Wood Ducks then swam farther away. In this case they swam across open spaces rapidly with the female in the lead; only on getting near stumps or in clumps of weeds did they stop and look back at the wagon. These ducks showed no fear at all of a big Black Vulture as it swept over only a few feet above them; and they seemed able to distinguish it from a hawk.

A pair of Wood Ducks seen on March 21, 1927, were quite devoted to each other and never separated very far, although constantly calling to each other in low tones. Although the Wood Ducks were in flocks during most of the year, they appeared to keep to themselves more than most other ducks, and I did not see them with any other kinds. Once I saw a grebe near a pair of Wood Ducks but it was evident the grebe was there only through its own curiosity.

The flight of Wood Ducks is rapid and direct, and their small size only serves to make it seem even more so. Since many of them live and nest in the forests, they are skillful in dodging trees, although it seems strange to us to see a duck in such surroundings. Sometimes they fly above the forests, following the course of the stream hidden below. They also fly out over the ponds and marshes, following the courses of open water as a rule. While flying, as well as while swimming, these ducks frequently call to each other. Their alarm-note is a low whistled "co-eek" repeated at short intervals. Usually the female utters it, at least at the start.

As Wood Ducks swim along through, or near, the water weeds, they glean seeds from the surface, but do not dive. One pair that I watched fed on the surface for two hours before the female began to thrust her head and neck under and even to tip up her whole body in her efforts to reach the submerged tidbits. Sometimes in the course of her feeding she flushed up insects that sought to escape, but she always caught them by swift little swimming rushes. Usually after feeding an hour or so, Wood Ducks rest and begin to preen either on the water or after mounting a partly submerged stump. At times, especially during the middle of the day, they stop feeding and go ashore to preen and sleep. As a rule they pair off and mate about the first of March in the Sandhills, but it is likely that many of the migrants are paired before coming up from farther south, although several pairs may unite to form small flocks.

Figure 16.   Open shrub-oak and pine forest east of Pinehurst, Feb. 1, 1926.   Favorite haunt of a pair of Red-headed Woodpeckers.

LESSER SCAUP DUCK

Marila affinis (Eyt.).　*A. O. U. No. 149*

Field Identification. A black and white duck smaller than a Mallard. Easily identified by its black head and blue bill. As a rule it frequents deep water and secures its food by diving.

Description. Head, neck, breast and upper back black; back and shoulders with wavy black and white lines so arranged that they appear light gray; spot on the wing white; belly white; bill blue. Female has white around base of blue bill; head, neck, breast and back brownish black; spot on wing and belly white. Total length 16½ inches.

Distribution. These are the commonest ducks in the Sandhills on *protected waters*. In winter these ducks are found from British Columbia, Nevada, Colorado, Lake Erie and New Jersey south to the Bahama Islands, Lesser Antilles and Panama; in summer they live north of their winter range as far as the Yukon River, Mackenzie, Hudson Bay and Ontario, but they are not known to breed east of the western part of Lake Erie.

Habits. These ducks are usually on small lakes and ponds, and are not found on streams and rivers. In fact, the only place I found them at all regularly was on the lake beside the Mid Pines Club. Here they were undisturbed and some individuals spent the entire winter there, from November to April. Sometimes Scaups feed near shore, sometimes even in narrow channels amid grasses and weeds in marshes, and again amid the butts of gum trees growing in the water. Quite often while quietly swimming on the surface, Scaups will lift themselves almost out of the water and while apparently standing on the surface will flap their wings vigorously. Where they are never disturbed, Lesser Scaup Ducks become very tame, and spend their time swimming, diving and even sleeping close to where automobiles are constantly passing. On the open water Scaup Ducks sleep with their heads folded back and under a wing in the customary position.

While sleeping, preening and moving from the feeding grounds these ducks work in unison. On February 2, 1927, a flock that had been feeding, slept for twenty minutes, during which time each bird gave an occasional kick to the water to counteract wind-drift, then they awoke, preened a little and went to diving and feeding again. At one time a small dog on shore attracted their attention, and they swam toward it with a female in the lead. For some time they showed great curiosity, but gradually lost interest and resumed feeding.

Lesser Scaups are, perhaps, the most social of our ducks. At times the groups scatter while feeding, but this scattering is only temporary and they soon gather again into one compact flock. Not only are they socially inclined with their own kind, but Lesser Scaup Ducks are often in company with grebes and sometimes with Mallards.

During the autumn of 1926, these ducks were rather numerous on the lake near Mid Pines Club. All through December the number remained about forty-five. About January 11, 1927, there was a sharp cold spell that froze the whole surface and they departed, leaving only one female duck behind. In time three drakes joined her, only to be driven away again by the second hard freeze on March 1. After that the number of Scaups gradually increased again until there were four females and a drake present on March 25, 1927.

Most of the favorite foods of these ducks are to be had only by diving in the deeper waters of the open lake, but some food is secured along shore and in shallower water. Sometimes these ducks feed by diving in water only a foot deep or a little over. At each dive they spring upward slightly, then forward and down. Their food in this case is probably vegetable matter. At times they skim from the water surface the seeds brought there by rains. Almost always after feeding, Lesser Scaup Ducks begin to preen while resting on the water, turning far over on one side, and then on the other, to get at their lower plumage. Then they are apt to go to sleep for a half hour before feeding again.

AMERICAN BITTERN

Botaurus lentiginosus (Montag.). *A. O. U. No. 190*

Field Identification. A yellow brown bird of the marshes, larger than a Crow and almost as large as a Buzzard. Their wings are small in comparison with the body and they have a slow, awkward, labored flight. They can be identified by their brownish color, everywhere streaked, and their light green legs.

Description. Upperparts a mixture of buffy brown and ochraceous, a little slaty on top of head and back of neck; a black stripe down each side of neck; underparts with creamy spots and brown stripes. Young birds are similar, but the browns usually darker in shade. Total length 28 inches.

Distribution. Although I did not actually see any of these birds during the winter they might occur in the Sandhills at that time. The first one seen was on March 12, 1927, and no doubt was a migrant. In winter Bitterns go as far south as Cuba and Guatemala; in summer as far north as Newfoundland, Keewatin, southern Mackenzie and central British Columbia. They make their homes from the Atlantic to the Pacific wherever there are swamps or wet meadows suitable to them.

Habits. The most striking thing about Bitterns is that, for such comparatively large birds, they are so seldom seen. To be sure they are never numerous in any one place, but there are usually one or two hidden in every suitable swamp or thick, reedy, grassy margin of a stream. They are not likely to be in the *thickets* that line so many North Carolina streams. When unalarmed they draw in their heads and long necks and stand quietly in a compact, hump-backed attitude. But when suspicious or alarmed, the long necks are stretched out and heads and bills pointed straight up to as high as the birds can reach. Until the suspicious object has disappeared the Bitterns maintain this attitude, and it is astonishing how well the bird's outline and striped plumage blends with the tall reeds by which they are usually surrounded. When they move off, Bitterns are apt to lower their heads and necks and hold their bodies horizontal.

When the flight is short, the heads and necks are outstretched, but in longer flights the necks are folded back upon themselves. I found places, in March, where a Bittern had dug out mouse nests on the high ground at the base of stumps; on the marshes they dug out frogs in the same way.

GREAT BLUE HERON

Ardea herodias herodias Linn.   *A. O. U. No. 194*

Field Identification. This is a big gray-blue bird with body larger than a Mallard Duck's, with wings so extensive that it seems larger than a Buzzard. When standing, the long bill, neck and legs are out of all proportion to the small, slim body; in flight the head and long neck are folded back in an S on the shoulders, the legs being stretched out stiffly behind.

Description. General color above blue-gray; below, white striped with buff and black and some slatish. In spring and summer, the head is crested with black plumes. Total length 42 to 50 inches.

Distribution. Although these are normally only summer birds in the Sandhills, they are occasionally seen there in very mild winters. In winter they are found as far south as the West Indies, Panama and Venezuela; in summer they go north as far as Prince Edward Island, northern Ontario, central Manitoba, central Alberta and British Columbia.

Habits. Although these birds are really scarce here, they would probably be more often seen if they did not move about and feed so much by night. Probably they would be more common if they were not shot at by every hunter who seems to think every large bird makes an excellent mark. Under these conditions the Great Blue Herons are more apt to be seen about absolutely protected ponds.

The movements of these birds are slow and deliberate until food is sighted, and then they are rapid and decisive. In the Sandhills Blue Herons are always solitary; but elsewhere they nest in colonies in suitable places. Here, we see them on the ground, but their nests are placed usually on the tops of tall trees. The flight of the Heron is powerful and swifter than the slow and deliberate wing-strokes would lead one to suppose.

Their favorite foods are small frogs, tadpoles, and minnows, but Herons will also eat mice and animals of similar size. As a rule, they swallow their smaller prey whole and do not either tear it up or beat it to pieces.

KING RAIL

Rallus elegans Aud. *A. O. U. No. 208*

Field Identification. A dark, ungainly bird smaller than a Crow and partial to small fresh-water marshes and the undergrowth along streams. They are darker and larger than other Rails and very reluctant to fly up from the low tangle where they skulk. Since they run under the grasses and brush and are expert at dodging they are very difficult to find and watch. When they are found they skulk away rather than fly. Even their flight is low and skulking, and much like the low running flight of an ungainly scared chicken.

Description. Upperparts and wings are varying shades of brown, some almost black; throat with white patch; neck and breast reddish brown; belly and sides darker brown, barred with contrasting white streaks. Total length 15 inches.

Distribution. A rare, scarce bird in the Sandhills in winter, more common in summer. In winter they live as far south as Cuba, Florida and Texas; in summer they go as far north as Connecticut, New York, Ontario and southern Minnesota.

Habits. My first introduction to this bird in the Sandhills was interesting, for I was driving with Dr. John W. Achorn to attend the organization meeting of the Southern Pines Bird Club. About a mile south of Aberdeen a branch covered by a dense thicket of bushes, cat-briars and wild grapes crosses the road. As Dr. Achorn and I neared this point a King Rail darted across the road in front of us.

AMERICAN WOODCOCK. Pl. 2, page 42

Philohela minor (Gmel.). A. O. U. No. 228.

Field Identification. A plump brown bird with a very long bill and larger than a robin. They are almost always to be found in the thickets along the numerous streams that flow through the Sandhills, especially in daytime; and not out in the open as that other long-billed bird, the Wilson Snipe, is. They are solitary, and rarely more than one, or at most two, are found together.

Description. Head mottled with various shades of brown; a dark line from bill to eye; upperparts cinnamon color, mottled, waved and intermixed with grayish, reddish and black; tail brownish black, tipped with gray above, silvery below; underparts reddish brown, more reddish on the sides; eyes large and dark brown; bill nearly three inches long. Total length, including bill, 11 inches.

Distribution. Woodcock are found in the Sandhills at all seasons of the year, but it is probable that the individuals seen in winter are different ones from those seen in summer. In winter some Woodcock are found as far south as Texas and southern Florida; and in summer some go as far north as Nova Scotia, southern Quebec, northern Michigan and southern Manitoba.

Habits. Since the Woodcocks' preferred haunts (Fig. 11) are only a fraction of the territory, if one is found others are apt to be near. A favorite thicket is usually tenanted by one bird after another should the earlier ones be shot or killed. They do not associate with other birds, although other birds might accidentally be found near them.

The food of the Woodcock is largely worms and small subterranean forms of animals which are secured from the soft ground and from mud near springs and streams. The bill of a Woodcock is long and the end of the upper half is flexible and so sensitive that it is used as a probe. During the short time that their bills are in the ground, the Woodcocks are able to feel their prey, grasp it and pull it out, or swallow it if it is small. In passing along the streams where these birds live, we often see their feeding grounds where they have perforated the top with small round holes the size of a lead pencil, while probing for food.

These birds pair off so early that they are one of the few birds whose nests might be found before the end of March. The nests are very difficult to locate, for they are only slight hollows in the fallen leaves, and the eggs themselves are brownish in color. In the Sandhills the eggs are laid as early in some cases as the latter part of February; and I have seen young birds as early as the first week in April. Since they are able to leave the nest soon after hatching, there is no chance of finding a Woodcock's nest by watching the old birds suspected of having young.

WILSON'S SNIPE

Gallinago delicata (Ord.). *A. O. U. No. 230*

Field Identification. A brown, sparrow-like bird with a very long bill and with a body that looks smaller than a Robin's. Its flight is erratic and it utters "sceep, sceep," as it springs up in alarm. Sometimes, when close, the rufous on the tail-feathers can be seen on the flying snipe. This bird is a lover of fresh-water meadows and swamps and is found both on marshes covered with tall weeds and grasses, and on open marsh where all the cover has been burnt, but it is not likely to be in brushy places as the Woodcock is.

Description. Upperparts dusky and mottled brown, a pleasing but irregular pattern; two dusky stripes on the crown and one extending back from the bill through each eye—between these dusky stripes are lighter ones; underparts soiled white, the chest, sides and neck spotted with dusky brown in rows; outer tail-feathers barred with black and white, inner ones black but barred with rufous near end and tipped with whitish. Total length 11¼ inches.

Distribution. Normally these would be only migratory birds passing through the Sandhills in spring and rarely in the autumn, but where there are springs to keep the ground soft and unfrozen one or two birds may stay all winter. In the spring the Wilson Snipe, on their way north, may be seen during warm spells in late February and in March. In winter they go south as far as Central America and the West Indies and even to Colombia and southern Brazil. In summer they are found in the northern United States and throughout Canada as far north as northwestern Alaska, and throughout Mackenzie, Keewatin and northern Ungava.

Habits. Wilson Snipe have even been seen out on burned-over land whose soil was soft but not necessarily marshy. They are almost impossible to see on the ground even where there is practically no cover. Where there is ample cover, they often lie hidden until almost trod upon, then dart up with a sudden "seep, seep" and fly away with swift, erratic flight. After flying a short distance their flight becomes more direct, but is still very swift. Usually when they fly up from the ground they rise against the wind and get under full headway very quickly indeed. When I flushed a pair on the marshes of Juniper Lake on March 19, 1927, they were separated, but after flying parallel courses for a few hundred feet, they gradually drew together and still more gradually, rising higher and higher in air, flew away over the fields and farms and about five hundred feet above them.

The food of the Snipe is largely worms extracted from the mud and soft soil. As with the Woodcock the Snipe's bill is long and the tip of the upper half is flexible and so extremely sensitive that the bird can tell in a fraction of a second if there is food to be had in the dark mud two inches below the surface, and completely out of sight. A Wilson Snipe is very active and quickly drives its long bill into the mud straight down with the full weight of the bird's body behind it. I once watched a Snipe feeding and at every stroke its bill went in clear up to its eyes. The strokes were continuous and rapid, like a woodpecker's, possibly eighty strokes per minute and each time in a slightly different place. In an hour this Snipe covered a space six inches wide and eight feet long. It secured food about every six strokes, there being a momentary pause each time to swallow it.

Many of the Snipe that pass through the Sandhills are already paired when they arrive from farther south, and no doubt continue their flight north in pairs.

KILLDEER. Pl. 11, page 272

Oxyechus vociferus vociferus (Linn.). *A. O. U. No. 273*

Field Identification. A brown, black and white bird the size of a Robin with the following distinguishing marks: two bands of black across the otherwise white throat and breast; rufous lower back; long, narrow wings; the ringing cry of "kill-dee, kill-dee."

Description. Forehead, a ring around neck, a band on breast, lower breast and belly white; front of crown above forehead, a ring around neck and a band on breast black; crown and back grayish brown; lower back rufous; tail-feathers rufous, and tipped with black and white. Total length 10½ inches.

Distribution. Although these birds are found in North Carolina at all times of the year, they are more common in the Sandhills from November to March and especially numerous in late February and early March. In winter Killdeers go as far south as Venezuela and Peru and stay as far north as California, Arizona, Texas, Indiana and New Jersey. In summer they migrate north to Quebec, Keewatin, southern Mackenzie and British Columbia. Some individuals, however, remain as far south as Mexico and the Gulf coast.

Habits. During the winter the Killdeers of the Sandhills are mainly on the golf course at Pinehurst (Fig. 12), and on the neighboring polo fields and race-course, but at times they are on the fields near the Pinehurst stock-yards. All four of these localities are open grassy fields affording the birds ample opportunities to run down and capture the small insects upon which they prey. Killdeers are on the golf links early in the morning, and later they fly before the first golfers to the nearby but undisturbed race-course. No doubt they spend the nights and early mornings on the golf links and the remainder of the day on the race-course, for the golf links afford a wider field for hunting insects. These birds are also on the polo field during the first half of December, but probably the more steady use of these fields later drives off the birds there as it does from the golf links. Three times in late January I found Killdeers in old, but rather open, cow-pea fields. Once in December and once in early March I found them on an old grassy cornfield. On February first there were three Killdeers on a wheat field, but only once in all my experience did I find these birds on a freshly plowed field. Not until March 12, 1927, did I find a pair of them on a wet or swampy habitat.

On the ground, Killdeers are wonderfully quick and alert. They do not hop, but walk and run with such speed and adroit dodging that it is useless to attempt to catch one. On cold, windy days and rainy, windy days, they prefer to face the wind both while on the ground and while flying. When chasing insects on rainy days they always end their run with a sharp turn and face the rain again. On warmer days, the wind may ruffle their feathers without discomfort.

Early in the winter Killdeers stay in couples and singles, promptly chasing away any third or intruding individual. But even during this period, on being alarmed, several couples will run together and fly away in a small flock. By the fifteenth of February, they are habitually in small flocks and so continue throughout the month. This, however, is during the first incoming migration movement. Usually after a flight, or after being alarmed, Killdeers remain in one spot, tipping their bodies up and down rapidly. This is an unconscious nervous act that gradually subsides as the birds grow less and less suspicious.

As a rule these birds pay no attention to other species. Not until March 1, 1927, did I see an exception. It was snowing hard that day and I found twelve Killdeers squatted near some feeding Horned Larks. Each lark had dug itself a hole in the snow. As they were busily picking up seeds, three of the Killdeers gradually "came to life," and flew over to see what the Horned Larks were doing. They actually drove the Larks out of their hollows, but were not interested in the seeds and soon returned to their former state of inactivity. This was not the only time I saw them near Horned Larks. In the same way I found temporary associations of the Killdeers with Meadowlarks, Doves and Robins; but I did not see a case of actual association with upland birds. Had there been other shorebirds in the neighborhood there might be a different tale to tell.

The flight of the Killdeer is light and airy, although at times very wavering and erratic. Usually they fly low and at a speed of about twenty-five miles an hour, but I have also seen them circle high in the air. Still, they are seldom seen flying in the Sandhills unless actually alarmed.

These Sandhills Killdeers do not at all deserve the name "vociferus." In all I saw more than two hundred, but only two gave their calls. Once in December a single individual intruded on a feeding couple and was at once chased away, the pursuer uttering low calls as it did so. Late in February some migrating Killdeers flushed from the Pinehurst Golf Links and flew away crying "kill-dee, kill-dee," with the usual mournful cadence.

When I first noted Killdeers about December 1, there were four couples near Pinehurst, and this number remained about the same until a cold, snowy period early in January reduced it to a single couple. The two latter promptly deserted the race-course where they had been staying, and moved over to the stock-yards. Here they subsisted on garbage in the hog-runs and on insects attracted by the garbage, from January 12, 1927, until February 2, when they moved back to the race-course. Three days later the number increased to eleven, due, I believe, to the arrival of the first wave of incoming migrants from the south. It then gradually increased to thirty-eight birds on the last of February. On March 1, 1927, the severest snowstorm known in this section for years drove the Killdeers away again for a second time. Most of them flew away, perhaps to a temporarily better climate, but at least twelve remained and moved over to a grassy cornfield near the stock-yards.

Nine birds weathered the storm in this vicinity, although they were out in the unsheltered field facing the driving snow and getting only a little shelter from the corn hills and occasional tufts of grass. After that storm they steadily decreased in number as they left, two at a time, on the northward migration probably.

Throughout the winter these Killdeers depend entirely on the small insects they catch in the grass. They walk over the grass until they sight an insect, and then quickly run it down and eat it. I found some birds feeding on scattered chaff and manure, and assumed they were catching insects there. For I noted then, and also at other times, that these Killdeers apparently did not eat seeds of any kind. I noted also that they do not *scratch* for insects, although one was seen to find a worm on the golf links and pull it out.

Normally, their food contains so much liquid, that I doubt whether they drink any water. At any rate I did not see them doing it. Neither did I see any of them bathing. But on rainy days, they did not object to the rain or seek any shelter beyond facing any wind that might be blowing. So far as the rain was concerned the Killdeers rather liked it, for I found them shaking themselves as if bathing in the falling rain and then preening afterward.

All through the winter, they were roughly paired. They might separate two or three hundred feet while feeding, but they always came together again soon. Still, the first actual mating that I saw was on January 28, 1927.

BOB-WHITE. Pl. 6, page 168

Colinus virginianus virginianus (Linn.) A. O. U. No. 289

Field Identification. Same length as a Robin, but the head and neck smaller and the body much plumper; dark brown in color. In the spring the whistled "bob-white" notes are characteristic. When a flock is flushed, it explodes into birds flying in all directions with very rapid wing-beats and swift flight. These birds are normally found in open fields, but they may take refuge in thickets in stormy weather, when frightened, or to roost at night.

Description. The male has the upperparts mottled reddish brown, chestnut, buffy and blackish brown; tail ashy-gray; front

Figure 17. Holly trees in Carolina Inn grounds, Pinehurst, Feb. 5, 1926. Well liked by Blue Jays.

of crown, a band from bill extending back to neck and a band on upper breast black; throat white; a broad white line from bill passing over eye to side of neck; lower breast and belly white, barred with black. Female has the throat, line over eye, and fore-head pale ochraceous-buff. Total length 10 inches.

Distribution. These birds live the whole year wherever found, but they seemed to be rather scarce in the Sandhills. They live only in eastern North America from southern New England, New York, Ontario, Wisconsin, and southern Minnesota and South Dakota south to northern Texas, the Gulf states and Georgia. South of this range there are other species of Bob-whites.

Habits. During the winter of 1925–6 there was a nice covey of Bob-whites inside the grounds of the Carolina Inn at Pinehurst (Fig. 17), and about the same time I found another covey on the edge of the Pinehurst Golf Links. These were tame and no doubt found a good living so close to man. On the other hand a covey was found later living in the densest and wildest of thickets far away from man's haunts. Bob-whites like weedy corners of corn-fields next to a tangle of blackberry briars, cane, cat-briars and brush into which they can retreat at a moment's notice. They also frequent the edges of cotton fields, especially if a corner be grown up to broom-sedge (Figs. 13, 14, 16, 19, 20, 22) and low brush. They live in alfalfa fields, especially in March, when the alfalfa is tall enough to hide them well. In good cover, they are not so wild and will often permit a person to almost step on them before flying. The birds that I found in the Carolina Inn grounds ap-parently spent their entire time there, even at night. On February 1, 1926, a covey of eight were found under a holly bush (Fig. 17) there just as they had roosted, all in a circle with their heads facing out. From there they ran rapidly out across the open ground to a cedar, looking very neat and trim with their bodies and heads held erect. Birds that had been shot at, flew to the nearest thicket; but tame birds merely flew a short distance and pitched down again into comparatively open shrubbery.

Where Bob-whites are not alarmed they run from brush, fol-lowing one another at short intervals, and wait a few minutes before darting on to the next cover; but under good cover they wander here and there as food or fancy dictates. Their wings are so comparatively short, wide and rounded, they give the birds an excessively speedy flight from the very start. This coupled with the tendency of these birds to fly to the densest thicket, is what saves them from their enemies. When we add to their natural enemies the host of sportsmen that find pleasure in the pursuit of the Bobwhite, we wonder at its ability to survive even after we allow for the large families hatched two or three times each year. Although they pair off and mate in April, they are always in flocks, or coveys, during the winter.

Their food consists chiefly of grass seeds, waste grain and berries during the winter. In addition, probably fifteen per cent. of their food consists of insects among which are numbered some of the most destructive farm pests—potato bugs, cucumber beetles, wireworms, corn billbugs, cotton boll weevils, army worms, bollworms and cutworms.

WILD TURKEY. Pl. 1; frontispiece

Meleagris gallopavo silvestris (Vieill.). A. O. U. No. 310a

Field Identification. Smaller than a domestic turkey and with a trimmer, wilder and more "gamey" look. They live mostly in, and near, swamps and river bottoms.

Description. Usually somewhat smaller, but may be distinguished from the domestic race chiefly by the chestnut instead of white tips to the tail-feathers and small feathers just above tail. These differences exist because the domestic turkey was derived from the Mexican sub-species (*Meleagris gallopavo gallopavo*). Total length of male 48 to 50 inches; weight 10 to 25 pounds.

Distribution. These fine birds have been killed out of most of their former range, which included the southwestern United States and all of the Great Plains north to southern Canada. They are still found over most of North Carolina wherever there are undisturbed forests of the kind preferred. In the Sandhills there are two or three groups totaling perhaps thirty birds in all. They are resident and non-migratory wherever found. Every effort should be made to preserve these birds.

Habits. Turkeys have largely retired to the deep swamps for they prefer to roost in trees standing in water; but occasionally they move out on the drier upland. When undisturbed they move about mostly on the ground, but at night fly to their roosts and in the early morning fly out again. On the ground they are quick in movement and strong runners. On the wing, they are quick, strong, direct fliers. Turkeys, except the hens with nests, are in flocks at all times.

In the spring (March in the Sandhills) the gobblers begin to strut and court the hens. Since an old gobbler is something of a polygamist he soon gathers a little harem of from one to four hens. This group scatters and the females find good, secure places on dry ground where they lay from ten to fifteen eggs in a slight hollow in the leaves. Fresh eggs may be found in May and the young birds appear toward the end of the same month. Within a few hours after birth, they desert the nest and follow their mother everywhere she leads them. She takes good care of them, fights for them when she can, hides them when she must, and shelters them from storms. Even so, they have many enemies and only a small proportion live to grow up to maturity. Nevertheless, man is their one great enemy; if Turkeys were given adequate protection no doubt they would increase again over practically every part of their old range where there is any wild forested land at all suitable for them.

MOURNING DOVE. Pl. 8, page 210

Zenaidura macroura carolinensis (Linn.).　　*A. O. U. No. 316*

Field Identification. A brownish bird (pigeon-like in shape, actions and flight) larger than a Robin but much smaller than a domestic Pigeon. These doves have a long, rounded, fan-like tail marked with black and deeply tipped with white, conspicuous just as the birds alight. Generally found on the ground of fields and not often in trees.

Description. The male has his upperparts olive-brown; crown of head bluish; sides of neck marked with iridescence; tail-feathers gray, banded with black and broadly tipped with white; breast vinaceous; belly light buff; legs and feet pinkish. Female birds are duller. Total length 12 inches.

Distribution. This is a common bird throughout the Sandhills at all seasons. In winter these Doves are found as far south as

Panama; in summer they live as far north as the most southern provinces of Canada and from the Atlantic to the Pacific coast.

Habits. There are not so many cowpea fields in the Sandhills, at least when compared with the cornfields, the cotton fields, or even the hay fields, and yet, wherever there is a cowpea field Doves are sure to be found congregating. But many Doves are also found in old cornfields (Figs. 18 and 20), especially the weedy ones, for they are after grass seed and weed seed rather than corn. Cornfields are mentioned because weedy cornfields are more numerous than cotton fields, and yet weedy cotton fields also attract these birds. The next most common resort of the Doves is the hay fields throughout the winter, although these birds are perhaps most conspicuous there in February. Fallow fields and weedy fields of all kinds—old watermelon fields, vineyards, grassy peach orchards, and old tobacco fields—are also sought out at times. Possibly because plowed fields are not numerous in winter, Doves were seen on them only occasionally. Doves fly so much from field to field and from feeding grounds to night roosts and back again that they frequently pass over houses and even over some of the larger towns.

Most of the wild lands of the Sandhills are covered by shrub oaks and sapling pines and here also are some Doves—usually only as birds flying over, but sometimes they descend to the grassy floor of the forest, although not in the denser woods. At times they perch in oaks, maple trees and on the lower limbs of tall pines. Sometimes they are perched on the very tip of a long-leaf pine, especially if there should be a dead limb there; occasionally on gum trees and liquidambars, and in the low blackberry briars, catbriars and brush thickets over streams. At other time they are in the brush and weeds at the edges of ponds and marshy places.

Doves walk with very short, quick steps, with their heads nodding forward and back in time to each step. At times resting birds are extraordinarily tame, but as a usual thing they are wild and difficult to approach. This is peculiarly the case when they are in large flocks, as they often are during the winter, when as many as three hundred may be together in a single field. These flocks are temporary and unstable, easily breaking up into couples and small groups; but it is an exception to find a single Dove absolutely alone. On the other hand they remain more or less paired all winter.

Although Doves seem to be gregarious they are seldom in company with other birds. I have seen them near Meadowlarks, Horned Larks, Rusty Blackbirds, Kildeers, Flickers, Bluebirds and Crows—more often the first named. But all these associations were temporary and could be readily explained by similar food or haunts.

When Doves fly up from the ground (and they usually start against the wind) they make a peculiar twisting, jerking start. After once getting under way the flight is swift, level and usually in long sweeping "S" curves, although sometimes much more direct. At times they prefer to fly against the wind, and they either enter a favorite field against the wind or they turn and settle down facing the wind. Their wings are long and pointed and when the birds fly past, the wings give a soft whistling sound.

Doves live in the Sandhills all summer, but their number is greatly increased in the autumn by the birds coming down from the north to spend the winter. They are well equipped to stand cold weather, but deep snows are hard on them because it covers their food. On March 1, 1927, when a severe snow started, there were Doves in an old cornfield near Southern Pines, doing their best to find comfort by crouching down in the lee of bunches of grass, and hunching themselves up with head and feet drawn in and feathers fluffed out. All the next day the storm raged and these birds kept hidden in the thickets. On the third day the weather cleared, although still very cold, and the Doves were actively moving about, but still all fluffed up. While the snow covered most of their food, they did the best they could with seeds kept above the snow on stems too long to be buried. During this and the succeeding day, they found small bare spots here and there where the wind had blown off the snow. Here they were able to get a few seeds, but their hunger was so great they permitted automobile traffic on a main road within twenty feet without taking alarm.

At normal times, Doves feed mostly upon small seeds, especially those from various grasses such as the "pigeon grass." Seeds are hunted out by the birds walking constantly about a small area and stopping at every favorable place before going on to the next little bunch of grasses. If they find a good place with plenty of seeds they may stop for several minutes. Early in the winter, Doves in the cowpea fields may eat the waste peas, but later they are after the grasses and the weeds that grow between the rows of peas. In times of scarcity they frequent hay stacks or barnyards for the sake of the seeds shaken out there. Doves seem to need water often and make special flights each day to a drinking place. These birds take dust baths and then fly up to low limbs of the oaks, maples or gums to preen. They like to take sun baths also.

TURKEY VULTURE. Pl. 9, page 236

Cathartes aura septentrionalis (Wied.). A. O. U. No. 325

Field Identification. The largest common flying bird in the Sandhills, much larger than a Crow, but not so large as a Wild Turkey. General color very dark brown; head and neck red. In flight the *tips and rear halves* of the wings underneath are gray; undertail gray and the tail itself longer than the Black Vulture's. Wings usually bowed in flight.

Description. Plumage black, but the feathers so much edged with grayish brown that upperparts are brown rather than black; tips and rear half of wings underneath gray; head and neck naked and the skin thereof bright red. Total length 30 inches.

When I first became aware that Turkey Vultures, or "Buzzards," as they are locally called, and Black Vultures were both common in the Sandhills I tried to distinguish them. This was easy if they could be seen on the ground, for there a good background enabled me to make out the red head and neck and the brownish plumage of the Buzzard, and the black head, neck and plumage of the Black Vulture. So it was natural that I should then try to see the red, or black, heads of flying birds. This, I could not do even when the light was good and my binoculars powerful, because the flying bird drew in its head until the lower neck feathers covered the red upper neck and head. Only on rare occasions could any red be seen. Usually the wings of a flying Buzzard were bowed, or held at an angle and not flat, and usually the tips of the wings were turned up or back from the general direction of the wing. But I sometimes found the wings were level and the tips pointing with the wing. The Buzzard usually soared or glided while the Black Vulture frequently flapped its smaller wings; but I soon found that the Buzzard sometimes flapped and the Black Vulture sometimes soared successfully for long periods. The Buzzard had a longer tail than the Vulture, but this was comparative and I could not be sure of it unless I saw the two species together. What I needed, and what every bird student needed, was a mark by which he could identify a single flying bird. The color of the head, the position of the wings, the manner of flight, and the length of the tail—all having failed me at times I began looking for a better field mark. Then I found that the Buzzard was grayer as it flew over me. The whole under surface of the tail was gray; and the under surface of the tip and the *rear half* of the wing was gray. On the other hand, only the tip of the underpart of the wing was gray on the Black Vulture. Furthermore, this gray tip frequently showed *on top* when the flying Black Vulture revealed the upperpart of its wing as it banked sharply.

Distribution. Common in the Sandhills and throughout North Carolina at all seasons. In winter these vultures go as far south as northern Mexico and Lower California; in summer they live as far north as New Jersey, Pennsylvania, Ontario and the Canadian boundary west to the Pacific Ocean; ranging from coast to coast.

Habits. Since Buzzards are very common and their flights in search of food carry them everywhere, they are seen in all sections of the Sandhills, and over all kinds of fields and forests. Wherever the Turkey Buzzards find a carcass or some carrion, quite a flock of these birds quickly gathers and remains as long as any scraps are left. Since offal of various kinds is found there, these birds congregate over the pig-pens near Pinehurst, and over all dumps. At times it seems as if Buzzards fly more over swamps and lowlands than they do over highlands. They are given to circling over farm houses in search of any scraps available there. At night they gather in a "roost," usually located on high trees in a low, or swampy, area in the depths of the forests. On the ground they are very awkward and move with a hunched-up, ridiculous, sidewise hop or a series of such hops. When perched on trees they present a clumsy, uncouth appearance.

Buzzards are quiet and dignified—if their food habits can be forgotten; they are gregarious on their roosts at night and at feasts.

Usually they are solitary while hunting and searching, but sometimes they circle and soar in comparatively large flocks. Once a flock of thirty-five was seen in the Sandhills, and on another occasion a flock of fifty-seven flew over the aviation field near Pinehurst.

Small birds have no fear of Buzzards and Vultures flying over, although they quickly take alarm if a hawk appears. A Buzzard will often sweep over Doves, Meadowlarks, Red-winged Blackbirds, Rusty Blackbirds, Cowbirds, Pipits, Field Sparrows, Song Sparrows, Mockingbirds and many others without alarming them in the least even if it be only a hundred feet above them. When Turkey Buzzards and Black Vultures at a carcass are disturbed, the Buzzards fly away first and all are usually on the wing before any Black Vultures get under way. At their feasts and sometimes on their roosts Turkey Buzzards and Vultures are together, with Black Vultures greatly predominating on the sea-coast. In the Sandhills, Black Vultures are seen more than twice as often as the Buzzards. Farther inland the proportion of Turkey Buzzards becomes greater and greater.

The flight of Turkey Buzzards starting from the ground is slow and labored and the wing-beats are heavy and so slow in effect that the birds usually have to hop along rapidly for some distance before they can rise at all. When actually started, their flight becomes more and more graceful and easy as the heavy wing-beats gradually decrease, and the birds are more and more supported by the sustaining power of their great wings. As "sailers," "soarers," or "gliders" the Buzzards are perhaps the easiest and most graceful of all American birds. Circling is a favorite evolution at all times, and at all elevations. At times Buzzards sail near the ground just over the trees and at other times are high in the sky. Sometimes low-sailing birds and high-sailing ones are seen at the same time and comparatively near each other. For a time I thought they usually fly low in the morning and higher in the afternoon. Perhaps this is so to some extent, but it is not invariable. When soaring Buzzards are watched closely, it is seen that the wings are in almost constant motion, turning and twisting slightly first one way, and then the other, evidently as the birds take advantage of different currents.

The wings of flying Buzzards vary in their angle with the body and with each other to utilize level, rising, or falling currents of air. On January 18, 1927, a Turkey Buzzard circled over, manifestly sustained by a rising current of air, because its wings were deeply bent upward as if to spill out the air. When going in one direction it held its wings at a markedly different angle from that on the return trip. The broad stretch of wing surface enabled it to take advantage of every wind and maintain its direction and speed, gliding and sailing by wind pressure. The next day the air currents were apparently not rising ones for the Buzzards' wings were held level and wing-strokes were needed occasionally. Sometimes the wings were almost level, or turned sharply up, again only tips turned up, or wings held straight out, and finally curved forward and back. Usually, though, all birds seen at any one time had wings in the same position when going in the same direction, and at the same angle. Under all conditions, these superb fliers were able to glide or sail right into the face of the wind. And this was so even on days of comparatively high wind, although I have seen winds strong enough to carry the Buzzards this way and that, the birds going very swiftly to leeward but very erratically.

At times Buzzards fly together in flocks and then they circle in and out in a long vertical spiral with endless interweavings and evolutions. These soaring flights sometimes continue for an hour or more without a single wing-beat being observed, but at other times there are several successive flaps between intervals of gliding. I have seen Buzzards circling over as early as 9 a. m. on the coldest mornings when the temperature was far below freezing. Unquestionably they do not move about much before that hour during winter days. But winter mornings are dark until comparatively late and I believe these birds require a fair amount of light to see their food on the earth far below them. For the same reason their hunting is usually over by 4 p. m. and they retire to their roosts soon after that hour.

Their food is almost always dead animals or carrion, and I have never seen one attack a living animal no matter how small. It is said that a Turkey Buzzard circling high in air will watch other Buzzards and as soon as it sees one swoop down for food it follows. The next bird sees this and follows in its turn, and so on until all the Buzzards of a large territory have followed each other to a feast that only the first one of their number discovered. Naturally a large feast will attract them quicker, but they also stop for and devour the bodies of rats, squirrels, snakes and rabbits. Because of the services rendered mankind by thus disposing of putrid animal matter, Buzzards are everywhere protected in the south by public opinion.

BLACK VULTURE. Pl. 9, page 236

Catharista urubu urubu (Vieill.). *A. O. U. No. 326*

Field Identification. A large black bird much larger than a Crow and about the same size as a Turkey Buzzard. In flight the black underparts, except *gray wing-tips*, are conspicuous. When a flying bird in good light turns sharply, the terminal gray tips of the wings show above as well as below.

Description. Plumage black; tip of wings underneath gray; head and neck naked and the skin black. Total length 24 inches.

Distribution. Common throughout the Sandhills at all times; in fact, more common than the Turkey Buzzard. In winter these vultures go as far south as southern South America; in summer they live as far north as Maryland, Indiana, Illinois, Kansas and western Texas. In the United States, they are Atlantic coast and Mississippi Valley birds only.

Habits. Wherever they find a carcass, or carrion, quite a flock of Black Vultures will soon collect and remain on the carcass, on the ground nearby, or in the neighboring trees as long as an eatable scrap remains. They also congregate about pig-pens and public dumps. At night they gather in a "roost" on high trees standing in low swampy areas. There was such a roost in the winter of 1926-7 midway between Southern Pines and Pinehurst, or at least that was its temporary location, for the Vultures are known to change them at times. This roost was located on the tops of three dead long-leaf pines in a bit of lowland. It is not known whether the trees were dead when the roost was established, or whether the birds killed them by excessive use. Twenty-five Vultures were the largest number known to be on this roost at any one time.

Since these Black Vultures cover a great deal of ground in their hunting flights, and in going to, or leaving, their roosts, they are seen at times over every part of the Sandhills whether field or forest, country or city. Indeed it is the usual thing for one or more birds to be in sight from every point at all times. Even so, they are a little more frequently seen over swamps and lowlands than over higher areas.

On the ground, or on the limbs of a roost, Vultures are very awkward and move with clumsy, sidewise hops, assisted by heavy flaps of partly opened wings when they are in a hurry. Since their bodies are heavier and their wings shorter, the flight of the Black Vulture is always more laborious than the Buzzard's. When perched on trees or when resting on the ground these Vultures present a hunched-up, uncouth appearance. Perhaps they are not so much given to roaming and flying for long hours in circles as the Buzzards are. Mature Black Vultures are not known to utter any sound beyond a low hissing when disturbed. They seem to like the company of their fellows and gather on their roosts in close companionship. Here they perch sunning, preening and airing their feathers during most of the daylight hours that they are not hunting or feasting. On even a small roost, twenty or thirty birds usually stay together.

At their repasts Black Vultures gather as long as there is room for another one to find a place. Since the Turkey Buzzards also gather, the two species are then more or less intermixed. In their flights and on their roosts both species are apt to be more or less closely associated, but there are no other birds with which the Black Vultures foregather. They never bother small birds, and the small birds—Wood Ducks, Blackbirds, Meadowlarks and Myrtle Warblers among others—seem to know this and to be able to recognize them as harmless.

Although Black Vultures and Turkey Buzzards are often seen flying together, sometimes the flocks of the two species are as sharply separated as if they had divided the territory between them. On the limb of a tree they face the wind, spread their wings and swoop off. Although the wing-strokes at the start are rapid, the birds reach full flight much more easily than they do from the ground. Black Vultures starting from the ground do so with a series of rapid hops. After about twenty or thirty hops, they rise slowly and laboriously, but gather headway and momentum at each wing-beat and are soon flying more and more easily and gracefully, after they are clear of the ground. All that has been said of the Turkey Buzzard's flight could be repeated here except that the flight of the Vulture has more frequent periods of wing-flapping, and the soaring is not quite so powerful and graceful. And yet the difference is not a marked one. On February 10, 1927, a bird flew over a swamp with frequent periods of wing-flapping. Yet it might have been either a Black Vulture sailing like a Buzzard, or a Turkey Buzzard wing-flapping like a Vulture. I'll own I was sorely puzzled. Later, after I had found a way to distinguish the two species, I noted a single Vulture that flew, sailed and circled overhead in every way like a Buzzard. A week later Black Vultures were seen flying low down over the ground, but soon circled higher and gradually soared and circled up and up until they were mere specks in the sky. And they did it with scarcely a beat of their wings—a true Turkey Buzzard's flight.

Black Vultures were probably not seen on so many days as the Buzzards were, but on the days that I did see them it was apt to be in comparatively large numbers. In the one month that I kept careful count I noted almost four times as many Vultures as I did Turkey Buzzards.

While the Black Vultures feed on carrion the same as the Buzzards do, they will not bother with as small a supply. But even so, the Vultures share with the Buzzards in the protection given by man because of their valuable services as scavengers. At feasts where the two species are together the Black Vultures often secure the best pieces because of their greater size and strength, which enables them to pull favorite pieces away from the smaller Buzzards. At the same time that I noticed this, I noted also that the Black Vultures did not seem so active while feeding.

Black Vultures spend a great deal of time either on their roosts or on other tall trees. While these trees are usually on low ground the outlook from them is very extended. Seemingly the Vultures on such a perch watch their fellows circling on their hunting flights. When they see a flying Vulture, or a Turkey Buzzard, swoop down for food, they fly up and follow it in order to share in the feast. Once I found a carcass as soon as the first Turkey Buzzard did, but soon after that a Black Vulture arrived and then several more in a long string until thirty had assembled. All these Vultures came from one direction and all were flying low. By following this direction back I found where they had perched. The next morning I was on hand early. The first Black Vulture left at 8:30 a. m., ascended in circles to a height of three hundred feet and then flew straight to the feast of the previous day. Another Vulture followed after a perceptible interval and then another until there was a long line of flying Vultures stretching from the roost to the carrion three miles away.

MARSH HAWK. Pl. 5, page 148

Circus hudsonius (Linn.). *A. O. U. No. 331*

Field Identification. A grayish or brownish Hawk of the open country and a little larger than a Crow. Usually this Hawk flies so low that it just skims the tops of grasses or low bushes. It can be identified by a white ring around the body just above the tail.

Description. The male's upperparts are bluish gray; feathers just above tail white; upper breast light gray; lower breast and belly white, spotted or barred with rufous. On the females and young birds the upperparts are brownish black, tinged with rufous; underparts ochraceous-buff widely streaked on the breast and narrowly streaked on the belly. Male: total length 19 inches; female: 22 inches. It should be remembered that Marsh Hawks in the brownish plumage far outnumber the adult males in the gray plumage. Perhaps ten of the former will be seen to every one of the gray Hawks.

Distribution. These Hawks visit the Sandhills in winter and may be seen at any time between September and May. In winter, some individuals go as far south as the Bahama Islands, Cuba and Colombia; in summer, they live mostly in Canada but go as far north as Siberia, Alaska, Mackenzie, Keewatin, Quebec and Prince Edward Island.

Habits. Although these Hawks do fly over marshes and wet meadows, their name is something of a misnomer so far as the Sandhills region is concerned. Here they are far more often seen hunting over farmlands and the very open parts of the shrub oak barrens (Fig. 16). It is but natural that low-flying birds like the Marsh Hawks should often be seen on very low perches such as stakes and fence posts as often as on taller trees.

Marsh Hawks are solitary in disposition except when paired or in families. They even seem to drive other birds away from their territory. While they do not regularly hunt and kill small birds they drive them about a good deal. One day in March as I walked along a tall hedge between two fields, I heard a Blue Jay's alarm cry repeated once or twice, and then saw a Marsh Hawk dart along the other side of the hedge. As it did so, White-throated Sparrows and Chipping Sparrows scattered before it without any being caught. I could not see that the Hawk really tried to catch any. Occasionally the bolder of the small birds turn the tables by chasing and tormenting the Hawk. But this is a trick that is not at all safe with such expert dodgers and twisters as these Hawks are, although their flight is not rapid. Sometimes they fly high, especially when traveling from place to place. Once near Jackson Springs, I saw a Marsh Hawk flying in circles well up over the forests and fields, although a reason for this high flight might have been a small bird flying near and tormenting it.

In hunting for food the Marsh Hawks fly to and fro over the meadows, fields and open forest. When they see their prey, they are extraordinarily quick at checking their course and pouncing down. In the Sandhills they prey almost altogether on mice and small rodents, and I neither saw nor heard of any visits to poultry yards. When they have caught their prey, they either eat it on the spot or carry it in their claws to a convenient perch.

SHARP-SHINNED HAWK. Pl. 3, page 64

Accipiter velox (Wils.). *A. O. U. No. 332*

Field Identification. A gray, sometimes reddish, Hawk but little larger than a Robin. Characterized by a long *square* tail and short rounded wings. Its flight is peculiar with its alternation of a series of wing-strokes with a period of gliding; but in pursuit of prey, the flight is by a rapid, continuous wing-stroke maintained without gliding.

Description. Adults have the upperparts slaty gray; tail nearly square, with blackish cross-bars and a whitish tip; underparts barred with white and pale rufous. Immature birds have the upperparts brownish black; underparts white, streaked or spotted with pale rufous-brown. Total length, male 11¼ inches, female 13½ inches.

Distribution. Rather common in the Sandhills throughout the winter. In winter, these fierce little Hawks go as far south as Panama; in summer, they live throughout the United States and Canada but are absent from the southeastern states east of the Appalachian Mountains.

Habits. Sharp-shinned Hawks are seen most frequently about hedges and near the thickets at the edges of fields (Figs. 13 and 14). They are seldom in very heavy forests and seldom out over the open fields. Quite often their coming can be foretold by the actions of the small birds who have reason to fear them. When a small bird sees one of these Hawks it utters sharp cries of alarm. These cries are understood by all birds and are promptly repeated; so that many birds repeating such an alarm may carry it along a hedge faster than the Hawk can fly. Occasionally a Sharp-shinned Hawk stops and rests on a tree limb, possibly to give the small birds' alarm time to die down. Blue Jays often find this Hawk and warn other birds by their vociferous alarms.

Not only are these birds the fiercest of our Hawks but they are also the most daring. On March 30, 1927, I was walking along one of the main streets of Southern Pines when a Sharp-shinned Hawk darted through and under the oaks and pines of a vacant lot. It actually passed between two residences and over a garage, then swooped at two or three English Sparrows feeding on the ground. This Hawk failed to catch a sparrow but swept on through the small trees. For a time I could follow its course by the birds' alarm cries that came back to me.

On March 19, 1927, a Sharp-shinned Hawk flew over the branch just south of Aberdeen. Soon it began to circle higher and higher over the fields and farms. At first it flapped its wings often, but later it began to soar and glide. Gradually it got up until almost out of sight and then drifted away, still circling and soaring, to the northeast. Most of this flight was without wing-beats and a fine exhibition of soaring flight. It may have had some mating significance.

The Sharp-shinned Hawk's usual flight is a swift dart through the brush and tree foliage. Sometimes they are near the ground and sometimes up in the foliage of the taller pines. The Sharp-shins do not circle and soar in pursuit of prey as some other Hawks do. Like true bushwhackers, they dart along a hedge and swoop suddenly on any small bird they see. They attack all kinds of birds, and they are so strong and fierce that they sometimes kill birds larger than themselves.

Unfortunately, these Hawks are rather common in the Sandhills, for they usually escape the traps and guns that catch and destroy so many of the larger Hawks that are really beneficial to the farmers.

COOPER'S HAWK

Accipiter cooperi (Bonap.). *A. O. U. No. 333*

Field Identification. A gray, sometimes reddish, hawk a little larger than a Crow. Resembles the Sharp-shinned Hawk but is larger and has a *rounded* tail.

Description. Similar to the Sharp-shinned Hawk but larger and the brown more blackish; corners of the tail rounded. Total length, male 15½ inches, female 19 inches.

Distribution. In winter these hawks go as far south as Costa Rica; in summer they occur from the southern limits of our country north to British Columbia, Alberta, Keewatin, Quebec and Prince Edward Island.

Habits. In every way this relative of the Sharp-shinned Hawk closely resembles that bird. Although rather more common all winter than most other hawks of the Sandhills, I did not see quite so many Cooper Hawks as I did Sharp-shinned Hawks. Those that I did see were in the oak and pine forests (Figs. 1, 2, 5, 16). Sometimes they alighted on the tops of the long-leaf pines, but their usual hunting flights were similar to the Sharp-shin's method.

The Crows seemed to have a special antipathy for the Cooper Hawks. On December 29, 1926, I was walking along the edge of the forest about a mile south of the Highland Pines Inn at Southern Pines, when suddenly I heard a Crow cawing loudly in the distance. Almost immediately it was answered by five other Crows all cawing noisily. After a few minutes the noise rose to a clamor and drew nearer to me. Then a Cooper Hawk appeared flying swiftly over the pine forest, closely pursued by ten very noisy Crows, flying behind and much higher in the air. Wise old Crows! They well knew the prowess of the quarry they were tormenting and that it could not get at them as long as they flew above it. But this hawk outflew the black mob and just beyond me it dived into a thick pine top until the Crows' clamor died out. On another occasion I saw a single Crow chase a Cooper Hawk over a swamp. This time the Crow could fly the faster, but always pursued and attacked from the rear. Again the hawk escaped by diving into a thick evergreen top.

RED-TAILED HAWK. Pl. 9, page 236

Buteo borealis borealis (Gmel.).　A. O. U. No. 337.

Field Identification. A large brownish hawk, much larger than a Crow and only a little smaller than a Turkey Buzzard. Its best identification mark is its red tail. This hawk is partial to rather heavy forests, especially along streams. When hunting they usually circle and soar high overhead.

Description. Upperparts usually dark brown, but varying often to lighter brown, marked with rufous and whitish; tail rusty red; throat white; upper breast streaked brownish so as to sometimes form a band; belly white, sometimes streaked. In immature birds the tail is the same color as the back, but crossed by several, more or less distinctly seen, darker bands.　Male: total length 20 inches; female: 23 inches.

Distribution. This hawk lives in the Sandhills at all seasons. Elsewhere it occurs all over eastern United States, and a few are found also in northern Mexico and southern Canada. Similar forms live in the western half of the United States.

Habits. Since they feed on a good many animals of the open fields, the Red-tailed Hawks are often seen circling over fields and farms. Sometimes they perch on the tips of the tallest pines. Because dead trees, dead stubs and dead limbs of living trees afford even better views of the surrounding country, these are still more favored by these hawks.

I did not see many of these big birds in the Sandhills and those that I did see were very wild indeed. No doubt this was because of the persecution to which all the hawks are subjected here. In this case it is not deserved, for the Red-tailed Hawks seldom bother poultry, but do destroy great numbers of mice and other noxious species. Evidently some small birds regard these hawks as enemies

Figure 18. A winter cornfield that is a great favorite with birds, especially White-throated Sparrows. Along road between Pinehurst and Carthage, Feb. 1, 1926.

for I once found one being tormented by four Robins. It protected itself fairly well in the top of a tall pine, but when it flew, twenty-six more Robins that had been concealed in the foliage, joined their efforts to the pecks of the first four tormentors that were now chasing the hawk. Still, as it is a favorite sport of a good many small birds to tease a bigger, clumsier one, this may have been all there was to this incident.

In flight Red-tailed Hawks are strong and graceful, especially when they sail or soar. Perhaps they are not quite so graceful as the Turkey Buzzards, but they are still very attractive features of the landscape. These hawks at times perform wonderful evolutions in the air, either one bird alone or several at a time. Such hawks mount up to a high altitude, then half close their wings and drop down on a steep incline at great speed only to reopen their wings and shoot up at an equal angle. This is repeated again and again while the hawks describe a series of deep "V's" as they gradually pass out of sight in the distance.

Red-tailed Hawks sometimes give utterance to shrill whistling screams, although I did not hear them often in winter. They are uttered both while the hawks are perched on a tree, and while in flight, and serve at different times as a call, a signal, or an alarm.

The food of the Red-tailed Hawks is mostly mice but they are not over-particular and I have seen them eat frogs, snakes, crawfish and grasshoppers as well. Sometimes one will kill a domestic fowl, but the good the majority do in killing mice and other undesirables more than counterbalances an occasional lapse of good behavior.

These birds nest very early and Mr. C. J. Pennock found a partly incubated egg on March 10, 1910, in a nest a half mile back of the Pinehurst Dairy. The nest is usually placed in the crotch of the limbs of a tall tree and is sometimes used several years in succession.

RED-SHOULDERED HAWK

Buteo lineatus lineatus (Gmel.). *A. O. U. No. 339*

Field Identification. This hawk is about the same length as a Crow but the heavier body and the greater spread of wing make this brown hawk seem larger. It is quite similar to the Red-tailed Hawk but lacks the red tail. The underparts are barred with rufous and the tail is barred black and white. It frequents the open fields and lowland areas.

Description. Upperparts mostly dark brown, varied with reddish, buffy and whitish; largest wing-feathers brownish black, barred with black and white; "shoulders" reddish brown; tail black, but crossed by four or five white bars and narrowly tipped with white; underparts reddish, barred with white. Young birds similar; tail grayish brown, barred with darker, upper part more or less reddish; underparts white. Total length, male 18 inches; female 20 inches.

Distribution. More frequently seen throughout the year than any other large hawk in the Sandhills. These are birds of the eastern United States where they range from the Gulf Coast north to Manitoba, Keewatin, Nova Scotia and Prince Edward Island.

Habits. Since these hawks hunt low for their food, they sometimes perch on low trees and telephone poles; and even at times on stakes and on the ground. When Red-shouldered Hawks fly from such low perches, they glide along near the ground with long, even, powerful beats of their wings. But they also fly high in air and frequently circle over in large soaring loops. On February 14, 1927, one was seen flying over or on gliding pinions. Frequently it turned and circled once or twice before resuming its rapid journey eastward. Only occasionally was there a slight movement of the wings, but the flight was strong, sure, gliding, and so graceful that I took it to be a Turkey Buzzard at first glance.

Although these hawks are the most common ones in the Sandhills, they are actually seldom seen. They have been the subjects of an unreasoning persecution on the part of the hunters and the farmers. They are not known to take poultry, or to kill Bobwhites, in North Carolina. But because they are larger than most birds and are rather unsuspicious, they are hunted and shot as enemies. They are really friends to the farmers, for three-quarters of their food consists of injurious mice, and the remaining items are frogs, snakes and insects. Economically considered, it is better to let all hawks go until one is able to identify the really injurious individuals.

SPARROW HAWK. Pl. 5, page 148

Falco sparverius sparverius Linn. *A. O. U. No. 360*

Field Identification. A small reddish hawk a little larger than a Robin and distinguished for its small size, its habit of perching on an observation post and watching for prey, its hovering over a field, the reddish color, and its long and narrow wings.

Description.　The male's upperparts are reddish, with many irregular curved black bars on his back; a black band near tip of tail; wings gray-blue and reddish; forehead and back of neck blue; underparts buffy, with belly and sides spotted with black; two vertical black splashes on side of head. The female's upperparts are reddish, with *small* black markings; underparts lighter than male's, and streaked with buffy. Total length, both sexes, 10 inches.

Distribution.　While they are present at all seasons, they are less common in summer. In winter these hawks are found as far south as eastern Mexico and Costa Rica; but in summer they live as far north as the upper Yukon River; Mackenzie, Keewatin and Newfoundland. A similar species inhabits the Rocky Mountains and west thereof.

Habits.　Although Sparrow Hawks are seen more often in the Sandhills than any other hawks, they can not really be called common. To a certain extent they share in the unreasoning persecution by guns and traps, so many times spoken of elsewhere. In this case again the persecution is unwarranted for the little Sparrow Hawks do a world of good to the farming interests. Inasmuch as they spend most of their time on prominent, although not necessarily high, perches watching for their prey, they are more often seen perched than in flight.

Quite likely the *favorite* perches of Sparrow Hawks are the tall dead stubs of pine trees, but they are seen almost as often patiently waiting on telephone poles. Sometimes they alight on telephone wires instead. At times they are at the very top of tall long-leaf pines; and at others they are on fence posts or fence wires. While they hunt mostly at the edges of weedy fields, these little hawks seem really partial to peach orchards (Fig. 7), especially where there are plenty of grasshoppers and beetles. It has been said that Sparrow Hawks are attracted for long distances by the smoke of burning grass in order to feed on the insects driven out by the fire. Although I saw many fires burning, I can not confirm this observation for I saw only one Sparrow Hawk near a fire, and one where the grass had been burned off a month previously. This species is not often seen in towns.

Sparrow Hawks are unsuspicious little fellows, often allowing a close approach, especially when they are industriously hunting small prey. At such times they spend many minutes patiently watching the ground below their perches. Sparrow Hawks are somewhat nervous. After each unalarmed flight they move their tails up and down slowly and regularly, continuing for as much as two minutes. This motion seems without volition on the hawk's part. Occasionally, it stops momentarily to allow the hawk to move or to scratch its head, but is resumed again immediately afterward. After an alarmed flight caused by a passing automobile the nervous motion continued longer.

Generally, the flight of Sparrow Hawks is low and directly connected with their hunting, but sometimes while flying from one hunting ground to another, they fly higher over the oak-and-pine forests. The flight is strong and sure but not rapid; it is apt to be level and straight but sometimes it is swooping in long undulations. When ready to alight, they approach their perches flying against the wind, previously circling if necessary to get to the leeward side.

Sometimes while flying, and while perching too for that matter, Sparrow Hawks give their call of "killy, killy." This is rapidly repeated and so characteristic that these birds are often known as "Killy Birds" or "Killy Hawks."

Although never very common, the Sparrow Hawks are evenly distributed throughout the Sandhills during every month of the winter. They are somewhat local in their haunts and may be found near the same field, or even the same part of the field, day after day.

They prey on mice and insects, many of which are highly injurious to the farms. They have several methods of hunting, all more or less preceded by long watchful periods. Usually the hawks simply swoop down from their perches, returning with their prey after catching it. A more striking method was shown by a hawk a mile east of Aberdeen. This bird quietly watched from a telephone pole but soon flew out and "hovered" over a weedy field before flying on to another telephone pole. In a few moments it shot down to the grassy field in a long swoop without hovering. Then back to its pole where it perched and watched for ten minutes. Then another long swoop to the ground and up again on the next pole where it watched seven minutes and swooped again without hovering.

But "hovering" is very characteristic of Sparrow Hawks. On February 22, 1927, a Sparrow Hawk was seen on a telephone pole but occasionally making trips out over a weedy corn-field. Here it frequently hovered, either swooping at the end of the hover, or flying to another place to hover again, or returning to its former perch on the telephone pole. Once it flew out over the field and alighted on the grassy ground. Here it remained motionless, except for constant turnings of its head in all directions, for eight minutes; then it flew two or three feet for an insect, then walked a foot or two; another silent wait, and then back to the telephone pole. Once it flew to the dead stub of a long-leaf pine, but later returned to the telephone pole. While this bird was "hovering," the motion of its wings was quite rapid but the body was held at such a high angle from the horizontal that the wings moved forward and back as well as up and down. The flight for short distances was with continuous and regular wing-beats, with a glide or a series of glides while approaching a contemplated perch or hovering position. The periods of observation on various telephone poles varied from five to twelve minutes. When finally alarmed by a passing automobile, this hawk flew out across the fields to a distant fence post of a wire fence where it remained for at least twelve minutes. During this longer flight, periods of wing-beating alternated with short glides.

SHORT-EARED OWL

Asio flammeus (Pont.).　　A. O. U. No. 367

Field Identification. A yellowish brown owl somewhat smaller than a Crow. The ear-tufts are not prominent, so that this bird is identified by size and general color, and by the fact that it is a *marsh owl*, seldom, if ever, alighting in trees. It has yellow eyes, but no breast barring like the Barred Owl.

Description. Ear-tufts very short; upperparts light brown streaked with darker; underparts more whitish, everywhere streaked with brown, the streaks wider on the breast and narrower on the belly; eyes yellow. Total length 15½ inches.

PLATE 4. HARDWOOD FOREST (OAKS, ETC.)

1: Yellow-bellied Sapsucker (male).
2: Yellow-bellied Sapsucker (female).
3: Flicker (female).
4: Flicker (male).
5: Red-headed Woodpecker (immature).

6: Red-headed Woodpecker (male).
7: Cedar Waxwing (male).
8: Cedar Waxwing (female).
9: Myrtle Warbler (male).
10: Myrtle Warbler (female).

(All figures about ⅕ life size)

Distribution. I found these owls in the reedy marsh at the head of Juniper Lake and they probably occur in similar open marshes throughout the Sandhills in winter. At that season they are to be found from California, Wyoming, Minnesota, Indiana, Ohio and Massachusetts south to Cuba, Louisiana and Guatemala; in summer they live north of the winter range as far as the Arctic Ocean. These owls also live in South America, Europe and northern Asia.

Habits. Unlike most owls, the Short-eared species confines itself to reedy and grassy marshes where it hides by day amid the thick grass and tall vegetation. Here, these owls remain hidden until almost stepped upon. On cloudy days they sometimes fly out of their marsh. In spite of this, they are properly night owls, at which time they are very active hunting and catching the mice and small animals upon which they live. On the other hand these owls can see quite well by daylight. Their flight is low, just skimming the marshes as a rule.

BARRED OWL

Strix varia varia Barton. *A. O. U. No. 368*

Field Identification. A gray forest owl larger than a Crow. Breast barred *across*, the sides and belly streaked *up and down*, and the line of change very sharply marked; no ear-tufts at all; brownish black eyes.

Description. No ear-tufts; upperparts brown, barred with buffy, or whitish; underparts buffy, the breast barred *across*, the sides and belly streaked *up and down*, with brownish black; bill yellow; eyes brownish black. Total length 20 inches.

Distribution. Common resident in the Sandhills at all times. The range of this owl extends south to Georgia, Tennessee, Kentucky and northern Arkansas; west to eastern Colorado, Wyoming and Montana; and north to Manitoba, northern Ontario, southern Quebec and Newfoundland.

Habits. These owls live both in the forests of the lowland and also in the oak-and-pine forests, but, because they are seldom disturbed there, they are more generally found in the dense forests along the streams and ponds. At one time I heard a great racket up in the tree-tops of a pine forest near Aberdeen. Upon investigating I found two of these owls flying from one long-leaf pine to another with half a dozen Blue Jays in hot pursuit. This time it was the Jays that were making all the noise; but these owls are rather noted for their hooting especially in late winter and early spring. Their notes are a resonant, deep-toned, somewhat questioning; series of "who-who-who." Usually they call in the evening, but sometimes in broad daylight.

The food of these comparatively large owls consists of rats, mice and other small mammals and I know of no instances here where they have disturbed domestic fowls.

These owls nest so early in hollow trees that their eggs might be found in late February, or almost any time in March. Usually two white eggs constitute a set.

SCREECH OWL. Pl. 9, page 236

Otus asio asio (Linn.).   A. O. U. No. 373

Field Identification. This bird is distinguished by being a small reddish, or grayish (the two color phases are not signs of either age, sex or season; sometimes occurring both in the same family) bird with length less than a Robin although the body is more chunky and the spread of wings greater. It has "horns" and its eyes are yellow.

Description. Ear-tufts conspicuous, one inch in length. *Red phase:* upperparts bright, brick red, with fine black streaks; underparts white, marked with black streaks and barred across irregularly with reddish. *Gray phase:* upperparts gray, streaked with black; underparts, white, finely streaked and barred with black, touched here and there with reddish; yellow eyes. Total length 9½ inches.

Distribution. This little owl occurs in the Sandhills at all times. It is found from Georgia and Texas north to Minnesota, Ontario and New Brunswick.

Habits. In the Sandhills Sereech Owls are occasionally seen in daytime in the thickest, darkest trees such as cedars, hollies and magnolias. But most of them prefer to spend the day in a hole in a tree or similar dark cavity. In the evening these owls leave their refuges and become more active. They are residents of the towns and cities as well as more rural districts and I have seen and heard them even within the limits of Southern Pines, Aberdeen and Pine Bluff. At night the Screech Owls hunt the trees for English Sparrows and the forests and fields for mice. Even in winter they can be heard giving their tremulous, wavering calls. Their common name is a misnomer, for their cry, although rather sorrowful and unearthly, is not at all a screech.

GREAT HORNED OWL

Bubo virginianus virginianus (Gmel.). *A. O. U. No. 375*

Field Identification. A big gray-brown owl almost as large as a Turkey Buzzard. It has prominent ear-tufts and a broad white throat patch.

Description. Ear-tufts nearly two inches long; upperparts ochraceous-buff marked with black; a white patch on the throat; remainder of under parts buffy, barred with black; yellow eyes. Total length 22 inches.

Distribution. This bird is a resident of the Sandhills at all seasons. South of us it is found as far as Florida and the Gulf states; west to, and slightly beyond, the Mississippi River; north to Ontario, Quebec, New Brunswick and Newfoundland. Farther west there are other varieties of this same owl.

Habits. These are birds of the heavy, least disturbed forests. Since a large share of such woods have been destroyed in the Sandhills, these owls are rather uncommon. Because the Great Horned Owls can see quite well in daylight, we do not often surprise them on their daytime roosts in the dense trees of the swamps. Like the Barred Owls, these birds have a deep-toned, far-reaching hoot that can be heard a half mile or more. The Great Horned Owls have also a loud scream that is very weird and startling to even the strongest-nerved hearer.

Possibly these are among the fiercest and most rapacious of American birds, if we eliminate the fiercest of the sea-birds. Their food consists of mice, rats, birds of all kinds, rabbits and game birds. Chickens and other poultry are not safe from them unless kept carefully shut up at night. Their destruction of useful birds is balanced somewhat by the good they do in killing harmful rodents.

This is the earliest nesting bird in the Sandhills, and its eggs might be found any time in February, or even in January of some years. Great Horned Owls do not build nests of their own but adopt a vacant nest left by a Crow or Red-shouldered Hawk. While they do not always return to the same nest a second time, a pair of these owls become so much attached to the territory where they live that they can usually be found near the same locality year after year.

BELTED KINGFISHER   Pl. 2, page 42

Ceryle alcyon alcyon (Linn.).   A. O. U. No. 390

Field Identification. A prominently crested blue bird spotted with white and larger than a Robin, with head and bill much larger in proportion. Always to be found near a pond or stream. It has a loud, rattling call, often uttered, and so typical as to make identification sure wherever heard. Flight is peculiar and characteristic; wing-strokes are even and strong for a series of ten to fifteen beats, then two to four quick, rapid strokes before resuming again the even spaced strokes. These alternations are repeated again and again. Another peculiarity is that the wings seem to be below the horizontal most of the time, and the lift up and the beat down are very quick.

Description. Both sexes have a high, ragged crest. On the male the upperparts are bluish gray with small white spots and markings; throat white; a white collar; a band across breast and the sides bluish gray; lower breast and belly white. Female with the breast band and the sides rufous. Total length 12 inches.

Distribution. Occasional during the winter in the Sandhills but more common in summer. In winter these birds go as far south as the West Indies, Colombia and Guiana; in summer they are found as far north as Alaska, Mackenzie, Keewatin, Quebec and Newfoundland.

Habits. Since the Kingfishers depend on fish for food, they must live near water. Even the range in winter is determined by how far north fishable waters stay open all winter. Hence near salt water, or along streams kept open by warm springs, Kingfishers may remain far north of their usual range. In the Sandhills the favored waters are usually open ones (Figs. 10 and 15).

Generally Kingfishers are seen on some elevated perch from which they can watch for prey. This may not always be the most prominent point, for I have seen a Kingfisher alight on a stake rising only two feet above the surface of a lake, with a wall of higher marsh reeds immediately behind it. Once I saw one fly up into a long-leaf pine at Silver Lake, Pine Bluff (Fig. 10), and I particularly noted that bird did not go to the highest limb but selected one that stretched out over the lake and closest to the water. On the other hand Kingfishers often pick out bare poles or branches where they can see for a long distance, and they seem partial to electric wires and telephone poles. They even alight at times on a wire fence if it stretches across a fishing ground.

Since the Belted Kingfishers usually catch their prey after watching for it from elevated perches, they frequently spend many minutes perched absolutely motionless, although keenly watching the water. But these birds have several nervous tricks. At the end of a flight they may simply tilt their tails sharply up and down two or three times. Again they may nervously raise and slowly lower their tails, and at the same time raise and lower there crests three or four times. Generally they dart along with a harsh rattling call, curve up to their perch, jerk up their tails, and raise and lower their crests.

The Kingfishers' flight is low and usually not over forty feet above the water. Sometimes they take an abrupt dive from their perch to within three or four feet of the water and then shoot along at that level to their next stopping place. Where they follow the sinuous course of a forest stream they may fly along close to the water and under the tree limbs, or they may rise twenty or thirty feet above the woods and fly there, although still following the stream. If flying low, they continue at that level right up to the time they wish to alight and then curve sharply up to the perch. Kingfishers fly a good deal, and I have seen one fly up and down Juniper Lake in what looked like a finicky attempt to find the best perch for a lunch on the minnow it carried.

The food of Kingfishers in the Sandhills is largely small minnows sometimes as much as five inches long, but generally chubs, suckers or other undesirable fishes from our point of view. These are usually caught by direct plunges into the water from observation points. On March 23, 1927, I saw a Kingfisher fly up the shore of

Juniper Lake to the marsh, and then up the inlet through the marsh. As it flew the half mile, it stopped and hovered about eight times. Just before stopping to hover each time this bird rose a few feet higher in the air than it had been flying. It hovered each time from twenty to fifty seconds, and averaged thirty-five feet above the water although the distance varied from twenty to sixty feet. As each hover proved unsuccessful in getting a fair chance at its prey, the bird flew on farther. Finally, the bird waited a little longer than usual, then closed its wings and shot swiftly down and into the water. In a few moments it emerged with a four-inch chub that it carried crosswise in its bill to a favorite perch on a dead tree. Since this fish was rather large, the Kingfisher beat it smartly against a limb to break it up. Previously I had seen the same bird swallow smaller minnows whole, although I noticed it always turned the fish around and swallowed it head first.

SOUTHERN HAIRY WOODPECKER. Pl. 3, page 64

Dryobates villosus auduboni (Swains.). A. O. U. 393b

Field Identification. A black bird spotted with white and smaller than a Robin; a scarlet spot on nape of the males; pure white outer tail-feathers. Like all woodpeckers this one is generally found on the trunks of trees.

Description. The male is black above, with a scarlet patch on the back of his head; a broad white stripe down his back; wings and "shoulders" spotted with white; outer tail-feathers white; one white stripe above the eye and another below; underparts white. The female lacks the scarlet patch. Total length 8½ inches.

Distribution. This bird is not very numerous in the Sandhills but it may be found there at all seasons of the year. This southern form lives from the Gulf states and Texas north to Missouri, Illinois and Virginia. Other forms live in practically all wooded parts of North America although the more northern varieties migrate south in winter.

Habits. While these woodpeckers are shy and usually seen on trees in the wilder places, they are not always so. On December 31, 1926, one was seen on the edge of the Southern Pines Country Club grounds and later one was found on some small bushes entirely apart from the forest. At times these birds are seen flying across the open fields from one lot of trees to another. The Hairy Woodpeckers are partial to the neighborhood of water, but they are also seen away from water often enough to indicate that this is only a tendency. They do not show a preference for any one kind of tree but are found on both living and dead shrub oaks, long-leaf pines, loblolly pine, sycamore, sour gum and sweet gum. They work on both trunks and limbs but usually at low heights, from the ground up to twenty feet above. On a vertical surface these birds work up, spiraling it and tapping it as they go. They move by a series of short hops, propping themselves each time with their tails. When hopping lightly along a horizontal limb they still use their tails as props. Perhaps their most astonishing feat is to spiral horizontal limbs, and to cling beneath them and hammer there with their backs down. Sometimes they work their way up to the very tip of slender shoots. Even in a heavy wind they cling to the violently swaying twigs while eating, but they stay only a short time before flying to a tree trunk to perch and rest before trying it again. Usually Southern Hairy Woodpeckers perch on a limb lengthwise, but sometimes they perch crosswise after the usual perching-bird style.

Shyness is more characteristic of these woodpeckers than it is of other small woodpeckers. Yet, on several occasions I found the Hairy Woodpeckers in the Sandhills comparatively tame and easy to watch. Still, I do think these birds are suspicious and prone to interpret every quick and unusual movement as one dangerous to themselves. As a rule, they are nervous birds that seldom stay long in one place. A solitary life seems typical of all woodpeckers except the Red-cockaded, so it is quite usual to find the Hairy Woodpeckers alone. Once, near Addor, I saw one with a Red-bellied Woodpecker, and once one was with eight Juncos in what was probably an accidental and temporary gathering.

The flight of these birds is strong and undulating, with fast-beating wings, and generally only from one tree to the next. Where the trees are not very close together, they swoop down to within a few feet of the ground and then fly with nearly level flight until they glide up to their next stopping place. Where they have to fly out across intervening open fields their flight becomes more undulatory, at times deeply so.

Insects, mostly grubs and beetles, are their favorite food, secured by searching the trunks and limbs of trees and by drilling into both living and dead trees. They do not seem to care much what kind of a tree, for they work on shrub oaks, loblolly pines, long-leaf pines and gums. They vigorously hammer each likely spot, moving up or down or sideways with rather long quick hops or "hitches" and closely examine every possible crevice in the bark. On February 28, 1927, a male was seen working on some small brush a foot or two above the ground, then it flew to a charred and dead stub of a shrub oak. Here it worked steadily for fifteen minutes pulling out small white grubs and borers. It drove its bill for three or four strokes up under a bit of bark and then pried the bark off with its bill as a lever. Then it attacked the semi-rotten wood so uncovered, directly. It did not seem to work so fast as a Downy woodpecker, but then it was so busy eating grubs that it did not have to dig much.

In winter the Hairy Woodpeckers vary their diet of insects with various berries and dried wild fruits. They are particularly fond of the small black berries of the sour gum (*Nyssa silvatica*). Soon after the early frosts the birds flock to these swamp trees and feast as long as the berries last.

SOUTHERN DOWNY WOODPECKER. Pl. 3, page 64

Dryobates pubescens pubescens (Linn.). *A. O. U. No. 394*

Field Identification. These are small counterparts of the Southern Hairy Woodpecker and about the size of a sparrow. Their outer tail-feathers are barred black and white.

Description. The male has a white stripe above the eye and another below; upperparts black, with a scarlet patch on the back of the head; middle of the back white; wings spotted with white; outer tail-feathers barred black and white; underparts white. The female has no scarlet patch. Total length 6 inches.

Distribution. These woodpeckers are common in all parts of Sandhills throughout the year, but less easy to find in summer. This form lives in the southeastern states from North Carolina to the Gulf and west to Texas. Other varieties of the Downy live in practically all the forested lands of the United States and Canada.

Habits. These little woodpeckers are more common than the Hairy Woodpeckers, and being more friendly and less shy, they are much more often seen. They are at home everywhere in the Sandhills from the lowest growth near the ground to the limbs high up in the tallest long-leaf pines, and from the most unfrequented wilderness to the dooryards of towns and cities. They are not inhabitants of the open fields because all their food is obtained on trees or bushes; on the other hand they do not live in the densest forests. They like thickets, and hedges, and the borderland between the forests and the open country. Since shrub oaks and pine saplings are the most common trees, their limbs and trunks are where Downy Woodpeckers are most frequently seen. But they are also found on gum trees and all kinds of planted shade trees. Frequently they are on small bushes of various kinds.

Downy Woodpeckers are very industrious when at work digging a home or when after grubs and borers, and seem able to maintain themselves in any position and to travel up and down or around the tree trunks and limbs. When they go down a vertical surface they drop down backward an inch at a time and catch a new footing before taking another drop. They can hang back downward even while working on the limb above them.

Downy Woodpeckers are comparatively tame, but if for any reason they do not like an intruder's appearance, they quickly hide by creeping around a limb or trunk. They are quite curious, too. One day a little Downy forgot, temporarily, its industrious life and flew over to see why a Sapsucker was "watching its wells" on the next tree.

Throughout their haunts in the northern states, Downy Woodpeckers are almost always with companions of the Chickadee-nuthatch-kinglet type. In fact all four are "boon companions." But here in the Sandhills they are as often alone as they are with other birds. Still, they are seen at times with Chickadees, Red-cockaded Woodpeckers, Brown-headed Nuthatches, Kinglets and Juncos. And these associations seem to be actual and usual, and not temporary and accidental ones as they are between most birds of different species. The Downy Woodpeckers are peaceable little fellows but other birds will impose on them. I have seen a Yellow-bellied Sapsucker and a mob of three or four English Sparrows near Pine Bluff chasing one about. But Downy was a fast flier and outflew all his tormentors each time. Their flight is undulating and typical of the woodpecker family. These woodpeckers have one trait of the Brown Creepers—they prefer to work *up* a tree and fly *down* to the base of the next one.

Perhaps a Downy Woodpecker does not really work any harder or faster for its food than any other bird, but somehow it seems that it does. I found one once on an inclined limb of a catalpa near the Highland Pines Inn and watched it work up ten feet in thirteen minutes. During that time Downy's blows fell good and hard at the average of a hundred strokes each minute except for a dozen momentary stops when a big bird flew over, or the Downy scratched its head. It was feeding on small white grubs which it secured at an average rate of four per minute. As it clung to the bark it spread two claws in front and two in the rear. Its bill appeared to be slightly open all the time. On a level limb Downy hopped along sidewise a little but while working on inclined or vertical surfaces it hopped straight up or down. But other Downy Woodpeckers preferred to work on smaller twigs and shoots of bushes, and even at times on stems of dried marsh plants.

These woodpeckers have the habit in the Sandhills of digging holes in which to sleep. One found a suitable place in the end of a dead limb of a large gum standing in a flooded swamp near Mid Pines Club. This limb had been broken and left a stub sticking out about five feet long at right angles to the trunk of the gum and about forty feet above the ground. It was about five inches in diameter where the woodpecker began work on it. Work was started on the under side of the limb about nine inches from the outer end on February 11, 1927, and the bird dug at it for forty-five minutes to such good purpose that the hole would then admit all its bill and half its head. As it worked it clung head down under the limb. Then it left its work to go foraging but came back in thirty minutes to resume work. During the next three days this woodpecker must have worked steadily for it then had a hole into which it could completely disappear. But the hole was not large enough nor deep enough, and the bird was still at work, continually popping in and out (backward) of its hole; usually when it backed out it carried a bill full of chips and shavings that it threw over its shoulder. As it did so, it glanced once or twice to either side as if to assure itself that all was well. Then back into the hole

Figure 19.   Broom-sedge corner, well liked by a variety of birds, particularly Field Sparrows, near Blue's Bridge, Feb. 2, 1926.

for another period of steady hammering. Apparently this woodpecker worked thus from thirty minutes to an hour after each half hour's foraging trip. Two more days of work completed the sleeping quarters in a snug cozy retreat. When finished, the hole was six inches deep, and the limb around it was but a mere shell. The opening being beneath the limb, it was sheltered from storms, and from any water running into it.

RED-COCKADED WOODPECKER

Dryobates borealis (Vieill.). *A. O. U. No. 395*

Field Identification. A woodpecker with black and white barring *across* the upperparts and a little larger than a sparrow. The white cheeks are conspicuous marks, but very few of the birds seen in the Sandhills during the winter had any red cockades at all. This bird is typical of the pine forests, especially about the edges near fields.

Description. Crown black, a small tuft of scarlet feathers on each side of the back of the head; back barred black and white; ear region white and separated from the white throat by a black stripe running down and back from the bill; underparts white. The female lacks the scarlet tufts. Total length 8 inches.

Distribution. Common in the Sandhills at all seasons. This species lives from the Gulf states north to Missouri, Tennessee and Virginia and is non-migratory wherever found.

Habits. Red-cockaded Woodpeckers frequent the shrub oak trees and loblolly pines at times, but seem more partial to the long-leaf pines, at least in this neighborhood. As a rule they work on the middle sections of trunks just below the lowest limbs, both on living trees and on dead trees.

Like most of the woodpeckers, these birds are expert at climbing vertical trunks by a series of hops assisted by the tails used as props. Red-cockaded Woodpeckers are so nearly always in small groups that when one is seen, two or three more are usually not far away. They have sharp calls more like loud sparrow alarms than woodpecker notes. In addition, their drumming on dead pine trunks is much more noisy than the small size of these birds would lead one to expect. So that between the calls and the drumming, these birds must be considered the noisiest small woodpeckers in the Sandhills.

Like most woodpeckers, these birds depend for food on the insects and grubs they can dig from the trunks and limbs of trees. As a rule they move upward as they work, giving a half dozen strokes or so at one place before moving on to the next. Perhaps their strokes are not so rapid as those of the Downy Woodpeckers, but otherwise the Red-cockaded Woodpeckers move and climb much like them. Like the Downy they prefer to work up only, and then fly down in going on to the next tree.

YELLOW-BELLIED SAPSUCKER. Pl. 4, page 114

Sphyrapicus varius varius (Linn.). *A. O. U. No. 402*

Field Identification. A black and white bird larger than a sparrow. Males have throat and crown scarlet; females have crown only scarlet. White streak *along edge of the wings*.

Description. Crown deep scarlet; back irregularly streaked with black and yellowish white; wing-feathers spotted with white; throat scarlet; breast black; sides marked variably with black; belly pale yellow. The female has a white throat. Young birds have the scarlet areas limited and dull; the breast brownish gray and specked with black. Total length 8½ inches.

Sapsuckers vary a good deal in winter. A good many are females and young birds and consequently show the dull colorings given above. But there are all manner of gradations between these plumages and that of the adult male. The amount of scarlet on the head varies; some birds having the whole crown deep scarlet, some having only the faintest scarlet tinge, others having the forehead scarlet, and still others having no scarlet at all on the crown. The throat patch varies less, but once in a while a bird shows only a scarlet chin or a reddish tinge where the scarlet throat patch ought to be. The color and markings of the upper-parts also vary, some birds having larger areas of yellowish or brownish white on the back. The amount of black marking on sides varies; some are barred, some are streaked, and some are a combination of the two. With the coming of spring, the plumage brightens and the full male breeding colors may be seen any time after the twentieth of January. After this change, the male Sapsuckers appear much more numerous than previously.

Distribution. Common in winter in the Sandhills. In winter members of this species go as far south as the Bahama Islands, Cuba and Costa Rica; in summer they live mainly in Canada, in the northern part of the United States, and in the Alleghany Mountains as far south as North Carolina.

Habits. During the winter Sapsuckers are most frequently on liquidambar trees, walnut trees and persimmons, but they also frequent cedars, gum trees, dogwoods and loblolly pines. They seem very fond, especially in January, of the trees with wisteria trained about them and frequently fly to the wisteria vines themselves. On oaks and pines these birds range from the bases far up into the highest limbs of the tallest trees. They are also seen on magnolias and in deciduous brush near streams. Some are found on privet bushes and occasionally on the trunks of apple trees.

When on vertical trunks and limbs, Yellow-bellied Sapsuckers usually move up by a series of hops or "hitches" an inch or two long. Occasionally they move down by short hops backward and downward, catching a new hold with claws and tail-prop, before making another backward hop. Not only do they move straight up and down, but they also go around the trunk, or limb, when moving in either direction. Generally, Sapsuckers perch length-wise of a limb, the same as woodpeckers, but often they vary this by alighting crosswise. These birds are skillful at clinging to even the smallest twig and are capable of hanging back downward and doing many aerobatic feats to reach insects and fruit. Sapsuckers keep their tails pressed against their supports, even when on a comparatively level perch.

Sapsuckers are usually tame, sometimes working in plain sight of a person less than fifteen feet away. At other times they are very wild and very skillful at keeping themselves hidden on the opposite side of a limb. Sapsuckers seem much more deliberate than other members of the family, except perhaps the Red-headed Woodpecker, for they are often seen resting in one spot as much as two minutes without movement of any kind. Even when drilling a tree they are comparatively slow and deliberate. At the same time, they are also restless and roving, perhaps even nervous, for I have seen them drill three or four holes part way through the bark of a tree without any reason at all that I could see. When feeding on persimmons and cedar berries they come and go every half hour.

During the winter of 1926–27, Sapsuckers were almost always alone. A Cardinal was seen once in the same persimmon as a Sapsucker; and other species, such as Downy Woodpeckers and Myrtle Warblers watched Sapsuckers at work. But there was no real association with them. While feeding in persimmons and dogwoods, the Sapsuckers often poach on the territory claimed by a Mockingbird and are usually promptly driven out. In Pine Bluff, a Sapsucker was seen battling over a privet bush with a flock of English Sparrows, but was able to hold its own against the mob. These birds are such fine little fighters that one has even been known to pounce on, and drive away, a Blue Jay! When forced to retreat, the Sapsucker's flight is rapid and undulating, typical of the woodpecker family. Yellow-bellied Sapsuckers in the Sandhills in winter are unobtrusive and quiet. Not until March 3, 1927, did I hear a note, and then once only, a clear sharp "cle-ur-r-r." These birds were common throughout the winter, about as much in evidence at one time as at another. They cared little about the weather, although on cold mornings they liked the sunny side of trees where they were also sheltered from the wind.

So much has been said and written of the bark-drilling and sap-drinking proclivities of these birds that the fact that they live on insects and wild fruits during a large part of the year is possibly neglected. From October to February I found the Sapsuckers eating insects obtained by exploring the crevices in the bark and by boring for them. During the same five months I noticed them picking insects from the surface of the bark, apparently small beetles. While hunting for such food, these birds worked from the bases of the trees to the highest limbs, but were most often in the limbs. During December and January the Sapsuckers were very fond of such berries as privet, sour gum, and persimmons. Some of the persimmon trees were great favorites, certain individual Sapsuckers going to them day after day, and often eating an entire fruit at one time. On other occasions the birds were more restless and only fed a few moments at a time, but even then returning again and again to the *same fruit* until it was all consumed. Usually after a Sapsucker had feasted five minutes on a persimmon, it flew to a small limb where it perched crosswise, wiped its bill vigorously and then rested for two minutes or more before returning to eat again. In all it took about fifteen minutes for a bird to eat an average sized wild persimmon. So much did these birds depend on this food that the load of persimmons on a favorite tree decreased visibly day by day. In fact it seemed quite usual for various species of birds to feast day after day on a few wild fruit trees until all the food was gone before moving on to the next supply. I found this to be the case with dogwood berries early in December, with sour gum berries and wild cherries in the middle of the same month, and with frost grapes during the latter part of December. Sometimes birds of other species ate the persimmons on the ground, but the Sapsuckers wanted their fruit to be hanging. If one accidentally knocked down a persimmon, it selected another pendant fruit. Eating persimmons hanging on a small twig required considerable agility, often resulting in the bird's clinging upside down under it.

During the latter part of January and early February I found the Sapsuckers visiting cedar trees regularly and feasting on the berries. They never ate more than fifteen or twenty berries at a visit, but a single bird sometimes visited the same cedar tree a dozen times in the same morning. Here on the cedar trees they did aerobatic feats again, but they also picked the berries up from the ground where they had fallen.

I did not notice any well-drilling until January 6, 1927, and then the holes extended only part way through the bark of a short-leaf pine. Later I found other Sapsucker drillings on trunks of loblolly pines that were also only partly through the bark. But at the same time that these shallow holes were being drilled, I saw the drilling birds catch insects. A week later, drillings were found on a long-leaf pine and from these a little sap had run out. On January 22, 1927, a male was seen drilling on a vertical limb of a walnut, but working intermittently with three to eight strokes at a time between rests. It did not move along the limb as a Downy Woodpecker would, but worked in one spot. He had a number of holes in this trunk, but they were not in rings or in any other regular formation. In drilling, this bird kept his bill closed. The first actual sap-sucking that I noticed was on February 18, 1927, and after that the birds drank sap from the trunks of liquidambars and walnuts. Later I found long-leaf pines, loblolly pines, persimmon trees and magnolias drilled; but nowhere did I see any extensive system of borings, or any permanent damage.

Before this sap-sucking begins, these birds find it necessary at times to drink water. On February 9, 1926, a Sapsucker was seen drinking from a crotch high up in a gum tree. On December 10, 1926, one flew to a hole in a gum tree and drank from a hollow filled with rain-water. On January 19, 1927, I noted another one taking a drink from a natural bowl high on the limb of a tree.

In accordance with the usual woodpecker custom, Sapsuckers preen and dress their feathers while clinging to the upright trunks of trees.

PILEATED WOODPECKER

Phlœotomus pileatus (Linn.).   *A. O. U. No. 405*

Field Identification. A predominantly black bird almost as large as a Crow, with undulating flight; a white bar on each wing showing in flight; a prominent red crest; bill large. A wild, shy bird that has retreated to the most undisturbed forests.

Description. Plumage blackish brown; whole top of head scarlet, the feathers forming a crest; a narrow stripe of white bordering this crest and separating it from the blackish brown ear-feathers; a stripe from nostrils down sides of the neck to the body is tinged with yellow before the eye and white below; between this stripe and the white throat is a scarlet stripe; bill horn color. Female with red markings more restricted. Total length 17 inches.

Distribution. The Pileated Woodpecker is resident in the Sandhills and may be seen at any season. This is the northern limit of this form which occurs south to Florida and west to middle Texas. North of us it is replaced by a similar form, the Northern Pileated Woodpecker.

Habits. I have seen these woodpeckers recently near Blue's Bridge and in the swamp at the head of Juniper Lake. In such places they are high on long-leaf pines, sour gums and cypress trees (Fig. 8).

Their flight is somewhat heavy, but it is undulating like that of other woodpeckers, although perhaps less deeply so. Since the groves of old-growth trees suited to these birds are now widely scattered, the Pileated Woodpeckers are forced to fly occasionally across fields and over farms. Those that I saw doing this, did not fly high, but when they neared their landing place they dipped down and swooped up to it. When in flight, I have heard them coming for some distance because of their loud, rolling "cow-cow" many times repeated.

I found the Pileated Woodpeckers operating on both living gum trees and dead pine trunks, from which they dug out big white grubs. These birds also ate insects of various kinds and sour gum berries (*Nyssa silvatica*). Pairing and mating take place in the Sandhills in March.

RED-HEADED WOODPECKER. Pl. 4, page 114

Melanerpes erythrocephalus (Linn.). *A. O. U. 406*

Field Identification. A red, black and white bird slightly smaller than a Robin; large white patches on the wings showing conspicuously in flight. (Red largely replaced by brown in winter.)

Description. Deep red on head, neck and upper breast; upper back and most of the wing-feathers bluish black; secondary wing-feathers white at outer ends; lower back white; tail black; lower breast and belly white; bill light ashy blue. Young birds have the red replaced by mixed grayish brown and brownish black; black tail usually tipped with white; white areas streaked and spotted with brownish black. Total length 9½ inches.

A good many of the Red-headed Woodpeckers seen in the autumn and early winter are still in the immature plumage, and consequently are "brown-headed" and not "red-headed." But in January, the plumage changes, and after that, all the birds show the mature plumage. Ordinarily we consider this bird to be very conspicuously marked; yet, when one presents its breast to an observer, and has the sky for a background, it will disappear from sight.

Distribution. Common locally throughout the Sandhills at all seasons. These woodpeckers live from the Gulf states and Texas north to New York, Ontario, Manitoba, Alberta and British Columbia.

Habits. Red-headed Woodpeckers are found on both dead and living sycamores, gums, oaks and long-leaf pines (Figs. 5 and 16); and on limbs and main trunks from the ground to the highest limbs of the tallest trees. Although usually on an upright surface they can alight on a flat surface when necessary, and sometimes they perch crosswise on a limb. Telephone poles are favorite living and resting places. Occasionally these birds are seen on the ground. Not only are they found in the open forests and on the farms, but they also live in the villages and towns of the Sandhills. Indeed they might almost be called the most "citified" of all the Sandhills woodpeckers. At times, they actually alight on our buildings, but sometimes they are very wary of a person walking. These birds are noted for staying at home. Wherever they have dug their holes in dead stubs or telephone poles, they will be found day after day. Some birds have three or four favorite trees scattered over a small area.

As a rule movements are quite deliberate, even while eating, and the birds frequently stop to look up and all about. In wood digging, their blows are powerful but comparatively slow. Like all the woodpeckers, the Red-headed ones are expert climbers. Perhaps these woodpeckers climb up or down or circle around a trunk more than most woodpeckers for they really seem to prefer climbing up a pole rather than flying up to the top. They are skillful at alighting on, or hanging to, a smooth vertical surface like a telephone pole. One Red-headed Woodpecker near the Mid Pines Club, was seen hanging to the edge of its hole for twenty-five minutes at least; during which time it did not move except to sway rhythmically sideways and turn its head. At one time it scratched its head with one foot while clinging with the other foot and propping itself with its tail.

For a bird whose reputation is that of being "active" this woodpecker is very quiet, at least in its winter home in the Sandhills. One day I noticed one enter its hole at 2:40 p. m., to rest out of a cold wind, and remain there until after I left twenty minutes later. Some of these Red-headed Woodpeckers were very tame. I remember one whose home was in an oak stub leaning over a busy motor road near Pinehurst, yet it merely glanced down as each car went by, scarcely twenty feet under it. But it was very critical and suspicious of any car that stopped, and I found another bird that was very doubtful of my efforts to see what it was doing. When I alarmed it, it dodged to and fro behind a pole, sticking an eye first out on one side, and then the other on the other side.

This particular bird didn't admire curiosity in me, but I have observed that Red-headed Woodpeckers in general exhibit the same trait at times.

Ordinarily these birds resent other birds being near them, and drive the intruders away. They seem to parcel out the territory to suit themselves and drive off all other Red-heads. So it is not strange that they remain solitary throughout the winter and do not form even temporary associations with other species. Indeed, most of their connections with other birds are warring ones. In the Sandhills the Red-headed Woodpeckers dig most of the holes in the telephone poles and the dead stubs or limbs of trees. Often the English Sparrows and the Starlings covet these holes without regard to whether the woodpeckers are through with them or not. The sparrows are the most persistent, but also the easiest for the woodpecker to eject. But the warfare with Starlings is more drawn out. A Red-headed Woodpecker had its hole near the top of a telephone pole near the Pinehurst Dairy. Here it was quietly perching on March 1, 1927, when a Starling flew over and alighted on the nearby wire. Then the woodpecker became uneasy, hitched itself down the pole, dived at the Starling and struck—but the Starling dodged. In a moment the woodpecker dived again and the two birds fluttered to the ground fighting. Instantly, the Starling disengaged itself and darted up to, and into, the disputed hole, with the woodpecker in hot pursuit. Once inside, the Starling had the advantage and easily kept the woodpecker out. After that day, fortunes varied, sometimes the Starling was in possession and sometimes the woodpecker. Finally the Red-head got a mate and between the two of them they managed to occupy the nest hole and keep the intruding Starlings out.

The flight of the Red-headed Woodpeckers is usually low and straight and from tree to tree, but in longer fights it is apt to fly gently undulating, but even then straighter and more direct than the average woodpecker. In many ways these woodpeckers seem quicker and more nimble than others, and certainly they spend a great deal of time chasing and catching numerous flying insects. Flying insects are an important source of food supply all through the winter, but with the increase of the number of insects in March this activity greatly increases. The observation post for fly-catching is usually the one in which the nest hole is situated. But I noted at least one bird that used four tall trees in succession for this purpose. On February 1, 1927, a Red-headed Woodpecker was seen clinging to the side of a telephone pole. Twice it left the pole, flew out twenty feet, caught an insect each time, and returned to the pole to eat it. Two weeks later another bird was seen to make six trips similarly out and back during six minutes, sometimes going more than a hundred feet from its perch. As the bird went direct to the insect, caught it and returned immediately to its perch, it seemed likely that the insect was seen each time before the bird started, indicating wonderful eyesight. While not engaged in thus hawking, this bird hunted the limbs for prey. Ten days later I found this bird watching for insects and making ten fly-catching sallies in a minute and a half. Its flights were from ten to one hundred and fifty feet in length and all the insects were from forty to sixty feet above the ground. One of the Red-heads seen fly-catching in December, returned to its dead stub where it drilled for grubs and borers in the usual woodpecker fashion, except that its strokes were heavy and deliberate. On another occasion, I saw one of these birds fly down into the road to catch and eat an earthworm.

Many of the same birds that were seen fly-catching were also eating acorns in January and February. Although the Red-headed Woodpeckers all seemed fond of acorns they may have utilized that food only when insects were scarce. Most, if not all, of the acorns were secured from the ground and carried in the bill to the top of a pole or suitable limb. There they were hammered by strong down strokes of the powerful bill until the shells fell away. While being hammered, the acorn was held by one foot firmly against the support, and the strokes were intermittent. Later I saw one of these birds take pieces of acorn meat from crevices in the pole; so this bird may store food in such cavities as it can find or chisel out for itself.

These woodpeckers are more fond of drinking water than most others, and they are among the few that can be attracted by a drinking fountain. On a very cold morning in January in Pine Bluff, one of these birds was seen by Mrs. Levi Packard to fly down to a pan of frozen water, stand on the edge, and chip out slivers of ice to eat.

Red-headed Woodpeckers chisel out holes for themselves, usually in telephone poles and in dead limbs, or stubs, of shrub oaks.

RED-BELLIED WOODPECKER. Pl. 3, page 64

Centurus carolinus (Linn.)　*A. O. U. No. 409*

Field Identification. A red-crowned woodpecker slightly smaller than a Robin; white and black barring *across* the upperparts; larger than the Red-cockaded Woodpecker; gray cheeks and throat.

Description. Top of the head and back of the neck bright scarlet; back and tail regularly barred across with black and white; small feathers just above tail, white; cheeks and underparts dull ashy white. Female has the crown grayish and the back of the neck scarlet. Total length 9½ inches.

Distribution. Occasional in all parts of the Sandhills at all seasons. These woodpeckers live in the eastern part of the United States from the Gulf states and Texas north to South Dakota, southern Minnesota, Ontario, New York, Pennsylvania and Delaware.

Habits. Red-bellied Woodpeckers are seen on the ground, low down on tree trunks, on the main trunks of large and small trees, and high up in the trees both on trunks, and on vertical and horizontal limbs. Frequently they are on oaks, more perhaps than on any other kind of trees. At times during the winter the Red-

Usually when they find a home to their liking they reoccupy the hole for several years. When they finally decide they must have a new hole they commonly choose another location in the same pole, or stub, if possible. These holes are generally about two inches in diameter and bored into the northeast, east, south or west sides. On telephone poles the tails of the birds perching at the entrance keep the wood below the hole worn fresh so that it is easy to tell which holes are occupied. In telephone poles the holes are between twelve and twenty feet from the ground; while there is a tendency to place the hole within a foot or two of the top, there are many exceptions. In the oak stubs the holes are from ten to sixty feet above the ground, but generally between one and two feet below the top of the stub. In winter these holes are used for shelter, and at times for roosting. After being abandoned, they serve for squirrels, Bluebirds, Starlings and English Sparrows.

bellied Woodpeckers are found in lowlands and swamps on the sour gum trees, but I saw these birds more often over dry lands, probably because I worked there more. On the ground, these birds are more at home than any other woodpeckers except the Flickers, but I never saw one attempt to move about much on the ground except by flying. While on the ground or any other flat surface they keep their tails braced against their supports just as they do on a vertical surface.

These woodpeckers work and hammer on the trunks of trees, on the boles of oaks, on boles high up in live or blasted pines, and on both living and dead limbs, usually working up, but working down also if they want to, using a peculiar partly-sidewise drop downward.

Red-bellied Woodpeckers appear to be always confident and assured. They are not disposed to molest the smaller birds, but toward the larger birds they manifest a disposition that keeps them all at a distance. Even the Blue Jays are driven away from choice food by these birds, in spite of the Jay's well-known fighting ability. Not only are these woodpeckers unsociable and solitary among themselves, but they do not gather with other species except in accidental, temporary associations. Such an accidental occasion was noted on December 21, 1926, when a Red-bellied Woodpecker and a Hairy Woodpecker were seen together in a sour gum after berries.

In flight, these woodpeckers are apt to progress step by step from tree to tree. In this respect, and in that it is undulating, their flight is much like that of other woodpeckers. In approaching a perch, the Red-bellied Woodpeckers usually glide and sweep up to it with the impetus already gained.

In most cases, these birds depend for food on borers and grubs, but I have seen them apparently eat insects, cocoons and insect eggs from the bark of trees. They eat acorns to a considerable extent, picking them up from the ground and carrying them off in their bills to a convenient place to hammer them. In winter, dogwood berries and sour gum berries are eaten as long as they last, although these berries are usually all consumed before Christmas. These woodpeckers take only a few berries and then fly away. But in ten or fifteen minutes they are back again for a few more berries, and again leave; and they may repeat these visits at intervals all day long.

Although other woodpeckers carry off and store bits of food, the Red-bellied Woodpeckers appear to do it more than any others in the Sandhills. These birds are rather easily attracted to artificial feeding stations, especially if suet be offered them. They will eat nuts and bread crumbs also, but not as greedily.

After the first of April they begin to assume the brilliant breeding plumage and a real pinkish tinge to their underparts, but they commence to pair before that, sometimes being seen in pairs as early as the middle of March. There is reason to believe that nesting begins late in April. These woodpeckers find a dead limb high in a long-leaf pine and proceed to cut an entrance hole into it and then carefully hollow out a cavity to a depth of eight or ten inches.

FLICKER.   Pl. 4, page 114

Colaptes auratus auratus (Linn.).   *A. O. U. No. 412*

Field Identification. A brownish gray woodpecker larger than a Robin. Undersurface of wings and tail yellow and showing in flight; white spot on back above tail, conspicuous in flight; a peculiar, undulatory flight; red and black markings on the head; broad, black crescent on breast; underparts with large black spots.

Description. Upperparts brownish gray, barred on back and wings with irregular broken black lines; bright scarlet band across the back of the neck; the underside of the wings yellow; lower back white; tail black above, yellow below; a broad black streak starting at base of bill and extending back on side of the throat; broad black crescent across the breast; upper breast brown; other underparts white, heavily spotted with black. Female is without black streaks on sides of her throat. Total length 11 inches.

Distribution. Common in all parts of the Sandhills at all seasons of the year. In winter Flickers go as far south as the Gulf coast and Texas; in summer they are found as far north as the limit of trees in northern Canada and Alaska, but many remain in all parts of the United States.

Habits. These woodpeckers are often seen on the ground. This is but natural for the ground in the Sandhills is warm and soft enough for ants and other insect food of the Flickers, even in winter. While largely ground dwellers, Flickers are always under, or near, trees, except when flying across an open from one tree to another. Both pine and shrub oak forests (Figs. 1, 2, 5) are inhabited, and even other kinds of trees serve if the ground in the vicinity is suitable for the Flickers' food. I saw more Flickers on pines than on other trees in the Sandhills, at all heights and from October to April. But Flickers were also on the trunks and limbs of various kinds of gums. Naturally the dead trees and dead limbs of living trees are favored, but perhaps not so much so as by other woodpeckers, for Flickers depend less on boring for grubs and beetles. Although Flickers are often on the ground under oaks and sapling pines, they are never found in very dense forests. Neither are they far out in the open fields. The places to look for them are in open forests with some underbrush, along streams, about ponds and in fields near a forest or grove of trees. Flickers like weedy old cornfields (Figs. 18 and 27) where they can dig in the soft soil and yet not be too far from forests and thickets. Often they are in waste corners where the broom sedge grows (Fig. 13 and 19), and sometimes in the wire grass under the shrub oaks. Often Flickers are seen in sweet gum trees (*Liquidambar styraciflua*), persimmons and cedar trees. While not so frequently on telephone poles, occasionally one is seen there. They are to be found in peach orchards often enough to say they at least like weedy orchards; and they are sometimes observed on the ground of recently burned-over shrub oak forest, but not often. In addition to these haunts, Flickers are seen on the rougher parts of golf links, in dooryards and sometimes even in quite large towns.

On the ground they are very much at home and readily move across it by rather long, easy hops. On one occasion a Flicker that I surprised near Aberdeen, sneaked off across the ground to a nearby cedar before it flew. Together with their ease of movement on the ground, they combine sureness and accuracy of movement on the high limbs of trees. Half the time at least, they perch crosswise on limbs, even on small twigs where one might suppose they would have trouble in balancing. On tree trunks they hitch themselves up by short jumps and keep their tails pressed against the trunk. They move downward by a series of queer, short, backward jumps.

They move around a good deal and are quite active, but often spend some time quietly perching, even as long as twenty-five minutes at a time. The disposition of the Flicker is somewhat social, for I frequently find them in groups, even in winter. I doubt if they actually associate with any, but I occasionally see them near, other birds. Once I saw three Blue Jays, a Flicker and a gray squirrel on the ground together. At other times I have seen Flickers near enough to Mockingbirds, Towhees, Cardinals, Blue Jays, Juncos, Robins, and even Doves in peach orchards and Meadowlarks in broom sedge corners to be considered in company with them, at least temporarily.

In flight, Flickers move in long bounding waves. There are a few wing-beats while going down, then a short glide carries them up, and there is a rhythmic quality to the whole flight that is very typical. Not only is this flight peculiar to the Flickers, but it shows the close relationship to other woodpeckers.

Flickers can hardly be called song-birds and yet they have several very pretty notes and calls. They have a loud, ringing ''peek'' call characteristic of the woodpecker family, and also a rolling ''zwick-ah'' that is peculiar to the Flickers themselves. Once a Flicker was heard calling ''z-zwick-ah, z-zwick-ah'' from the limb of a tall pine near the Pine Bluff postoffice and a moment later another Flicker appeared on the trunk of a neighboring pine. On another day I heard one calling in the top of a tall gum, but it was so hurried that the call sounded like ''zwicky'' repeated six or seven times. In the spring of the year, Flickers seem to feel their limitations in the way of making music, so they drum out rolling tattoos on hard dry tree trunks and tin roofs.

Flickers stay in the Sandhills all winter, but the infrequent snowstorms cause them lots of trouble in finding food. On January 10, 1927, I found quite a little coterie of birds had scratched the leaves under a dogwood tree until they had a space twelve feet in diameter more or less cleared of snow. Here, among other species of birds, were two Flickers foraging among the leaves for fallen dogwood berries. These berries were probably eaten until weather conditions became better for insect catching. Even during the winter, ants are fairly plentiful for the Sandhills Flickers, especially on warm days. One day at the edge of the golf links at Southern Pine Country Club, a Flicker was seen hunting across the ground amid leaves fallen from the oaks and needles from the pines. He thrust in his bill experimentally at every step or two across the

Figure 20. Old cornfields in winter, a favorite bird haunt, especially for Juncos and Field Sparrows. About a mile south of Highland Pines Inn, Southern Pines, Feb. 20, 1926.

ground. When he found a promising place he scratched away the leaves with his feet, and then quickly dug a hole with his bill to uncover the ant nest he had discovered. Flickers are given to alighting on the ground and picking and digging in it for ants by striking swift blows downward with the bill and the whole force of head, neck and body behind it. While ants are the most sought-after food, the Flickers have not altogether abandoned the traditional method of woodpeckers and may often be seen digging on the trunks of loblolly and long-leaf pines or on white oaks. In addition to dogwood berries, the winter Flickers also eat sour gum berries and cedar berries. Flickers will often consume fifty cedar berries or more at a meal, thereby differing from other woodpeckers that take only six to twenty berries at a time.

These birds can be attracted to artificial feeding stations with shredded meat, suet or meal worms; but a saucer of water seems more effective, even in winter. The water should be an inch or so deep, for their bills are long and they like to put them well down into the water. Probably, such a saucer of water will soon be used for a bath, as they like to bathe, and they appreciate a dish with a non-slippery bottom. After bathing, Flickers usually fly up to the nearest perch to preen and dress their feathers.

''Drumming'' on hollow stubs or tin roofs is an important part of the mating activities, but still more prominent is the ''dancing,'' for Flickers bob, dance and courtesy in true cake-walk style. They dance on either dead or living trees, and although there is not much movement to the feet, the bodies are bent from side to side and there is a constant jiggling motion. The heads are tilted back at times and the bills pointed up at an angle of sixty degrees with the necks outstretched. The bills, heads and necks are kept in constant motion, reminding one of a musical director's baton. There are intervals of rest alternated with the periods of motion, and the whole dance lasts perhaps five minutes. During the dance the birds perch crosswise of a limb or cling to an upright one, or may change from one position to the other during the display. Although there are indications of this dancing all through the winter, true courting does not begin until the first of March and then the dancing becomes more vigorous. In the case of Flickers, the females do much of the dancing, but there is another form of mating activity where the males take the lead. Here, the pair of birds fly together to a thicket or a grove of trees where the female alights. The male alights on the trunk two or three feet below her and creeps slowly up with wings open and fluttering, and with tail spread. Usually the female flies just before he reaches her. Then he follows and they repeat at the next place they stop.

PHOEBE. Pl. 6, page 168

Sayornis phoebe (Lath.). *A. O. U. No. 456*

Field Identification. A small dark bird a little larger than a sparrow with darker crown; black bill; two inconspicuous white wing-bars; white outer tail-feathers. The only flycatcher that winters in the Sandhills.

Description. Upperparts grayish brown; crown darker; wing-bars white and distinct, although not prominent; outer tail-feathers white, except at the tip; underparts white, tinged with yellow, and with some brownish gray on the breast and sides; bill black. Total length 7 inches.

Distribution. Common in the Sandhills at all seasons of the year. In winter Phoebes are found as far south as southern Mexico; in summer they live from Texas, northern Mississippi and Georgia north to Nova Scotia, New Brunswick, Quebec, Ontario, Keewatin and Alberta.

Habits. As a rule Phoebes prefer very open forests, or fields either bordering forests or having hedges running across them. They do not care for large fields where there are no bushes or elevated perches from which to watch for prey. And they are decidedly not a dooryard bird in winter. Phoebes usually perch low, within four or six feet of the ground, to watch for prey, but sometimes as high as thirty feet. These perches include pine saplings, shrub oaks, small gum trees, low bushes, stumps and tall weeds—which, although good for observation, are not always the most prominent perches. Sometimes Phoebes hunt out across wet and marshy lands and here they perch on occasional willow shoots or the tallest reeds. In old cotton fields and cornfields they use the tallest stalks left standing. If no better perches present themselves, they will use electric wires and fences.

Usually these small erect birds are seen perching quietly, but having decided it is time to move, their movements are quick and decisive. When perched, especially just after a flight, a Phoebe's tail moves up and down evenly and regularly about an inch each way. At the same time, its head is in constant motion, turning this way and that. As a rule, these birds attend strictly to business and are so indifferent to persons that they will permit a close approach. At least this was the way they impressed me during the winter; that is, indifference rather than friendliness. I mention this particularly, because in their summer homes, Phoebes are dooryard birds that make friends with the house people. During the winter these birds are almost always solitary, seldom even two birds being near each other. Nor are they seen with any other species.

Living as they do largely on insects, Phoebes have developed their powers at sudden starts and pouncings and quick, dodging flights. When going from place to place, they fly low and direct, a few feet above the ground, with a sharp rise as they reach the new perch. Flights are short and only from perch to perch and the birds are apt to stop several times in crossing even a narrow field.

During the winter the Phoebes were silent, and not until March 17, 1927, did I hear one utter a "phoebe" note, and then, once only.

The Phoebes' usual method of hunting is to perch quietly on some favorable perch until an insect makes its appearance. If the insect is on the ground it is promptly pounced upon and carried off to be eaten; if the insect is flying it is just as promptly chased and quickly caught in spite of all its twists and turnings. In common with other birds that adopt this method of hunting, the Phoebes' eyesight is quick and keen. Sometimes passing insects are seen as much as a hundred feet away, and when insects are numerous short flights are made every few seconds. Occasionally Phoebes are seen in cotton fields; and they are known to eat cotton boll weevils.

Evidently berries form a conspicuous part of the Phoebes' food from December to the middle of March. Early in the winter they eat dogwood berries and later they take those of sumach. Berries are usually eaten a half dozen, or so, at a time, and may be secured by the birds alighting on the twig bearing them, or by hovering in front of a cluster while they pick them one by one.

Phoebes take flutter-baths throughout the winter in the shallow edges of streams. After bathing they fly up on a bush or a low tree and shake themselves thoroughly in the warm sun, but seem to do much less preening at such times than birds of other species would.

HORNED LARK. Pl. 11, page 272

Otocoris alpestris alpestris (Linn.). *A. O. U. No. 474*

Field Identification. Difficult, for the "horns" do not show in winter before March first. These are small brown birds somewhat larger than sparrows. They have black tails edged with white; they feed only on the ground in large open fields; when they fly up from the ground, they nearly always utter a series of "cheeps," and make a wide circle only to return to alight near the starting point. There is no way, in the field, of telling this species from the Prairie Horned Lark, although both have been positively identified from near Southern Pines. The only time I have seen this form in the Sandhills was during, or immediately after, a snowstorm; but this may be accidental and this bird may occur at other times also.

Description. Forepart of crown, a mark from bill downward to side of throat, and a patch on the breast dull black; on some birds the throat is yellow; head, neck and spot above tail brown; back grayish brown; "shoulders" vinaceous; tail black margined with white; lower breast and belly white, the former more or less spotted with dusky; sides vinaceous. *In spring and summer only,* the black markings are clear black; a black tuft (the "horns") of elongated feathers on each side of crown; forehead, line over the eye, ear region and throat sulphur yellow. Total length $7\frac{3}{4}$ inches.

On March 1, 1927, I noticed the distinctive markings about the head were just becoming bright and clear. Four days later they were still brighter and in a few cases the "horns" were beginning to appear.

Distribution. I have seen these larks on the fields between Southern Pines and Montevideo Park, and on the fields near the Pinehurst Dairy and the Archery Club. These birds go as far south in winter as the Ohio Valley and Georgia; in summer they live as far north as Boothia Peninsula, the head of James Bay, Labrador and Newfoundland.

Habits. I have seen Horned Larks only in fields where the grass has been mown down so close that there was no cover whatever to obstruct their view. On the ground, they walk, and only once have I ever seen one hop and then I thought that particular one might have been injured. Ordinarily, they can run quite rapidly and even cross quite a large field without taking wing; but I have never seen one on a tree limb, or even perched as high as the top of a fence post. As a rule, these larks crouch down close to the ground so that they sometimes become very un-birdlike and difficult to see.

At times they are tame and unsuspicious enough to permit of close approach. On March 5, 1927, I passed a flock on the ground so tame they permitted automobiles to pass within fifteen feet. Later, I parked my car in an open field near the Pinehurst Archery Club. Soon a flock of twenty-nine Horned Larks came flying in, but, on seeing my car so close, they would not fly to the feed about me but alighted forty feet away on the surface of the snow. Here they rested a few minutes until the more venturesome ones, followed gradually by the others, ran over to the feed and soon all of them were feeding about me. When I got out of the car, they flew away, but immediately came flying back, and settled down before I had gotten back into the car. Horned Larks are sociable and when one bird appears the whole flock comes soon afterward, for they are always in flocks here, containing from eighteen to eighty-five individuals. On the other hand, they do not associate with other kinds of birds although this species is sometimes with Prairie Horned Larks in large mixed flocks.

The flight of the Horned Larks is light and easy, with some wavering motion. Usually their flocks are rather loose and yet compact enough so that the birds are all together and probably under one directive force. Their cheeping call is a shrill little ''tsee-tsee-der-e-e-e,'' similar to that of Pipits and yet easily distinguished, at least in the Sandhills.

Although these Horned Larks appear with cold storms they are not entirely impervious to temperature and weather. On March 1, 1927, I found a flock of thirty-seven in an old cornfield.

The majority faced the wind and worked up against it, many stopping in the furrows under the lee of tufts of grasses. When under this shelter, they began scratching the snow away and soon worked themselves down into little hollows in the snow. Here they scratched and dug for seeds. Sometimes one fed as long as fifteen minutes in one place. After the storm I found these same birds crouched close to the ground of wind-blown bare spots feeding, seemingly with the feathers of their breasts and bellies actually touching the ground. These Horned Larks scratched the bare ground both with their feet and with quick little side sweeps of their bills. Later in the day I found other Horned Larks feeding in the hay seed and chaff swept out of a barn. In this same chaff were a few grubs and at least two of these were eaten. Once I saw one of these larks stop at the edge of a little pool of melted snow and take a drink.

PRAIRIE HORNED LARK

Otocoris alpestris praticola Hensh. *A. O. U. No. 474b*

Field Identification. Similar to Horned Lark, from which it cannot be separated by plumage character in the field. I have seen this smaller form earlier in the winter when the weather was warmer and it is not associated in my mind with snowstorms as the larger bird is.

Description. Like the Horned Lark but smaller and paler. Total length 7¼ inches.

Distribution. In winter these larks go as far south as Texas, Tennessee and Georgia; in summer they live from Connecticut, West Virginia, Ohio and southern Missouri north to Manitoba, Ontario and Quebec. Here in the Sandhills they are winter birds only, from early December to the last of February.

Habits. They are birds of the open fields and are not found in forests or brush of any kind; and they do not even like long grass if they can find fields free from it. They do not alight on the limbs of trees, but once I saw one alight on the top of a fence post. Such fields as polo fields, race-courses, aviation fields and golf links (Fig. 12) are the places where these birds are found in the Sandhills. Occasionally they visit the peach orchards, where their presence is wholly beneficial (Fig. 7).

On the ground, Prairie Horned Larks walk and run rapidly after insects, but when feeding on seeds they squat down and sometimes remain in one place for several minutes. Normally these birds are very quiet and tame. When mildly alarmed they crouch flat on the ground and trust to their neutral color for concealment. When actually frightened, they spring up with sharp whistled notes, and fly off only to hesitate and swing about (first one bird and then another and finally the whole flock) and return to near the spot from which they started.

Prairie Horned Larks are sociable little fellows always seen during the winter in flocks of from six to two hundred birds. They do not associate with other birds in the Sandhills except accidentally with Meadowlarks, Killdeer Plover, Mourning Doves and Rusty Blackbirds.

When these larks fly up, they start suddenly, quickly and all together. Their long wings beat in slow, gliding strokes, but the flock turns and maneuvers sharply at times. When they fly, they face the wind; when they are ready to alight they are apt to circle around, fly low over the ground, and alight facing the direction from which the wind is blowing.

Prairie Horned Larks remain all winter. They were originally birds of the western prairies, but as larger and larger fields appeared they gradually established themselves farther and farther east.

Evidently, these birds depend mostly on seeds for food during the wintertime. Sometimes they come about barns and frequent freshly manured fields for spilled oats and waste hay seed. Prairie Horned Larks also eat insects that they pick up, or catch by running. Once I saw one catch a white grub, thrash it sideways on the ground and finally eat it.

Prairie Horned Larks rather enjoy rains. During hard showers they keep right on feeding but stop every few minutes to shake vigorously.

BLUE JAY. Pl. 3, page 64

Cyanocitta cristata (Linn.). *A. O. U. 477*

Field Identification. A blue and white bird larger than a Robin, with blue crest, and a black band on back of the neck and across breast. One can hardly mistake the Blue Jay "in them baseball clothes of his'n" for any other than the bold free lance he is.

PLATE 5. Cutover Hardwood Swamps

1: Red-winged Blackbird (female).
2: Red-winged Blackbird (male in winter).
3: Sparrow Hawk (male).
4: Sparrow Hawk (female).
5: Marsh Hawk (male). (Greatly reduced.)
6: Marsh Hawk (female). (Greatly reduced.)
7: Rusty Blackbird (immature in winter).
8: Rusty Blackbird (adult male in winter).
9: Swamp Sparrow.

(Figures 1–4 and 7–9, about ⅛ life size)

Description. Upperparts various shades of grayish blue; forehead black; face and throat whitish, outlined by a narrow black line; head crested; wings blue, spotted with white, and smaller feathers barred narrowly with black; tail blue, narrowly barred with black; underparts dusky whitish. Total length 12 inches.

Distribution. A common resident in the Sandhills at all seasons; in fact these birds are resident wherever they live except in the extreme northern part of their range where they are slightly migratory. They live in the Gulf states; west to Texas, eastern Colorado and Nebraska; north to Alberta, Keewatin, Quebec, New Brunswick and Newfoundland.

Habits. Blue Jays are inhabitants of the forests and of the borderland where forests and fields meet and alternate, but are seldom out in very large fields. These birds are so bold and venturesome they rarely retreat to thick bushes for protection as other birds do. Jays prefer the limbs near the tops of the long-leaf pines when the wind is not too strong, and are more in pines than in all other kinds of trees combined. You may find them at all elevations; at times on the ground after acorns and ground insects; again in the oaks; and again they are on the tops of the tallest trees. Although not so often in the bushes and thickets, there are many exceptions. Sometimes the hollies (Fig. 17) and magnolias are alive with birds, and among these are usually some Jays. Occasionally Jays are in or over peach orchards, but there appears to be nothing there especially attractive to them. They not only live in the wild districts, but come quite as often to towns and cities.

Jays in flying from place to place are apt to go bird by bird in long strings, although evidently more or less in one troop. When on the ground, they make their way in a series of long hops and these hops are a little sidewise as well as forward. Usually, they perch in trees in orthodox fashion, but at times one is seen clinging sidewise on the trunk of a pine. Jays have prominent crests, not always erect, but sometimes laid back flat on the crown. They have many of the ways of Crows, showing the close relationship between the two species. At all times they are bold, aggressive birds, apt to tyrannize over such other birds as will permit it, or can not help themselves. But this bold disposition serves them well when it comes to finding new sources of food. For they are the quickest of all birds to find a new feeding station.

Throughout the winter, Blue Jays are extremely noisy, beginning early in the morning and often keeping the racket up all day, and as they are usually in hearing of each other, their noise covers large areas. They even scream in the evening. As one old negro told me: "Every Friday the Blue Jays go to Hades to tell what people are doing on earth." Only, I never missed any Jays on Friday, or on any other day for that matter.

But all this noise has one good purpose, it notifies all other species within hearing. One day, the White-throated Sparrows quickly darted out of sight when a Blue Jay screamed. Another time a Jay just north of Pine Bluff school gave a single alarm on the approach of an automobile, and sent all the Juncos to cover. Once, five noisy Jays in the trees near a rose tangle called my attention to a sleeping cat on the ground beneath them. Jays are full of insatiable curiosity and they are often seen trooping to and fro when something attracts their attention. One Blue Jay, after watching a woodpecker eat suet, tried it, but desisted after only one peck. On another occasion a continuous stream of Field Sparrows to a water-bath attracted the attention of a pair of Jays that flew over to see what all the excitement was about.

Blue Jays do not associate with any other birds at any season of the year, but because they are everywhere and are so very active, they are often seen in the same places as other birds. The most remarkable group I remember was a Blue Jay, a Towhee, a Cardinal, a Catbird and a Brown Thrasher all in the same small thicket. But when even one Jay and one Cardinal are together they make a striking contrast in color. On one exceptional occasion I found a Blue Jay and a Brown Thrasher drinking out of the same pan of water together. In practically every ease, these temporary associations were due to protection, shelter, food or water, drawing the different birds.

There is continual warfare going on between the Blue Jays and the Cardinals, Brown Thrashers, Mockingbirds, Tufted Titmice and smaller birds. While I have no doubt the smaller birds often wish dive things on the Blue Jays, they could hardly be considered enemies because so impotent against the larger birds. The Red-bellied Woodpeckers are even more at odds with the Jays. Mockingbirds are often chasing the Jays in and out through the trees and as far away as they can. Apparently all these instances might be explained by home territory, rivalry and food rivalry, perhaps guarding food in the case of Mockingbirds. But with hawks and owls the Jays' antipathy perhaps takes on a touch of the love of mischief and excitement. On February 10, 1926, one mile south of Highland Pines Inn, I heard four Blue Jays giving alarm calls in a thicket. There I found them excitedly tormenting a Sharp-shinned Hawk. The hawk stood the mob as long as it could and then darted out and away. After that the commotion gradually died down.

The flight of Blue Jays is rather slow and comparatively level and direct. These birds have a curious habit of carrying their heads high as they fly. Flight is usually low, or through the tops of the tallest pines at most; but sometimes they are seen flying over high up above the trees. The flight is usually from tree to tree rather than for long distances.

Although most of the numerous sounds that Blue Jays make, are disconnected and properly classed as calls, some are musical enough to be called short songs, such as the "johnny-cake" call. As makers of varied and distinctive calls the Blue Jays rank high, but they are so noisy! The racket is bad enough when two or three birds participate, but much worse when they begin to scold in groups. At times, especially when the birds are excited, as many as fifteen will be calling and scolding at once. Even when feeding they sometimes stop and call loudly between bites. All this noise has something to start it, probably, but in only a few cases did I have time to investigate. On March 1, 1927, the Jays were calling and scolding as usual all day up to the time it began to snow. Next day there was eighteen inches of snow on the ground but I heard no Jay calls all day. The following day was clear but very cold with the thermometer at twenty degrees, and, although I saw several Jays, I did not hear a single note. On March 4, the weather began to warm up and the Jays began to scream again and gradually returned to their old ways.

Sometimes the Jay calls mingle with the calls of other birds—a Titmouse, a Towhee and several Jays calling all at once make quite an avian pandemonium. At times we wish Jays would keep quiet when more musical birds want to sing. I remember once I was very much exasperated to hear a Brown Thrasher singing whenever there was a lull in the Blue Jay chorus.

The "johnny-cake" call, although I do not know its significance has always had a pleasing sound to me and I count it the most musical of the Jays' repertoire. It requires considerable effort on the birds' part for their whole bodies quiver with the strain, and the different notes are fairly coughed out. The other calls and whistles are so numerous that it is safe to attribute any strange call to these versatile birds. The commonest of all is a loud, far-reaching "d-jay, d-jay, d-jay, d-jay." Sometimes this note is a rally call. At its sound, Jays will quickly gather, swarming from all directions and screaming as they come. A much gentler note, and one as pleasing in its way as the "johnny-cake" call, is a whistled "ker-wheedle, ker-wheedle, ker-wheedle," repeated over and over again. It strongly suggests the "tea-kettle" note of the Carolina Wren. Blue Jays have been accused of mimicry and this may be a good instance.

Although cold weather dampened the Jays' vociferousness, I noted no other departures from their usual behavior except that they attended all day long strictly to the business of getting food. They fluffed out their feathers and hid their feet in them, or stood on one foot as they ate. They also sought the protection of the thickets and brush when actually forced to it on very cold days.

The Blue Jays in the Sandhills are resident as a species at all times, but there is some coming and going of individuals. In late February, I noted that there had been an out-flight of Blue Jays for they were manifestly fewer than they had been previously.

Blue Jays get food at all elevations above the ground and at times they are on the ground itself for acorns and ground insects. They are fond of acorns and a large supply will draw them. These acorns are usually gathered from the ground and carried up to the limb of an oak or pine, generally oaks, because those trees are the nearest and have more convenient crotches on which to work. Sometimes the acorns are picked from the twigs where they grew and are then carried in the birds' bills. When a suitable place is found the acorn is either jammed into a crack or held against the limb, or in a crotch, with one foot while the bird strikes strong, straight, downward blows with its bill partly open, a regular pile-driver effect. This soon removes the shell. In the winter when it is the custom of southern gardeners to rake up the leaves, they scratch the ground in a way that is very attractive to the Jays, probably because of insects and seeds uncovered. Sometimes the birds even fly down before the gardeners finish work.

Once I found some Jays on a scale-infested pear tree but I did not actually see them eating the scale insects. But these birds do eat other insects at times. When hunting insects on the ground, they usually search through the grass but they are not above imitating the methods of other species. On December 28, 1926, at least one Jay was seen scraping away the leaves and pine needles with its bill much as a Brown Thrasher usually does. Sometimes they pick the ground after the manner of a Flicker. One day a Mockingbird found an insect on the ground, but a Jay flew down and took it away. Occasionally a Jay makes flycatcher-like sallies from the spring foliage of an oak. In addition to the foods already mentioned, Blue Jays often resort to the dogwoods in December to eat the bright red berries. They are common about old cornfields in December, January and February, and they extract kernels of corn from the nubbins and waste ears left on the stalks.

The Blue Jays frequent our artificial feeding stations where they seek bread particularly. These birds also eat grain, cracked corn and cheese. For a long time I wondered where they put all the supplies they carried off, but finally found they were storing bread, and I presume other supplies, in tree hollows and old woodpecker holes. One was even seen burying a bread crust on the ground under fallen leaves. The presumption is that the Jays go back after such supplies later, but I am not at all sure of it. Jays do not care so much for suet and yet I have records of their eating it as it lay on a feeding station. Later I noticed that they became more fond of suet at about the time nesting began, probably owing to its quick availability. On March 1, 1926, a Mockingbird flew from a feeding station with a piece of bread, but was immediately set upon and robbed by three Blue Jays, that were so prompt it seemed as if they must have been waiting. On February 21, 1926, a White-throated Sparrow tried to carry off a bit of bread only to be robbed in the same way by the blue-coated bandits.

While the Blue Jays do not drink as much as some other birds, they drink more or less regularly all winter and still more when the weather grows warmer in early summer. I sometimes see them bathing in the shallow water of a stream, but most of my observations have been made with some small earthenware saucers placed on the lawns and kept filled with fresh water. These were actually put out for the birds to drink from, but it was not long before they were used for bathing. Sometimes the Jays flew direct to the saucers and had a bath, but at times they took a drink first and followed with a bath. At these baths, they got thoroughly soaked, making a more complete job of it than other birds did. They would then often fly into an oak to shake and preen.

Jays become more and more quarrelsome as mating and nesting time approaches, and I used to think them less noisy, but more careful observation does not bear this out. It is difficult to tell just when mating actually begins but it is about the middle of April in the Sandhills. In March I saw two Jays on a pine sapling with nesting material in their bills. But this seems almost too early for serious building, for the earliest actual nest found was on April 18, when I discovered a nest in an oak. It was in the fork of a limb about five feet from the trunk of the tree and seventeen feet from the ground, and under a thick mass of foliage. It was made of oak twigs for a foundation, with interwoven twigs, rootlets and a few bits of moss forming the nest cup. It contained two brownish ashy eggs with distinct, darker spots on the larger end. I did not see anything of the nest owners while I was investigating, but a few minutes later one of the Blue Jays was back and on the nest. A gray squirrel ran up the tree and the bird was after it quickly; it did not actually strike the squirrel but it was close enough and active enough to be threatening. This nest later had four eggs in it. The female was on the nest on April 20, and, although the bird left the nest when I appeared, there was not much excitement over my intrusion. The set of eggs was then complete and brooding commenced that same day.

CROW. Pl. 8, page 210

Corvus brachyrhynchos brachyrhynchos Brehm.

A. O. U. No. 488

Field Identification. A glossy black, rather large bird. Ravens are so very unlikely in the Sandhills that there should be no confusing those birds with the smaller Crows. The "caw, caw, caw" call of the Crow is distinctive.

Description. Entire plumage black, with deep blue or purplish glints in certain lights; underparts duller. Total length 19¼ inches.

Distribution. Considering their abundance elsewhere, Crows are comparatively scarce in the Sandhills, but may be seen at any time. In winter Crows are found throughout the United States and in summer they live north as far as Mackenzie, Keewatin, Quebec and Newfoundland.

Habits. Crows are such travelers and fly about so much that they may be seen flying over all kinds of forests, fruit orchards, fields, swamps, thickets and lakes. They do not restrict themselves to country districts, but are seen practically every day flying over even the largest towns and cities in the Sandhills.

In the forests, Crows are apt to pick out the tallest long-leaf pines to perch on, no doubt because of the extensive outlook there. But they also alight on lower pines, oaks, gums and dead trees; and even at times they are seen on thickets over a stream, on oak bushes, and in old fields grown up to broom sedge and sapling pines. At times they seem to actually prefer recently burned-over ground. In addition to wild areas, Crows are often seen on the aviation fields and golf links. These birds are wary and likely to perch first on shrub oaks and pines to look over the country before flying out into the wheat fields, oat fields, potato fields, cotton fields and hay fields. But they show a decided preference for freshly plowed areas and resort to them again and again. I have seen these birds in the Sandhills on freshly planted oat fields and where the fresh, green oats were one to three inches high. Although I watched and searched carefully I could not see that the birds were disturbing the plants, and I really thought they were after worms. Contrary to the usual idea of Crows, I noted only one single bird in a corn-field during the two winters' work. On the ground, they walk slowly and sedately along with heads nodding slightly forward and back. Sometimes they hop awkwardly forward with their bodies turned a little sidewise at the same time.

Here in the Sandhills in winter, Crows are more or less solitary or in small groups; they do not gather together into great flocks as they do in so many other places. Two groups of ten birds each, a group of eighteen birds, and a group of twenty birds were the largest flocks of Crows seen. Furthermore, in the case of the twenty Crows they did not appear like one flock, but more like a loose aggregation temporarily assembled. Sometimes in driving across the country a single Crow is seen on a tree or other prominent perch. Yet later, more birds may be found feeding nearby, so that it would seem as if the lone bird might be a sentinel on guard.

Although the antipathy of Crows toward hawks and owls was well known to me, I had never seen it shown towards a Black Vulture. But on February 10, 1927, I found a Black Vulture roosting on a swamp tree at the head of Juniper Lake, with a Crow cawing loudly on the tip of a pine about a hundred yards away. This certainly sounded like a Crow's rally call and three other Crows actually came flying over soon. But the four did nothing more about it and in a few moments abandoned such tame sport. When after hawks and owls, Crows perform a valuable service to other birds by warning them of the danger.

The flight of Crows is not rapid and the wing-beats seem actually slow and measured. As a rule, they do not fly in compact flocks, but are more likely to follow one another at intervals. Even when flying from place to place the line of flight is only high enough to clear the tops of the tallest trees. When flying slowly, they move in long, slow undulations, but when they move hurriedly, their flight is more direct. If the wind is brisk, Crows fly closer to the ground to minimize its effects. When they rise from the ground, or alight, in a breeze, they do it facing the wind.

One of the amazing things about Crows is their ability to utter so many different calls, and so many different intonations to those calls, that they seem able to communicate ideas to one another. Certainly all Crows know the rallying call and one will recognize another's food call. Our own ability to understand them is very limited, but even to me the sharp "caw-caw-caw" of the hawk-chasing Crows (see under Cooper Hawk) sounded like "hawk-hawk-hawk." Crows visit the pig-pens at Pinehurst, and if they find food, they begin sounding their calls and other Crows will soon respond and come to the feast. If one wants to caw while flying it will stop its wing-beats and glide during each call; that is, if it is not in too much of a hurry. At times Crows are very noisy, and at other times they are just as noticeably silent.

In winter, the feeding habits of the Sandhills Crows are wholly beneficial, their food consisting of waste grain, insects, mice, frogs, dead fish, carrion, and many other items of both vegetable and animal origin. They do not collect in marauding flocks to raid the grain fields, but quite often they are attracted to fields where

Figure 21. Carolina Inn, Pinehurst. Under these evergreen trees the Towhees liked to scratch the sandy soil. Feb. 5, 1926.

stable manure has just been spread. There, they appear to be after grubs and worms, and perhaps find some waste grain to eat. Crows will frequently carry off the smaller pieces of food in their bills, often to a considerable distance. At other times they hold the food to the ground first with one foot and then with the other while they tear it apart with their strong bills. Occasionally, they are seen drinking at springs or pools, or at edges of small streams, but they make more use of rain-water caught in cavities high up in the trees.

About the first of February Crows perform certain evolutions in flight high in air; that appear to be connected with pairing and mating. As they fly along each pair by itself goes through a series of maneuvers; rising, falling, swooping, sailing, with mimic attack and defense. The two birds are never far apart, but closely follow each other and constantly change leadership. As they fly high above the pine tops, they keep up these maneuvers as long as they remain in sight.

STARLING

Sturnus vulgaris Linn. A. O. U. No. 493

Field Identification. This is a short-tailed blackbird with a body slightly smaller than a Robin's. They have long wings, a long yellow bill, and a spotted appearance. They walk with short awkward steps, and erect bodies; their legs are set so far apart that there is a decided waddle as their bodies swing from side to side and their heads move forward and back at the same time. Starlings fly in straight level lines with rapidly beating wings, very much like a Meadowlark. The resemblance is even greater at the end of the flight, when they glide for some distance on set wings.

Description. In winter the entire body is black, shaded with brown above and whitish below; spotted everywhere with yellow spots; bill long and yellow. Male *in summer* has his body black with green and purple reflections; spotting not as conspicuous as in winter. The female is less brilliant than summer male but spots larger, especially on underparts. Young birds are grayish brown. Total length 8½ inches.

Distribution. Occasional in all parts of the Sandhills at all seasons and increasing in number. These are the descendants of

European birds intentionally introduced into New York City in 1890, and since increased and spread until their number has reached hundreds of thousands, and individuals are found west to the Mississippi River and as far north as Maine and southern Canada.

Habits. During the winter from November to March there was a flock of about fifty Starlings almost constantly about the Pinehurst stock-yards, aviation field and Pinehurst Dairy. These three localities all adjoined each other, and sometimes the Starlings were in one section of the area and sometimes in another. During the winter they were in the stock-yards, about the barns, out in alfalfa fields, in wheat fields, and occasionally on plowed ground. They often alighted on oaks and pines, perching close together and covering the top limbs rather densely. At times these birds were seen on board fences and on both the wires and posts of wire fences. But Starlings were more often seen on the ground than all other places combined. About February 20, 1927, this flock began to split up into pairs, and after that they were in all sections where fields and forested areas were mixed.

Their walk is peculiar. When seen coming toward one, they remind us of a walking duck, although the waddle is not quite so pronounced. When they are in a little more hurry, Starlings hop on the ground, usually a little sidewise, like a Crow. They can also stride along quite rapidly enough to be called running. When in flocks on the ground there is a continual movement both by the birds walking and by the birds in the rear flying up and over to a place in front. While moving forward, Starlings have the peculiar habit of hopping up in the air from eight to twelve inches and forward at the same time a foot or more. These hops are rather frequent, four per cent. or more of the flock being in the air at the same time.

Although these Starlings are not at all wary or suspicious, they are like other birds in taking alarm whenever an airplane flies over them. At such times they fly about uneasily until the noise of the machine grows less in the distance. In the wintertime, at least, Starlings collect in compact flocks that eat, sleep and move about together. Not only do these birds seem very socially inclined among themselves but they usually join the big blackbird flocks. They sometimes join the Meadowlarks in the fields and seem to like to be with them. But it is a liking that is not reeiproceated. They are more restless than the Meadowlarks and when a compact flock of Starlings fly off, or pass by, the larks do not join them. Sometimes the Starlings are by themselves and their restless movements often cause their big flock to split up temporarily into many flocks containing from two to six individuals.

While they are together the Red-winged Blackbirds, Cowbirds and Starlings move and wheel in one flock seemingly under a single command. In flight and on the ground relations are amicable between all three species. When perched in the trees, the Starlings often break out into a confused medley of hoarse clucks and croaks that seems their closest approach to a song.

Neither cold weather nor rain bother the Starlings. During cold weather they are perhaps a little more restless and active; during a rain they merely shake themselves a little at times. Throughout the winter they keep in dense flocks composed of both sexes.

As this flock of fifty probably includes all the Starlings in the Sandhills at present, they are not numerous enough to affect grain or fruit. As yet, they appear to confine their feeding entirely to wild seeds, waste grain, insects, and garbage of various kinds. In fact they forage rapidly over fields, stubbles and barnyards where they act more as scavengers than the native blackbirds do. Starlings sometimes carry off food in their bills but it is doubtful if they store any away for future use. Once I found the Starlings closely clustered in a pool of water where they bathed as close together as they could pack themselves. Then they preened while standing on the ground, on stones, on weed stems and on the wire and posts of a nearby fence.

Toward the end of February, 1927, the big flock of Starlings began to break up into pairs and scatter, although two pairs stayed in the neighborhood as late as March 24. In their nesting operations, they come into direct competition with our native birds. These foreign birds nest in holes in telephone poles and trees and usually monopolize holes used previously by woodpeckers and bluebirds.

Two nests were found in a telephone pole about a mile south of Southern Pines where two pairs of Starlings were carrying straws and nesting material into old woodpecker holes in an electric pole about fifteen feet tall. The two holes were located respectively one foot and three feet from the top. Both pairs of birds were carrying straws, but only the pair claiming the lower hole carried the material in, and the other pair were driven away whenever they attempted to enter either hole. Probably these holes were originally made by Red-headed Woodpeckers, or possibly by Flickers. Occupied nests are easy to find for the Starlings use no *camouflage* but fly straight and direct to their homes. Sometimes they perch in their nest holes looking out with their heads and half their bodies outside the opening. On March 18, 1927, a pair of Bluebirds were found nesting in a hole in an old oak stub, but a pair of Starlings flew over, drove the Bluebirds out, and one of the Starlings went into the nest hole and occupied it.

COWBIRD. Pl. 8, page 210

Molothrus ater ater (Bodd.). A. O. U. No. 495

Field Identification. A blackbird larger than a sparrow, with the males having heads and necks brown and eyes brown.

Description. The male's head, neck and breast are brown; rest of plumage black, showing some iridescence in good light. The female is dark brownish gray with lighter underparts. Total length 8 inches.

Distribution. Occasional throughout the winter in all parts of the Sandhills. In winter these birds are found south of the Ohio and Potomac valleys to the Gulf coast and central Mexico; in summer they live north of the Sandhills as far as New Brunswick, Quebec, Ontario, Keewatin, Mackenzie and British Columbia. This species ranges from coast to coast although replaced in some places with other varieties of Cowbirds.

Habits. During the winter from November to February, 1927, there was a flock of sixty Cowbirds almost constantly about the fields near Pinehurst stock-yards. This flock was composed of both sexes and remained together all winter, but began to split up and scatter about the tenth of March. While these birds were usually on the ground, they often alighted on low oaks and pines in compact groups. At other times, these birds were seen on telephone wires, on board fences, and on both wires and posts of wire fences. Occasionally a Cowbird was seen on the race-course or golf links, or about a stable. Still, it was quite evident that they gave no heed to herds of stock nearby, but frequented the upland fields with other blackbirds by preference.

Cowbirds on the ground ordinarily walk, and hop when in a hurry. In a field or stubble, these birds feed while walking with heads nodding to and fro. In such places they feed on seeds and when they find a favorable place, they settle down. When through in one place, individual birds fly up and over the rest of the flock to a new place in front. In the mixed flocks of blackbirds and Cowbirds, it was usually the Cowbirds that led the way in this onward movement.

Cowbirds fly in dense compact flocks. Usually, in the trees they all face into the wind, if there is any breeze at all. An airplane going over always starts them to flying about uneasily. Some birdbook writers seem to imply that Cowbirds are such despicable characters no other birds will associate with them. This is not quite accurate for the Sandhills. Here the Cowbirds are with Redwinged Blackbirds, Rusty Blackbirds, Starlings, Pipits, Meadowlarks and Grackles all winter, and no antagonism nor avoidance is shown. On February 15, 1927, a male Cowbird was even seen near the race-course to join a little flock of eight Killdeers without the slightest objection on the part of the latter. Actually, the Cowbirds are fond of gathering in flocks, both with their own species and with the other birds just mentioned. In these mixed flocks of several species, they fly much as the other blackbirds do. Cowbirds are silent during most of the winter, but toward spring they begin to utter clucks and "cluck-see-e-e's." One day in March a flock in a small tree broke into a medley of notes resembling the tinkling chorus of spring Redwings.

During the winter, the number of Cowbirds remains quite constant but early in March more birds begin arriving from the south. For a time the Cowbirds increase in number, but after the middle of the month they begin to leave for the north. Cowbirds feed on weed seeds and insects of various kinds. Sometimes they are in the cowpea fields, but they seem to be after weed seeds rather than peas.

Cowbirds bathe and preen much like other birds. Here again their tendency to gather close together is well shown, for they bathe in flocks in shallow pools and so crowded that the water can scarcely be seen between the birds.

RED-WINGED BLACKBIRD. Pl. 5, page 148

Agelaius phœniceus phœniceus (Linn.). *A. O. U. No. 498*

Field Identification. A blackbird slightly smaller than a Robin. Identified by the black color and scarlet "shoulders" of the males, and the streaked and spotted black of the females accompanying them.

Description. Male has the "shoulders" bright scarlet bordered by buff; rest of plumage black, but upperparts touched with rusty. In young birds the feathers of the underparts are tipped with whitish and the "shoulders" are dull orange red mixed with black. Female birds have the upperparts streaked and spotted with rusty and buffy; the "shoulders" sometimes tinged with reddish; underparts conspicuously streaked with black and white. Total length 9½ inches.

Distribution. Common in the Sandhills at all seasons. These birds are found throughout eastern United States south of Nova Scotia, Quebec and Ontario, except in Florida and along the Gulf coast. In the winter all Redwings north of Kentucky and Maryland migrate to points farther south. Farther west these blackbirds are replaced by other varieties of the same species.

Habits. During the winter from Christmas until March, 1927, there was a flock of two hundred Red-winged Blackbirds almost constantly with the Cowbirds about the Pinehurst stock-yards. Although they were usually on the ground, they often alighted on low oaks, sapling pines and even on tall gums, clustering close together on the very top in compact flocks. Occasionally flocks of Red-winged Blackbirds were seen elsewhere, particularly about old cowpea fields. Early in the winter, and again after the winter was over, I found these blackbirds about old cornfields (Figs. 18 and 27), freshly planted oat fields, and swampy places, but I did not see them there during the winter.

When on the ground, these blackbirds walk or hop. Usually they hop when in a hurry or to escape a pursuing blackbird. Sometimes their hops are a little sidewise as well as forward. When feeding on a field or stubble, they advance steadily across it by walking. While some individuals may stop and stay in a favorable place for a time, the majority of the flock move on by the flying up, and over, of small groups of ten to thirty birds from the rear to a position in front. There is no concerted leadership in this movement, but it is probable the birds use a continual trial and retrial by venturesome individuals with the majority following if these scouting birds seem to find food. Although usually in motion, Redwings sometimes stop after eating and rest motionless for as much as thirty minutes.

Like the Cowbirds, the Red-winged Blackbirds fly in dense flocks, and usually alight first on a tree before joining other Blackbirds on the ground. They are very fond of collecting and spending the winter in big flocks. And this social inclination is further shown during December, January and February by their including other species such as Cowbirds and Rusty Blackbirds in their flocks; by their tendency to join Meadowlarks, Pipits and Purple Grackles; and by their allowing Starlings to join them. Red-winged Blackbirds fly with rapid wing-beats but they are so skillful and move in such orderly flocks that they wheel and whirl in unison although each individual bird is constantly changing its position in the flock. While the flock moves steadily onward each bird undulates up and down, or swings from side to side, and gives to the flock a flowing appearance. When ready to alight, the flock drops down facing the wind, or if not in the right position, they wheel and circle so that they can do so. During the winter, most of these birds were silent and it was not until January 28, 1927, that I heard them whistling and chattering as they so often do when in flocks. On February 1, 1927, a little of the piping, tingling chorus, so characteristic of spring, was heard. This chorus increased little by little until it attained full spring volume about the middle of March. On March 16, the males were singing a musical tingling chatter with touches here and there of the ''konk-la-ree'' notes. Three days later they were giving clearly whistled notes. All of this spring singing was done from the tops of leafless trees such as oaks and gums. During the winter the number of Red-winged Blackbirds remained quite constant, although there were temporary variations each day. But early in March more birds began arriving from the south, and at about the same time it became evident that some of the winter birds were leaving. Throughout the winter and until about February 20, the flocks were composed of equal numbers of both sexes. After that date the sexes divided and were then seen for a few days in flocks each composed of only one sex. Probably the snowstorm of March 1–3, 1927, brought them together again. Then all the females disappeared and only males were seen in small groups. After the middle of March, only male Redwings were seen, near the marshes and swamps where the nests would be later. No doubt these males were summer birds that had come from farther south and were then awaiting their mates.

Seeds of various kinds and a few insects caught in the grass and herbage constitute the winter food. In December and early January the Redwings are fond of the dried fruits of the sweet gum. These birds are often in fields where stable manure has just been spread, eating waste grain, insects and worms. Here they scratch with their feet, and throw trash about with their bills after the manner of Brown Thrashers. Later, in the spring, the Red-winged Blackbirds perch on water reeds and cattails and catch small insects as they emerge from the water.

One day I found a dense flock of a hundred and fifty Blackbirds bathing in a shallow pool. There they bathed, crowded as closely as they could get, in a steady stream of birds until all had had a bath. Then they preened on the ground, on stones, on weed stems and on fence wires and posts.

MEADOWLARK. Pl. II, page 272

Sturnella magna magna (Linn.). A. O. U. No. 501

Field Identification. These birds are brown above and yellow below, and larger than a Robin. They have white outer tail-feathers showing conspicuously in flight but not visible when the birds are on the ground or perching; black crescent on the breasts; long bills. Flight is strong and very straight and consists of an alternating series of four to ten beats of the wings and periods of sailing. When about to alight, they glide with bowed wings to an easy landing. During flight, the white tail-feathers are conspicuous, but after alighting the tails are twitched three or four times and the white tail-feathers then close under the brown ones.

Description. Prevailing color of upperparts various shades of brown and buffy; crown with a buffy line through center; outer tail-feathers mostly white; throat, breast and middle of upper belly dull yellow; a black crescent tinged with buffy on breast; sides and lower belly whitish. In summer the colors are clearer and brighter and the markings more distinct; less brown, and more black and white in the plumage. During the latter part of January, larks may be seen in all stages of plumage; but they change rapidly after that, and by March 1 all are in bright spring colors. Total length 10¼ inches.

Distribution. Common in all parts of the Sandhills from October to the end of March. At that season other individuals of the species are found as far south as the Gulf states and as far north occasionally as southern New England and the Ohio River; in summer they live as far north as Minnesota, Ontario, Quebec and New Brunswick. They range west to the Great Plains but beyond that area their places are occupied by the Western Meadowlarks (*Sturnella neglecta*).

Habits. Sometimes the Meadowlarks are in one locality and sometimes they are in another, but usually they frequent hay fields, wheat fields, alfalfa fields or old cowpea fields. One flock of eighty birds remained together from November until the first week of March but then began to break up and scatter. Although these birds are usually on the ground, they often perch on oaks and pines, on board fences, and on both the wires and posts of telephone lines and wire fences. Occasionally, a few Meadowlarks are seen on race-courses or golf links, or about a stable. Still it is quite evident that these birds frequent the upland fields more than other locations. In addition, larks are often scattered over a great variety of other haunts. They are so often in old fields grown up in weeds and broom sedge (Fig. 13) that they are known as "old-field larks," in many places. They are found often enough on recently burned-over fields to indicate that they rather like such localities; and sometimes they are in old weedy cornfields (Fig. 27), especially in February, in weedy vineyards and peach orchards. From the old fields filled with broom sedge to the broom sedge in shrub oak forests (Fig. 2) is an easy transition, and next to the old fields these are perhaps the favorite haunts.

But it seemed strange to me to see Meadowlarks high up on the topmost limbs of tall long-leaf pines. I never did get used to seeing larks in the forests, no matter how open, and one day I found one in the wire grass of an extensive open oak-and-pine forest (Fig. 5) at least a quarter of a mile from the nearest field. Strangest of all to me was the finding of these birds throughout the winter in such towns as Addor, Pine Bluff and at least the outskirts of Southern Pines. But in spite of this, I did not find even these town birds tame. Actually, they were neither very wild nor very suspicious.

On the ground, Meadowlarks are usually quite active, walking and running here and there, but settling down in one place when they find a supply of food. While moving about and searching, these birds keep their heads down and their bodies low, but at times they stretch up to their fullest height. If they then see something alarming they begin an occasional flitting of their tails, and may fly later. Meadowlarks are quite nervous birds and this tail-twitching is often seen, especially as the white tail-feathers show a little at each movement. When alarmed, or when going to new feeding grounds, they sometimes fly in flocks, but are apt to start one at a time and fly in long strings. Amongst themselves, Meadowlarks are socially inclined and are usually in small flocks all winter, but there are many exceptions. There are also many differences in their relations with other birds. On January 12, 1927, a flock of twenty Meadowlarks joined a big flock of blackbirds, but did not follow them later when the blackbirds flew away. This actual joining with a blackbird flock was an exception, for the Meadowlarks usually did not join them and were really indifferent to their presence. On the other hand flocks of these larks were often joined by Starlings, Rusty Blackbirds and Purple Grackles; and were found temporarily with Doves, Horned Larks, Killdeer Plover, Flickers, Juncos, Blue Jays and Robins.

Meadowlarks are usually silent during the winter, but one was heard singing on the ground on February 16, 1926, and another was seen singing on the top of a tall pine on February 19, 1926. These birds have short, sharp, explosive alarm notes that may be translated as "d-zit," "peent," or "kip." These are uttered both from the ground and while in flight, and are very apt to be given just after alighting.

During the winter the number of Meadowlarks remained quite constant, although there were temporary variations each day. But in February it became noticeable that some of the winter birds were leaving. They seem able to stand cold weather, but snows cover their usual food and then these birds may be found in very unusual places on any little patch of bare ground they can find, and about barns and stock-yards.

During the winter in the Sandhills the Meadowlarks depend largely on seeds and waste oats for food, but also catch caterpillars, cutworms, earthworms, and as many kinds of insects as they can. These foods are secured on the ground and in the short stubble and grasses. At times these birds seem to give preference to seeds and at other times to feed almost entirely on insects even during the depth of winter when insects might be supposed to be scarce. For securing the two different kinds of food, the Meadowlarks use quite different methods. When after seeds they hunt through the grass and weeds, stopping occasionally to gather seeds from the standing or fallen stalks. When they find places where the seeds are numerous on the ground, they both scratch with their feet and dig with their bills. If there is a wind blowing, they usually fly to the lee side of the field and then advance on foot across it and against the wind. This is apt to scatter the flock, especially as one individual often has better luck than another, and the unsuccessful ones usually hunt up new places for themselves rather than share the first ones' success. Even when scattered over a large field the flock retains its organization, and when one bird leaves, the others usually follow one by one at short intervals until all have left. When they are feeding on insects the Meadowlarks move more rapidly, and perhaps separate more. Then, they do not search the ground or dig with their bills, but they look very closely at the bases of the bunches of grass as they pass by. At times they appear to find insect-catching very profitable at the stock-yards and near barns.

Occasionally a Meadowlark takes both insects and seeds indiscriminately. Such a bird came walking through the "rough" at the edge of a golf links; like a Flicker, it thrust its bill into the soil experimentally every step or two. At the foot of a tuft of grass it dug out two white grubs and ate them, then it walked over to a spray of dried everlasting, pulled it down and ate several seeds while holding the stalk down under one foot.

I did not see any larks taking flutter-baths in pools, but I did often see them walking and running about in the rain. They appeared to be thoroughly enjoying these shower baths, many of them shaking themselves and preening while standing in the short grass and stubble.

PLATE 6. ABANDONED FIELDS WITH GRASSES AND WEEDS

1, 2: Bobwhite (male, female).
3: Field Sparrow.
4: Phoebe.
5: Goldfinch (male in winter).
6: Goldfinch (immature male in winter).
7: Goldfinch (female in winter).

8: Song Sparrow.
9: White-throated Sparrow (adult male).
10: White-throated Sparrow (immature).
11: Vesper Sparrow.

(All figures about ⅙ life size)

RUSTY BLACKBIRD.   Pl. 5, page 148

Euphagus carolinus (Müll.).   A. O. U. No. 509

Field Identification. A blackbird slightly smaller than a Robin, and marked with pale yellow or white eyes. The males are black and the accompanying females are slate colored.

Description. In winter the plumage is bluish black with the feathers of the upper parts widely tipped with rusty or rufous; a buffy line over eye; in spring and summer the entire plumage is a uniform glossy black. The female is slate colored above and duller below; in spring and summer entire plumage more glossy. Eyes of both sexes are pale yellow or white at all times. Total length 9½ inches.

Distribution. I did not find this Blackbird at all common in the Sandhills but occasional flocks were seen throughout the winter. At this season other individuals of this species go as far south as the Gulf coast; in summer they live in our extreme northeastern states, and in Canada as far north as northern Ungava, Keewatin, northern Mackenzie and Alaska. In the western United States the Rusty Blackbirds are replaced by other forms.

Habits. During the winter from November to February there was a flock of fifty Rusty Blackbirds almost constantly about the fields near the Pinehurst Dairy. This flock was composed of both sexes, but began to split up and scatter about the first of March. Although these birds were usually on the ground, they often alighted on low trees—oaks, pines, gums, dogwoods and syca-mores—and on board fences and the wires and posts of wire fences.

Occasionally they are seen on race-courses or golf links, and often about streams or the thickets over streams. Still it is quite noticeable that these birds prefer the uplands with other black-birds more than any other locality.

Rusty Blackbirds on the ground walk, and run nimbly, with a nodding of their heads forward and backward in time to their own steps. As compared with other blackbirds, this species is perhaps tamer and certainly more quiet, composed and dignified. When hunting across the ground, members of the flock are con-tinually walking and running, and frequently individual birds fly a few feet to a position at the front. While Rusty Blackbirds fly in dense compact flocks all winter, and appear to enjoy the society of other members of their own kind, they are less apt to join other species. When in flocks composed of several species, the Rusty Blackbirds usually split off into separate flocks composed of their own kind. But at times they vary this and join flocks of Meadowlarks and Starlings; but on the other hand Starlings, Cowbirds and Red-winged Blackbirds more often join the Rusty Blackbirds. During the winter these Blackbirds are also seen temporarily with Bluebirds, Juncos, Doves and Horned Larks.

While the flocks of Rusty Blackbirds are more dense and compact than most other species, they are not so much so as those of Red-winged Blackbirds. A flock in flight moves steadily onward, but the individual birds undulate up and down, or swing from side to side, so that the relative positions constantly change and give the flock a rippling appearance. They fly either against the wind or with it. In the latter case, just before alighting on ground or trees they wheel and come up to their perches against the wind. In its minor points, the flight of these birds is thrush-like. Rusty Blackbirds are quiet during the winter, but the song also suggests a thrush rather than a blackbird.

During the winter the number of Rusty Blackbirds varies a good deal from time to time. At about the middle of February they begin to leave, presumably on their regular migration. By February 5, 1927, the males were in spring plumage but perhaps not as bright as they became later.

These Blackbirds have a more varied diet and they feed less on the ground than other blackbirds; and varied diet is probably the reason that they are more widely scattered. In addition to the seeds, waste grain and insects usually eaten by all blackbirds, the Rusty Blackbirds add fruits from the sour gum in December, January and February, and dogwood berries in January. In February, Rusty Blackbirds feed in cowpea fields on insects, but do not disturb any waste peas that may be present.

PURPLE GRACKLE

Quiscalus quiscula quiscula (Linn.).   *A. O. U. No. 511*

Field Identification. A brilliantly colored black bird larger than a Robin. The purple, or blue, heads and necks are distinctive; so are the yellow eyes of the males, the iridescence of the plumage, the straight level flight, and the long bills. After the middle of February grackles are seen tending strongly toward the bronze form. Probably both forms are present then, the Bronze Grackle being a migrant in North Carolina. Habits are the same for both forms.

Description. The male's head, neck and upper breast are purple; back greenish; wings and tail purple or bluish black; all the upperparts show a varying amount of bluish, greenish or purplish iridescence; underparts are dull black; eyes pale yellow. Females are duller but may show a trifling amount of iridescence. Total length 12–14 inches.

Distribution. Rare in the Sandhills during winter and summer, but more common during the migrations. In winter, members of this species range south of the Delaware valley as far as Georgia, Alabama and Tennessee; but in summer they live as far north as Long Island and the Hudson valley, and west as far as the Alleghany Mountains.

Habits. A Purple Grackle stayed with the blackbirds near the Pinehurst Dairy and across by the stock-yards during the winter of 1926–27. At times it was seen in the roadways, on bare ground, in clover fields, in alfalfa fields, on grain stubble, and under the plants of an old pea field. Although generally on the ground, this Purple Grackle sometimes perched on dead trees, poles, fence posts and fence wires. During the migration period in late February and early March other Purple Grackles visited the dooryards of Aberdeen and Pine Bluff.

When Purple Grackles are on the ground, they walk with heads moving forward and back, and bodies swinging from side to side in rhythm with their footsteps. If a wind is blowing they prefer to face it, for, whenever the grackles walk with it, the wind tumbles their tails, wings, and long feathers most disconcertingly. Occasionally, these birds jerk up their tails quickly and then lower them more slowly. Aside from this nervous movement of their tails, grackles are deliberate, erect and dignified in their movements.

The Purple Grackle seen near Pinehurst Dairy was alone most of the winter, but after the arrival of others about the middle of February, they were always in small flocks. Toward other species the grackles are unsocial but are sometimes seen temporarily with

Starlings, Meadowlarks, Red-winged Blackbirds and Cowbirds. Even when they are with these birds, the Grackles often walk away from them or fly away from them, or allow them to fly away. Their flight is comparatively slow, with slow wing-beats, and nearly level, but with very slight undulations up and down. At times, grackles give voice to chucks and chuckles and metallic clacks rather attractive in their way, but hardly a song.

On February 17, 1927, the wintering grackle (a male) was joined by four more grackles (a male and three females). Two days later there was an additional female grackle and on March 1 the number had increased to eight, but two weeks later the last grackle left. In spite of the fact that these birds go so much farther south, Purple Grackles keep to shade and out of the hot sun even in February in the Sandhills.

During the winter grackles eat seeds, waste grain and such insects as they can find. Occasionally they secure a scrap of food from the pigpens and fly off with it in their bills. Usually they hunt carefully through the grass and stubble, but sometimes they stop and throw leaves and trash out of their way as Thrashers do. At times they chase insects and even make little hops into the air for small insects flying past.

PURPLE FINCH. Pl. 10, page 262

Carpodacus purpureus purpureus (Gmel.). *A. O. U. No. 517*

Field Identification. A sparrow-like bird slightly larger than an English Sparrow. The females and young are streaked gray-brown like sparrows, but the males are reddish. Aside from the colors the best marks are the forked tails with each half rounded, and the large bills.

Description. The male has his body streaked with blackish brown and tinged with more or less reddish, most marked on the head and breast; upper back brownish and with very little reddish tinge; lower back brick-red; wings and tail brownish, but many of the feathers edged with reddish; outer tail-feathers longer than the middle ones; two indistinct wing-bars; belly whitish; bill large and black. Females and young males are very different and look like sparrows. Upperparts grayish brown, finely streaked with black; underparts white and streaked irregularly with brown; a whitish line over the eye. Total length 6¼ inches.

Figure 22. Broom sedge and low brush, favorite haunts of Cardinals, Field Sparrows, and Song Sparrows, a mile south of Aberdeen.   Feb. 20, 1926.

Distribution. I found these beautiful birds in only a few places in the Sandhills during the winter. At that season other individuals of the same species are found as far south as Florida, the Gulf states and Texas; but in summer they live as far north as British Columbia, Alberta, Ontario, Quebec and Newfoundland.

Habits. The presence, or absence, of these birds from certain sections is governed in winter by the food supply, particularly privet berries and cedar berries. Since these are cultivated in various dooryards, that is where Purple Finches are found. They are not here restricted to the heavy damp woods at all. In the spring, they are often seen high on sour gums and tupelos, tearing the leaf buds apart. Instead of walking on the ground, these finches hop from place to place. In the trees they are alert and hold themselves more nearly perpendicular than most other birds. But if conditions require it, they can perform as many gymnastic feats as Chickadees usually do. They are expert at clinging to wind-blown foliage even when they are violently swayed to and fro. At times Purple Finches erect their crests, but these are not very prominent and not usually noticeable.

At times they are nervous, but this is exceptional, for they generally are content to stay in one place while eating and seem unusually tolerant of any other birds that may be near. Even on the ground they feed for several minutes in one place and then move quickly and surely to the next place where they settle down and go to feeding again. In the cedar trees, they vary their procedure a good deal some days occupying the lowest limbs but perhaps the next day on the very highest ones. Possibly it is a preference for sunshine and warmth that draws them to the top on some days.

Sometimes a single finch is seen alone during the winter, but usually they are in small flocks of two to seven birds, containing both sexes. They do not really associate with other birds for companionship, but similar haunts and food take them temporarily near Robins, Hermit Thrushes, Cedar Waxwings, Fox Sparrows, White-throated Sparrows and Towhees.

The flight of Purple Finches is straight and direct. While their rapid wing-beats give the flight a somewhat jerky appearance, they descend to a landing place with airy, sweeping grace. As they alight, each finch turns and faces the direction from which the wind is coming. During the latter part of January, the Purple Finches eat cedar berries and can then be found every day and practically all day on trees where there is a good supply of these. Their usual method is to pick the berries direct from the twigs where they grow, but sometimes they fly down to the ground for fallen berries. There, they depend entirely on surface supplies and do not scratch like the Fox Sparrows and Towhees that may be near them. One day a tame Purple Finch near the Highland Pines Inn, allowed me to get a very close view while he was eating the cedar seeds and discarding the pulp. The cutting away of the pulp was done by rolling the whole berry to and fro in his sharp bill until the seeds worked out and were swallowed. This particular bird ate cedar berry seeds steadily for thirty minutes without a pause. Next to cedar berries, I found these finches most frequently eating privet berries. They also eat dogwood berries in early January.

On one occasion, a female finch was seen to mount forty feet up into a walnut tree and shake herself in the misty, falling rain. After that she carefully preened her feathers although still exposed to the softly falling rain.

ENGLISH SPARROW

Passer domesticus (Linn.)

Field Identification. This common sparrow of the town and city streets is marked by chestnut shading of the upperparts, the black throat and breast of the males, and by the "kis-sick" note.

Description. In the male the upperparts are a mixture of streaked black and chestnut; "shoulders" chestnut; a white wing-bar; lower back ashy; throat and breast black; belly whitish. Female has upperparts of grayish brown streaked with black; underparts dirty gray. Total length 6¼ inches.

Distribution. I found small colonies of this species in all the larger towns and cities, but they were not common in the outskirts of these same towns and not seen at all in the country districts. These birds are native to most of Europe and Asia; they were intentionally brought to the United States and planted in Brooklyn, N. Y., in 1851 and 1852, and have since spread to all parts of the

United States, and Canada, until there is scarcely a village or even a hamlet still free of them.

Habits. English Sparrows confine themselves to the city streets as a rule and the only other places that I noticed them were near the Pinehurst Dairy barns and the barns at the Pinehurst race-course. Usually when feeding stations or bathing fountains are established in the towns, these sparrows are slower than the native species to find them, but finally they appear and then they are hard to discourage. On January 31, 1926, there was a partly albino English Sparrow on the streets of Pinehurst. Both wings were half white, especially the longest wing-feathers, and when this bird flew these white wing-patches gave it some of the appearance of a Mockingbird.

The habits of the English Sparrows in the Sandhills are very much the same as they are everywhere; they are noisy, dirty and destructive to other birds. I noticed no native birds actually consorting with the English Sparrows. Most of their contacts are antagonistic ones. Some native birds like the White-throated Sparrows, Red-headed Woodpeckers, and Mockingbirds chase the foreigners away, but even so, the English Sparrows are persistent and it must be discouraging to our native birds to find their rivals flying right back again as soon as they cease their pursuit. Another characteristic of the English Sparrow that discourages our native birds is the tendency of a defeated sparrow to gather a flock of its species and come back. But the English Sparrows have at least two active enemies, in the Sharp-shinned Hawks and Screech Owls that sometimes invade the towns and raid the English Sparrow flocks. The worst trait of these sparrows is their appropriation of martin houses, bluebird houses, wren houses and woodpecker holes for their own use. Near the Pinehurst race-course a Red-headed Woodpecker had its home in a stub of a broken shrub oak. On February 2, 1927, this bird was on guard nearby, when a female English Sparrow attempted to investigate the nest, but was twice driven off. She came back each time, and even entered the hole once while the Woodpecker was away momentarily. By virtue of persistent watching and constantly driving her away, this Woodpecker finally succeeded after several days in discouraging her, at least for the time being.

GOLDFINCH. Pl. 6, page 168

Astragalinus tristis tristis (Linn.). *A. O. U. No. 529*

Field Identification. An olive-tinged bird smaller than an English Sparrow. It has black wings with white wing-bars, and a characteristic undulating flight.

Description. Adult male in winter has upperparts of grayish brown tinged with olive; wings and tail black; white wing-bars; "shoulders" yellowish; lower back gray; throat and breast dull yellow; belly whitish. Females in winter have their wings and tails less black. Adult males in spring and summer are bright canary-yellow, with crown, wings and tail black, and white wing-bars. Females in spring and summer are yellowish brown above; wings and tails blackish; no crown-caps; dull yellow below. Total length 5 inches.

The changes from winter plumage appear gradually after the first of March; a yellow tinge appearing first on the upperparts and slowly spreading and becoming stronger.

Distribution. I found this a rather scarce bird in the Sandhills where it occurred only in winter so far as I could find out. In winter, Goldfinches go as far south as the Gulf coast; but in summer they live to the north of us as far as Newfoundland, Quebec and Manitoba.

Habits. Sometimes a Goldfinch is seen alone, but usually these birds are in flocks of from two to fifty individuals. Goldfinches are birds of the open fields and of the brush and weed patches at the edges and corners of cultivated fields (Figs. 13, 14, 18, 19, 20, 22, 27). They particularly like old hay fields, old fields lying fallow, and weedy fields of all kinds. Occasionally they are seen on the golf links. The broom-sedge-and-brush corners are favorites with these birds, but wherever they are found, they are never far from thickets or shrub oak forests into which they can dart when danger threatens. While never seen in any very dense woods, Goldfinches often alight on trees in the oak-and-pine forests, and sometimes on sweet gums or sour gum trees.

On the ground, Goldfinches move with quick, agile hops. They are somewhat nervous at times, but they evidently enjoy the company of their fellows. They also enjoy joining flocks of other sparrows, where the white wing-bars of the Goldfinches show rather contrastingly with the others. Goldfinches adapt their flight more or less to that of the other sparrows and do not then exhibit an undulating flight. Neither do they show undulations in making short flights, for then they are apt to be airy, hesitating, and somewhat jerky. In flocks of their own species they may follow one another at intervals or fly in a dense flock with gentle undulations. At no time during the winter did I see the bounding, deeply undulating flight so typical of summer Goldfinches. Nor did I hear one sing while flying, although I did hear one singing while perched on a bush on February 17, 1927.

During the winter the food of the Goldfinches consists largely of seeds of various kinds that they obtain from the plants themselves, or glean from the ground or surface of the snow where the seeds have fallen. In the broom-sedge they often fly up on the stalks and "ride them down." They also eat seeds from the catkins of alders, and tear apart the buds of the red maple. Once I saw a Goldfinch eating the seeds of a sweet gum, and once the seeds from the sour gum.

PINE SISKIN

Spinus pinus (Wils.). *A. O. U. No.* 533

Field Identification. A sparrow-like bird smaller than an English Sparrow. Yellow edgings of the wing-feathers show in flight. Unlike Goldfinches, they have heavy streaking over all underparts; unlike Redpolls, they have no blackish on throats.

Description. Upperparts brown, streaked with black; larger feathers of the wings and tail edged with yellow, and with yellow bases; underparts buffy white, streaked with blackish. Total length 5 inches.

Distribution. This is a rare bird in the Sandhills in winter when it is at the southern limit of its range. It is not even common in either the mountains, or the northern parts of North Carolina. In summer it goes as far north as Canada and even into New Brunswick and Nova Scotia.

Habits. In the Sandhills, the Siskins' movements, and even their more presence, depend on food. As long as food is plentiful farther north, these birds do not occur here at all. They are sociable little birds always in flocks and frequently with other sparrows of similar tastes. In the Sandhills their preferred foods are the seed catkins of alders and birches, but they also eat sweet gum seeds and probably many others. While extracting seeds they perform all sorts of gymnastics on the terminal clusters of seeds and go through as many contortions as Chickadees might.

VESPER SPARROW. Pls. 6 &7, pages 168, 184

Poœcetes gramineus gramineus (Gmel.). *A. O. U. No. 540*

Field Identification. A brownish gray sparrow, same size as an English Sparrow, with outer white tail-feathers showing conspicuously in flight.

Description. Upperparts brownish gray, streaked with darker; wings brownish black; two white wing-bars; "shoulders" bright rufous; tail dark brown, the outer feathers mostly white; underparts white; the breast and sides streaked with brown. Total length 6 inches.

Distribution. While these birds are found in winter in all parts of the Sandhills, they are erratic—abundant at times and notably scarce at others. In winter the Vesper Sparrows occur as far south as the Gulf coast and Texas; but in summer they live as far north as Cape Breton Island, Quebec, Ontario and Keewatin.

Habits. Vesper Sparrows much prefer old weedy cornfields (Figs. 18 and 27), although they are often in the hedges and thickets bordering such fields. In addition to these localities I have seen them in alfalfa fields, on freshly plowed fields, on the ground under dewberries and peach trees, in dooryard shrubbery, and in shrub oaks at the edge of a field.

On the ground they hop, but they can do it so rapidly for at least a short distance that it looks very much like running; sometimes they walk a few steps. As they hop along they give an occasional flit of their wings and stop now and then to pick up a seed. On a low perch such as a fence post or a dewberry stake they dip their tails when alarmed or nervous. Occasionally, one is seen alone but there are generally others not far away, and they are far more often seen in small groups of from two to a dozen. Like most sparrows they join with others to form flocks, including Juncos, Field Sparrows, Savannah Sparrows and Goldfinches; and are also seen with White-throated Sparrows, Chipping Sparrows and Bluebirds.

Vesper Sparrows have a peculiar habit, when a person comes too near, of hopping along a few feet in front and then flying on before, but low and near the ground, only to drop down into the path again. Here they wait until they are again almost stepped on and then flit a hundred feet or so farther on, only to repeat again and again until either the unintentional pursuer leaves the path or the sparrow reaches the edge of its territory. In the latter case it circles over the fields to one side or the other and goes back to where it started. Even when flying over an open field, the Vesper's flight is low, uneven and hesitating. Sometimes the flying birds vary their flight by alighting on a fence or a low shrub oak.

These sparrows are seen in the Sandhills throughout December to the first of March, and after that for a month their number is greatly increased by migrant Vesper Sparrows from the south. It is doubtful if any remain later than the first week in April. During the time they are in the Sandhills, they live on weed seeds of various kinds that they either pick from the plant stems or glean from the ground.

SAVANNAH SPARROW. Pl. 7, page 184

Passerculus sandwichensis savanna (Wils.). *A. O. U. No. 542a*

Field Identification. A grayish brown sparrow smaller than an English Sparrow. The yellow lines over the eyes and the striped appearance of the head are characteristic; breast striping is narrower than the Song Sparrow's; tail is short. A ground-dwelling sparrow.

Description. Upperparts brownish black, streaked with darker on the back; tail brownish black with each feather edged with whitish; a pale yellow line over the eye; underparts white, narrowly streaked with blackish. In summer the color is lighter and less tinged with ochraceous. Total length 5½ inches.

Distribution. I found this Sparrow rather common at times throughout the winter in the Sandhills. On the other hand, Mr. C. J. Pennock says he saw only a few in 1910. The Savannah Sparrows go as far south in winter as Mexico, the Gulf coast, Cuba and the Bahama Islands; but in summer they live as far north as northern Ungava and central Keewatin.

Habits. During the winter in the Sandhills these are sparrows of the marshes and *wet* meadows more than any other habitat, and they are not found in forests of any kind, no matter how open they may be. On the marshes they may be out in the open or among the marsh weeds and water grasses, but are not apt to be over ground that is actually flooded at the time. Where a part of the marsh grasses have been cut or burned away, these sparrows are out on the open wet ground nearby. After the marsh at the head of Juniper Lake had been burned over, I found the Savannah Sparrows with other sparrows in the low bushes at the former edge of high water. In spite of this preference for low wet ground, Savannah Sparrows are sometimes found on drier locations—on plowed fields, in weedy fields, in hay fields, or at the edges of corn-fields near a wet ditch or spring (Fig. 27). They are usually on the ground, but I have seen one on a charred bush a foot above the ground, another on a low stump where it was singing, once on a small bush, and once on a swamp tree at least twenty feet above the ground.

Almost all Savannah Sparrows are bright and alert and a few are very tame, although on a partly burned marsh they were wild where there was no cover and quickly dodged back into the weeds that had escaped burning. Probably the recent destruction of their accustomed cover caused them to be excessively cautious for a time. Usually, when they fly to the tall marsh weeds, they drop out of sight at once, but sometimes they perch sidewise on the swaying stems of water weeds and cling there for a short time. When feeding on the ground, Savannah Sparrows walk along slowly and take very short steps; when they are in a little more hurry, they hop. But they are quick at dodging and they can dart along the ground as quickly as mice and they appear to be actually running, but the gait may be only a succession of quick low hops so rapid that one can not distinguish the actual method. Ordinarily these sparrows are quiet and self-possessed, but after being alarmed they are nervous when they alight again, and often keep their tails slowly tipping up and down. These birds are almost always in colonies of a half dozen individuals up to a hundred, possibly be-cause the restricted nature of their preferred habitat rather crowds them together. They do not join other species as much as most sparrows do, but they are seen occasionally with Juncos, Song

Sparrows, Field Sparrows, White-throated Sparrows, Vesper Sparrows, Goldfinches and Chipping Sparrows.

Generally, Savannah Sparrows remain in sight such a trifling amount of time before they dive headlong into the marsh weeds, that it is very difficult to tell just what their flight really is. Actually it is hesitating, jerky, erratic, and just clears the top of the grass or weeds by a foot or two. In fact Savannah Sparrows do everything but fly in a straight direct line.

They have a pretty little insect-like trill of a song given as early as the middle of February. Savannah Sparrows mount on fallen logs or low stumps, or even on stakes, throw back their heads, puff out their chests, turn their breasts toward the sun, and then remain motionless while they give their whole attention to singing. Their song may be scarcely louder than a husky insect's song, but it is quite musical at that. These birds also have a quite explosive "tip" used as an alarm note. The food of Savannah Sparrows during the winter is largely the seeds of various grasses and weeds which they obtain by hunting over the ground and through the aisles bordered by water plants.

GRASSHOPPER SPARROW. Pl. 7, page 184

Ammodramus savannarum australis Mayn. A. O. U. No. 546

Field Identification. A sparrow that is smaller and chunkier than the English Sparrow; with unstreaked underparts and with yellow markings and shadings on the wings. Tail-feathers equal in length but each one pointed.

Description. Upperparts a mixture of black, gray, buffy and chestnut; crown with a buffy line through its center, bordered by blackish; bend of wing yellow; a whitish wing-bar; tail-feathers equal in length and noticeably pointed; underparts whitish, but tinged with buffy, especially on breast and sides, not streaked. Total length a little less than 5½ inches.

Distribution. While I did not, myself, see this bird until March 1, 1926, it may winter in the Sandhills. Not only is it a rare bird in North Carolina, but it is also very elusive and hard to find even where comparatively common. It spends the winter to the south of us, going as far south as the Bahama Islands, Cuba, Yucatan and Mexico; it summers north of the Sandhills as far as Wisconsin, Ontario and southern New Hampshire.

Habits. These hard-to-find little sparrows are inhabitants of sandy, grassy fields and tall grasses, especially broom-sedge (Figs. 13, 14, 19). They are expert hiders and remain unseen until almost trodden upon, and then dart away low and near the ground until they find suitable places where the grass swallows them up again. They do not perch on bushes and are not found in the forests, but sometimes they mount to a fence top to sing their weak little insect-like songs.

HENSLOW SPARROW. Pl. 7, page 184

Passerherbulus henslowi henslowi (Aud.). *A. O. U. No. 547*

Field Identification. This bird is smaller than an English Sparrow. It is reddish brown with narrow breast streaks; has a large bill, olive-green marks on the head, and tail-feathers narrow and sharply pointed.

Description. Upperparts brown, streaked with blackish and rufous, and dotted with whitish; the crown, cheeks and back of the neck buffy olive-green; sides of crown blackish; bend of wing yellow; tail-feathers reddish, narrow, sharply pointed, and the outer ones much the shortest; underparts white, narrowly streaked with black; bill very large. Total length 5 inches.

Distribution. A rare winter visitor to the Sandhills. In winter members of this species are found as far south as southern Florida and Texas; but in summer they live as far north as Minnesota, Ontario, New York and New Hampshire.

Habits. Henslow Sparrows are mostly found on broom-sedge lands (Fig. 19), but they are also to be seen on dry stubble fields, at the edges of small ponds, and in the burned brush at edges of burned fields. Usually they are very secretive and lie hidden in the grass until one almost steps on them, then they dart quickly away for a few feet only to drop again into the tall grasses. One morning I suddenly found one on a low bush quietly watching me and apparently filled with curiosity. When it flew off with a rapid-wing-beating, jerking flight to the protection of some weeds and brush at the edge of a small lake. A Henslow Sparrow or two were seen in the big mixed flocks of Juncos, Song Sparrows, Field Sparrows, Chipping Sparrows and Savannah Sparrows when they were gathering in the spring.

WHITE-THROATED SPARROW. Pls. 6 & 7, pages 168, 184

Zonotrichia albicollis (Gmel.). A. O. U. No. 558

Field Identification. A brown sparrow slightly larger than an English Sparrow and easily identified by the white and gray markings about the head and the yellow spot in front of each eye. A sparrow of the hedges and open forests.

Description. The adult usually has a dull yellow line from the bill to a point above the eye ; a wide black stripe on each side of the crown enclosing a narrow white stripe between them ; a broad white stripe runs backward from the end of the yellow above the eye ; back reddish brown, streaked with black and whitish ; bend of the wing dull yellow ; lower back gray-brown ; two obscure white wing-bars ; tail gray-brown ; throat white ; underparts gray, breast darker and often streaked obscurely with blackish ; sides brownish. Young birds have the center crown-streaks brownish gray flanked by chestnut ; throat-patch less sharply defined and often lacking. The winter birds show both adult and juvenile colors and all gradations between. After April 1, the yellow, black and white markings become bright and distinct, the throat acquiring a well-defined squarish white patch. Total length 6¾ inches.

Distribution. I found these sparrows very common throughout the Sandhills all winter. At this season some White-throated Sparrows are found as far south as Florida, the Gulf states and Mexico ; but in summer they live as far north as northern Mackenzie, Keewatin and Ungava.

Habits. As a rule, these birds shun both the heavy forests and the middle of the open fields if without hedges or dense weedy growth. They are essentially ground-frequenting birds, but often perch in the thickets and on the lower limbs of trees. They like thickets, brush piles and thorny growths to retreat to for protection. They may be actually in the brush, or more often on the ground beneath. While these birds are more frequently on bare ground or on ground covered by fallen leaves, they are sometimes in the growths of wire grass and broom-sedge. Occasionally, the White-throats fly up into the smaller oaks, but not so often into the pines, though I have seen one sixty feet above the ground in the foliage of a long-leaf pine. They are also found in blackberry thickets,

PLATE 7. HEADS OF SPARROWS

1: Chipping.
2: White-throated.
3: Henslow.
4: Grasshopper.
5: Savannah.
6: Vesper.

7: Fox.
8: Swamp.
9: Song.
10: Bachman.
11: Field.

(All figures about ⅔ life size)

thickets over streams, tangles of brush and vines, wild grape jungles, dogwood and sumach hedges, cane and briar tangles, and in cat-briar thickets. These dense retreats are still more favored where they are at the edge of fields, or better yet, between fields (Figs. 13, 14, 19, 20, 22). Cornfields and cotton fields, particularly if very weedy (Figs. 18 and 27), are so much liked by these birds that a rather low weedy cornfield bordered by thickets is perhaps the best place of all to look for them. I have seen these sparrows on ground over which fire had recently swept, but I could not say they actually favored it.

Sandy sidewalks, if not packed too hard, are favorite places to scratch for food. Particularly so, whenever a gardener rakes them and thereby opens the ground up a little for the little searchers. No doubt for a similar reason these birds are sometimes on freshly plowed ground. These sparrows are greatly pleased when the leaves are raked up under hollies, cedars and magnolias because these thick trees give them nice protection from rain and enemies (Fig. 17, 21, 24, 26). So much do these birds like thick shrubbery, that if we would attract them about our homes, we should plant these artificial thickets for them. But these sparrows do not avail themselves of our society beyond the food, and the facilities for getting food, that we provide, and only once has one of these birds seen by me on a porch.

White-throats depend largely upon scratching to uncover food. Like the Fox Sparrows, they give a triple scuffle with spread feet, and a quick jump backward to throw out the dirt behind them. At times these birds will scratch for as much as an hour without a pause beyond that necessary to pick up the food.

On the ground, White-throated Sparrows hop, sometimes moving across a yard by a series of short hops; in the trees, they perch quietly on the limbs, or hop from limb to limb through the foliage. When a flock flies off, they sometimes go all together and sometimes one at a time. The appearance of the White-throated Sparrows is almost always trim, neat and erect, except that when feeding they nestle close to the ground. In search of feeding grounds, these sparrows roam about in flocks, now here, now there; and are much more often on the wing than the Song Sparrows are. In fact the White-throats seem to move in waves, and when one arrives on the feeding grounds it is sure to be followed by more.

Yet, when they are actually feeding they move about less than the Song Sparrows do.

During the winter, the White-throats' disposition seems as social as usual with sparrows, for they are found in small flocks of four to sixty individuals, although they often occur singly or in twos. But, in spite of this fondness for each other's society, these sparrows chase each other away from feeding grounds at times when they are more tolerant toward other species. The White-throated Sparrow is one of the few small American birds bold enough to eat quietly with ten to twenty English Sparrows around it. In fact they even go farther and actually drive the English Sparrows away at times. I have also noticed that the White-throats are even bolder and less subject to distant alarms than the English Sparrows feeding beside them. But even these White-throats are frightened when the big Jays dash up, although I think this is due more to the size and carelessness of the larger birds rather than to actual fear.

With birds so common in so many different places as the White-throated Sparrows are, it is difficult to say just how much they enjoy the society of other species. They are often alone and seemingly indifferent to other birds. Yet they are so often in flocks with other species, and so often seen traveling with them that I think they actually associate with some of the other sparrows, such as Juncos, Towhees, Song Sparrows, Cardinals, Fox Sparrows and Field Sparrows. But their gathering with other birds seems more accidental and probably is only temporary. On January 12, 1927, the Juncos arrived first, one or two at a time, on a bit of bare ground under a dogwood tree. Then came Fox Sparrows. Finally after the last Junco arrived the first White-throated Sparrow came, and then the White-throats continued to arrive until there were fifty of them present, replacing the Juncos who had left one by one.

White-throated Sparrows are subject to all the enemies of small birds, and, in addition, have a special few of their own. Naturally such bold, pugnacious little fellows stir up the other birds to retaliate. Towhees also are pugnacious and they drive the smaller White-throats from their feeding grounds. Mockingbirds chase away those eating the dogwood berries that the larger birds claim. Once I saw a gray squirrel try to catch a feeding White-throat, but the bird easily dodged and flew away.

The flight of the White-throated Sparrow is quick and direct. Birds in a flock usually fly one by one between two feeding grounds a short distance apart. When alarmed, they dive headlong into the nearest thicket. Sometimes they fly direct to the higher foliage of a tree, but they are more apt to fly up to the lowest limb and then jump up limb by limb to the top.

The song of these sparrows is clear, somewhat plaintive, and very pretty, and is usually delivered from a perch in weeds, from a blackberry briar, or from a low bush, but rarely from a tree. This song is not loud, but it is a clear whistle that carries a long way. They sing a little all during the winter on the warmest days, but do it softly at first. After the middle of January their songs become stronger and more common until the first of April opens the real song season of these sparrows, and then they sing at all hours of the day.

During the winter, the White-throated Sparrows are one of the most abundant birds in the Sandhills. Curious to say, that although these birds dislike cold weather, they almost always feed in the shade if possible. Even on cold days in a keen wind, they still stay in the shade. During rains, they usually seek shelter under thickets or dense garden shrubbery. On very cold mornings, they are the first birds to appear. At first they perch quietly on limbs or briars protruding from a thicket at the edge of a field. As they wait for the sun to warm them up they puff out their feathers until they look like little balls. During an unusual snowstorm some White-throated Sparrows hunted seeds in a weedy cornfield a mile south of Southern Pines, by going under overhanging bunches of grass, and even into little hollows where the arched-over grasses kept off the snow. Later that day I found where they had been searching in the fallen leaves and had scratched off all the snow from quite large bare spaces. Here, and also beside sticks and logs and at the bases of trees, they were seen scratching merrily. One little fellow stopped once or twice to pick out with its bill the ice and snow that had accumulated between its toes. When four inches of snow came later, the White-throated Sparrows mostly retired to scratch the ground remaining bare under the shelter of certain oaks; and on the next day with the temperature at twenty-two degrees above zero they scratched only in the leaves under these oaks.

The food of the White-throated Sparrows consists of small seeds that they pick up, augmented by seeds and insects uncovered by scratching. Since the White-throats are often with Fox Sparrows, it seems as if they might have learned this scratching from them. On January 11, 1927, after a Fox Sparrow had scratched in one place for a time, a White-throated Sparrow promptly moved into the vacated place and scratched as hard as the Fox Sparrow had. Although this scratching is done mostly under thickets and shrubbery, it is also practiced out in the weedy cornfields and weedy cotton fields. In such places they are apt to pick out places previously covered by little piles of grasses and waste vegetable material. Plowed fields, also, are searched in the same way. In addition to the grass and weed seeds devoured, it is quite likely that beetles and other small insects, and insect eggs and pupæ are secured, as these sparrows deliberately search for insects later in the winter. In addition to picking up such seeds as they find on the ground, I have seen White-throats hop up, alight on seed stalks, "ride them down," and hold them under foot while they picked off the seeds.

These sparrows vary their diet by eating many dogwood berries in January. These are picked from the tree, gathered from the ground under the trees, or uncovered by scratching away the fallen leaves that cover them. They usually eat only the pulp, rejecting the seeds. They are also very fond of sumach berries in December, January and February. As a rule, these birds eat only a few sumach berries at a time and pick them direct from the bush. Wild grapes are another favorite during the last week of December, when they are at their best, but are generally neglected at other times. The pulp of the wild grapes is eaten and the seeds rejected. In addition to these berries, persimmon pulp, smilax berries and cedar berries are eaten. Once I found the White-throats under some sour gum trees at the head of Juniper Lake, but I did not actually see them eat any of the berries. The only cultivated berries that these sparrows were seen eating were those from dooryard cedars and privet bushes.

Probably these sparrows are the easiest of birds to attract to artificial feeding stations by scattering small seeds, cracked grains, bread crumbs, doughnut crumbs, grits or coarse corn meal. It is better, however, to scatter this material on the ground at first, for

Figure 23. A Sandhills stream, or ''branch,'' with gum swamp in background, well liked by Cedar Waxwings. Little River, between Pinehurst and Carthage. Feb. 4, 1926.

these birds will not so soon find the food on an elevated platform. Water is also very attractive, even more so than with some other birds. They like water both to drink and to bathe in, even during the very middle of winter. Naturally they prefer the water a little warmed on a cold day.

Not only do the White-throated Sparrows bathe during the winter in baths prepared for them, but they take advantage of natural facilities also. They get very wet every morning in the dew, or melted frost, on the grass; and appear to take these dew baths intentionally by making their way through the grass. Beneath the tangled grass, they flutter their wings, striking the grass and nearby herbs, so that their loads of dew are shaken down upon them. After these dew-bathers get good and wet, they fly up on a sunny bush to shake themselves and preen their feathers. One day in a drenching rain, I was watching what birds I could find under some shrubbery near the Carolina Inn at Pinehurst (Fig. 17). Naturally, I thought all birds were then as wet as they could be. But to my surprise, a White-throated Sparrow darted out into the street to take a flutter-bath in a temporary puddle! It did a good, effective job of it, too.

CHIPPING SPARROW. Pl. 7, page 184

Spizella passerina passerina (Bech.). A. O. U. No. 560.

Field Identification. A gray sparrow smaller than an English Sparrow, and distinguished by the unstreaked ashly breast, by a black line through the eye, by the rufous crown in spring and summer, and by the markedly grayish appearance.

Description. A grayish line over the eye and a black line behind it; top of the head and the back gray, streaked with black and a little rufous; lower back slaty-gray; wing-bars, if any, obscure; underparts grayish white but whiter on throat and belly; bill brownish. In spring and summer, beginning about the first of March, the crown turns rufous, and the forehead and bill black. Total length 5½ inches.

Distribution. A rather uncommon winter visitor to the Sandhills but more common after the spring migrants begin to arrive in March. In winter, Chipping Sparrows are found as far south as Texas, central Mississippi and Georgia; in summer they live as far

north as Cape Breton Island, Quebec, Ontario, Keewatin and central Saskatchewan.

Habits. To those of us to whom Chipping Sparrows are
familiar, and that includes almost everyone with any acquaintance
at all with birds, the "Chippies" in the Sandhills seem strange.
In the first place they are uncommon and must be sought out. Although they are occasionally around houses and dooryards, those
are not their usual haunts. To find the Chippies we must go to the
fields, sometimes far from man's habitations, and look for them in
the hedges and thickets bordering weedy cornfields (Figs. 18 and
27) and cotton fields. Here, in the thickets over streams, in the
overgrown hedges between fields, and where the blackberry briars
and cat-briars covered with wild grape vines make impenetrable
retreats, the Chipping Sparrows will be found. Sometimes they
work out into fields of broom-sedge (Figs. 13 and 14) or into weed
tangles in a field. Occasionally they are observed in the edge of a
plowed field. But in all such open locations, they are always ready
at an instant's warning to fly into the thickets or into the edges of
the forests. Here they generally seek safety near the ground, but
are sometimes seen in oaks, long-leaf pines and gums. Sometimes
Chipping Sparrows enter peach orchards. When the migrant
Chippies come up from the south in early March they are tame, and
are then sometimes seen about dooryards where they find secure
retreats in the hollies and magnolias.

They are quick and spritely and prompt to rise from the ground
when alarmed. While on the ground, they hop across it as they
feed. Although they crouch low on the ground when actually feeding, they move with rather long hops and do not look so much like
running birds as some sparrows do. They often perch quite motionless for some time on bushes.

Chipping Sparrows usually occur here in small flocks of from
two to twenty individuals. Not only are they prone to gather in
flocks of their own kind but they also join flocks of Juncos, Field
Sparrows and Song Sparrows. Though seen at times with other
sparrows, these gatherings are probably merely accidental and
temporary. Chippies fly with rapid wing-beats in an airy, jerky,
uneven way that is slightly undulating throughout longer flights.
As a rule they perch on a prominent observation point before
launching themselves out across an open field.

The song of the Chipping Sparrows is a simple little monotonous trill, "chippy-chippy-chippy-chippy" repeated over and over again. It is sung from a perch on a low thicket, or on shrub oaks, usually from six to twelve feet above the ground. This song is heard on warm days in February, although the chorus does not become strong until after the migrant Chippies begin to arrive in March.

The food of the Chippies is largely small grass and weed seeds varied with such insects as the birds can find. Most of these are picked up as the birds hop across the ground, but sometimes they stop and scratch. Sometimes they seek food on ground recently fire-swept, and again they make flycatcher-like sallies out from a thicket after small flying insects. On a very cold day following a snowstorm, I found some Chipping Sparrows eating broom-sedge seeds, picking them mostly from the top of the snow and also jumping up and riding down the stalks projecting above the fallen snow. Chipping Sparrows can be easily attracted to feeding stations by practically any kinds of small seeds and crumbs from the table, and they will also eat suet. They are very fond of preening on low bushes and on weeds sticking out into the sunshine of a warm, protected nook.

FIELD SPARROW. Pls. 6 & 7, pages 168, 184

Spizella pusilla pusilla (Wils.). A. O. U. No. 563

Field Identification. A reddish sparrow smaller than an English Sparrow. It has a reddish bill, a black eye in strong contrast with the gray line over it, and two white wing-bars. It is very partial to the broom-sedge areas.

Description. Bill reddish brown; top of head reddish; a broad gray line over the eye; cheeks and back of the neck gray; back reddish brown, finely streaked with dark brown and grayish brown; two white wing-bars; underparts gray, tinged with reddish on the breast and sides. In spring and summer, the colors are brighter and more distinct. Total length a little more than 5½ inches.

Distribution. Field Sparrows are very abundant in all parts of the Sandhills at all seasons of the year. In winter these birds are found as far south as the Gulf coast; but in summer they live as far north as Minnesota, Michigan, Quebec and southern Maine.

Habits. As its common name indicates this is a "field" species. That is, it is not an habitual tree-loving species as so many sparrows are. But this must not be taken to mean that these birds should be searched for out in the middle of open fields, for they are essentially sparrows of the weedy *edges* of fields near dense hedges and thickets into which they can disappear at a moment's notice when alarmed (Figs. 13, 14, 19, 20, 22). They are also the most common birds in the sedge corners and the larger stretches of broom-sedge, but here again they prefer the edges near convenient thickets. Broom-sedge is usually on comparatively high ground, but these sparrows also show a liking for low fields and the thickets along streams and ponds if there be a suitable field within a few feet. These sparrows seldom come into towns, but once I found some Field Sparrows on a waste lot near the Pine Bluff post-office. Sometimes I have seen them in peach orchards, especially if somewhat weedy, but in every such case the Field Sparrows have been with Juncos, and the latter birds are noted for their presence in the orchards. As both birds feed on weed seeds and small insects their presence is advantageous to the peach trees. I believe also that the Field Sparrows fly with the Juncos into the shrub oak forests whenever they are found there. In these forests the Field Sparrows often perch on tree limbs, but it is unusual to see them on telephone wires.

On the ground, the Field Sparrows depend on hopping to carry them along and they actually travel quite considerable distances across the ground instead of flying between points as most birds do. On some occasions they use short, bounding hops, and then again, I have seen them hopping, but at the same time scooting so rapidly along the ground that they looked like running birds. While they are out in the open, these sparrows are so watchful and nervous that it would seem as if their lives are a constant succession of alarms. Frequently the feeding birds crouch flat and turn their heads as if watching for flying hawks above them. As a rule, they are quiet and spend much time perched motionless on low bushes with their heads drawn back until their bills almost rest on their breasts. They have a curious custom of pursuing larger birds, especially Bluebirds. The first time I noted this was on December 29, 1926, when a single Field Sparrow pursued a flying Bluebird a hundred yards without apparent reason. The next time, the Bluebird started from the ground and flew up to the top of a tall long-leaf pine. The sparrow started from near the same place about ten feet behind the Bluebird and chased it almost to the top of the tree, again without apparent reason. A month later I saw a Field Sparrow chase a flying Phoebe in the same way. The Field Sparrows did not try to attack or torment the pursued birds in these instances.

Field Sparrows are very gregarious all through the winter and often gather in quite large flocks of a hundred or more individuals. But these flocks are small compared with the combined flocks of Juncos and Field Sparrows that roam the fields. In fact it is noticeable that very few Junco flocks are seen without there being at least some Field Sparrows included. Field Sparrows also gather with White-throated Sparrows and Song Sparrows; and are seen temporarily with a variety of small birds. Perhaps the most remarkable flocks seen by me in the Sandhills was one containing 320 Juncos and 150 Field Sparrows on February 27, 1926; one containing 55 Juncos, 23 Song Sparrows, 6 Field Sparrows, 3 Chipping Sparrows, 4 Savannah Sparrows, a Henslow Sparrow and a pair of Cardinals on February 28, 1927. When in flocks, Field Sparrows fly comparatively low in a series of short flights. In mixed flocks with Juncos, they fly in a long continuous stream of birds that may take several minutes to pass a given point. One big flock of 115 Juncos and 30 Field Sparrows on December 17, 1926, made their way through an open strip of pines containing broom-sedge and catkin-bearing bushes. First came half of the Juncos, then the Field Sparrows predominated among the traveling birds, and finally the remainder of the Juncos.

When Field Sparrows get ready to sing, they mount to a bush a few feet above the ground, throw their heads slightly back, erect the feathers on their foreheads and throats, and sing with their bills barely open. It is a dainty little trill, all the more pleasing because it is sung at intervals all winter long. Even as early as December 10, 1926, a few notes were heard. In addition to songs from low bushes, I have seen these sparrows singing from a limb of a dogwood protruding from a thicket and about twelve feet above the ground, from a bush twenty feet above the ground, and from a blackberry briar eight feet above the ground.

Since these birds are residents at all seasons in the Sandhills they have learned to adapt themselves to all the various weather changes. When the cold winds blow they seek shelter in a thicket or under its lee in the warm sun; when it snows their food is borne aloft by the tall stalks on which it grows. The number of Field Sparrows increases greatly during February and early March probably because of additional birds coming up from the south; but soon after the first of March some begin leaving for the north and the birds present gradually decrease in number to the comparatively few that stay and nest in the Sandhills.

That they can stay all the year round in the Sandhills, especially throughout the winter, is due to large supplies of their favorite food being always available. This food is largely grass and weed seeds, especially the seeds of the broom-sedge, of which they are very fond. A large share of the broom-sedge seeds are picked up from the ground where they have fallen; but these birds also have a trick of flying up and perching on a stalk. As it bends down to the ground under their weight, they walk out along the stalk to its head, where they pick out the seeds while standing on the bending stalk to hold it down. This trick they repeat again and again throughout the winter; and it is even used on snowy days to ride down the broom-sedge sticking stiffly above the snow. These Field Sparrows are also fond of picking up seeds from the ground of weedy old cornfields and cotton fields. Although they often stop in one place for two or three minutes when they find plenty of food, they do not scratch the ground as so many sparrows do. Sometimes they are found on ground recently burned over, but it is not believed that there is any special attraction for them there. I have seen one now and then on a sumach bush, but I have never detected one actually eating the berries. But I have seen a perching Field Sparrow suddenly fly out from such a perch and catch a small insect flying past. Probably they also eat a good many small insects while picking up seeds from the ground.

Since Field Sparrows are not normally dooryard birds, they are rather difficult to attract to feeding stations, but sometimes a few will come with Juncos. When they do come and find supplies of small seeds and small bread crumbs, they may return again and again until they become quite regular visitors. Perhaps the best way to attract field sparrows to comparatively open dooryards is to provide an ample supply of clean water in shallow pans or fountains, for these sparrows are very fond of bathing, especially after the weather commences to grow warm in April.

SLATE-COLORED JUNCO.　Pl. 8, page 210

Junco hyemalis hyemalis (Linn.).　A. O. U. No. 567

Field Identification.　A dark little bird the same size as an English Sparrow.　The dark slaty hood is sharply separated from the white belly; the white tail-feathers are conspicuous and show as an inverted V in flight.　The bill is flesh colored.

Description.　The male has head, throat and breast covered by a slate-colored hood extending down the back where it becomes tinged with grayish brown; belly white; sides grayish; tail almost black, the two outer feathers and part of the third white; bill flesh color.　The female has upperparts browner and her throat and breast paler.　In spring and summer the colors of both sexes are clearer and not so much washed with brownish or rusty.　Total length 6¼ inches.

Distribution.　This species is abundant everywhere in the Sandhills throughout the winter.　At this season the Slate-colored Juncos are found as far south as the Gulf coast; but in summer they live as far north as the limit of trees in northern Canada and are not then found south of the Canadian border except on a few of the highest mountains of New York and New England.

Habits.　These birds are much more partial to forests than the Field Sparrows, so much so in fact that they are to be found in oak-and-pine woods at quite a distance from any fields or openings. They are sometimes seen in quite heavy pine woods and even down in the lowlands where the gums and deciduous trees grow.　On the other hand, they are also birds of the *edges* of open fields, particularly the old weedy cornfields (Figs. 18, 20, 27) and cotton fields (Figs. 6 and 9), and are sometimes seen on the grassy fields and golf links (Fig. 12), but in all such places they like to be near thickets into which they can quickly disappear when danger threatens.　They are also birds of the broom-sedge corners and patches of high weeds (Figs. 13 and 14) and are quite often in the peach orchards (Fig. 7) and grape vineyards, especially the weedy ones. In fact they are the only birds, with the exception of the Bluebirds and the Shrikes, that are frequent in the orchards.　These dark little birds are as often to be found in towns and cities as they are in the country.　Indeed the Juncos come the nearest to being universal throughout all kinds of habitats in the Sandhills of any birds I know. The only places I can recall where I did not find them were in the open marshes, the cypress swamps, and the densest long-leaf pine forests. In spite of this seeming avoidance of swamps they like to be near springs, streams, ponds and wet ditches. Juncos are often seen on the freshly burned-over areas. Sometimes they are out on freshly plowed fields, where they hop quickly in and out of the furrows, presumably picking up small insects. Once I found a small flock well out in an old stubble at least two hundred and fifty yards from the nearest trees, but later they flew directly to these trees when alarmed.

While they are much more usually seen on the ground, they frequently perch on bushes, preferably from seven to twelve feet high, and they also perch in the highest trees as much as sixty feet above the ground. They show no preference for any particular kind of bush or tree, for I have seen them in all kinds, both wild and cultivated. The lower perches are used as observation posts and at times for sun baths. While on a perch, or when quiet on the ground, the white tail-feathers do not show, but flash out brightly whenever a Junco takes wing.

On the ground, Juncos hop like Field Sparrows, often traveling considerable distances where most other birds would fly. When making these journeys, they may actually be in one large flock, but still they hop along one or two birds at a time, or perhaps in small groups, seemingly detached from all the other members of the flock. Most of these birds travel quite leisurely, but they can hop along quite rapidly if necessary. Even when on their feeding grounds Juncos are true rovers, hopping rapidly along with only momentary pauses wherever they find food and then on again to rejoin the rest of the flock.

It is evident that the Juncos are very sociable little fellows, for they are seen in flocks, sometimes as many as five hundred birds, throughout the winter, roaming here and there, and where some birds of the flock go, all are sure to follow. In almost every flock there are at least a few Field Sparrows, but White-throated Sparrows in these flocks nearly as often. Perhaps the Juncos associate with a greater variety of small birds than any other birds do. Of course this is but natural in view of the great number of different habitats that they frequent and of the abundance of these birds. Juncos are seen consorting with almost all sparrows, and quite often with many other small birds. Sometimes the chance nearness of a screaming Jay will warn a flock of a danger the Juncos do not themselves see. Perhaps the worst enemies the Juncos have are the Sharp-shinned Hawks that dart through the bushes and seize them unawares.

In one way, the Juncos carry out in flight a trait they show on the ground. The flocks do not move in compact units, but straggle along with its members in ones and twos or small groups sometimes separated a hundred feet or more from the nearest of the other members of the flock. Yet, they quite evidently all belong to the same flock for they start from the same point, travel at the same speed, and all go to the same places. They travel this way through the forests, along the thickets and hedges, and over the open fields; and the only times they bunch together is when they fly in sudden alarm. Even after such an alarm, they fly back to the feeding ground they have just been seared from, one or two birds at a time. A Junco's flight is usually short and from point to point across a field or through a forest, rather than one long continuous flight. On a few occasions I have been able to measure their speed alongside my auto at twenty-four miles per hour, but of course I could not be sure they were then doing their best.

Juncos have rather monotonous, tinkling little songs generally sung from the limbs of bushes or the lower limbs of shrub oaks. They are not often heard during the winter, but after the middle of February they are much more frequent.

Since they are primarily northern birds they are skillful at seeking food and shelter during the occasional snowstorms that visit the Sandhills. Usually they are the first birds to be seen after a very cold night, but on the other hand they are very apt to seek shelter in thickets during the cold storms and winds. On January 10, 1927, there was a snowstorm, and during that day I found the Juncos crossing the cornfields by a series of short flights, frequently stopping a few moments on the corn stalks and then flying down to the ground to feed on seeds picked from the top of the snow. Sometimes they went under the tufts of grass covered by the snow. The next day they spent some time warming up in the weak sunshine. The following day was still colder and there was considerable snow left on the ground. So I went early to a favorable feeding ground for Juncos under a dogwood tree. Soon a band of these birds arrived, first alighting one or two at a time in the leafless dogwood tree and then flying down to the ground to feast on the fallen berries. They continued to arrive until there were seventy of them around me. With them came seven Fox Sparrows. After feeding a few minutes the Juncos began to leave as the snow melted away, uncovering more and more food elsewhere. But the movement was very gradual, the birds going one by one and only a few steps at a time, moving slowly across the fields to the hedges on the far side. During the next snowstorm, the Juncos flocked to every bare spot of ground that remained uncovered, to the sumach bushes and to the patches of broom-sedge, where they picked seed from the snow's surface or rode down the stalks for the seeds that still adhered to the tops. Although able to forage for themselves during storms and the coldest weather, Juncos always prefer warm sunny corners sheltered from keen early morning winds.

The Juncos' usual method of feeding is to hop across a field, picking up whatever seeds they can find. I watched carefully many of the thousands seen until I was almost ready to say they never scratched, but finally I began to see one or two at a time scratching ground and kicking away the waste material just as the Fox Sparrows and Towhees did. At times I thought they really liked to forage on freshly burned-over ground. During the winter the Juncos eat the seeds of broom sedge, crab-grasses, pigeon grass, and countless other similar seeds. They eat the pulp of dogwood berries, but reject the seeds, sumach berries, occasional sips of persimmon pulp, berries of the sour gum trees, and privet and cedar berries. No doubt they also eat many insects while searching for seeds and berries, but as field identifications of insects eaten by birds are difficult to make I noted only the following: On January 12, 1927, a Junco caught a bluebottle fly, of which it ate the legs first, then the wings, and then broke up and ate the body. On February 5 and again on February 10, 1927, Juncos were seen to spring up two or three feet from the ground and catch flying insects they had frightened.

As destroyers of vast quantities of obnoxious weed seeds, Juncos are of untold benefit to the farmers of the Sandhills. These birds pick out as their favorite feeding grounds the weediest of the cornfields, cotton fields, peach orchards and vineyards. Evidently the weeds are the important items, for they do not disturb the cultivated plants. But once I saw a Junco feeding in the blossoms of a peach orchard. Even then I really thought the bird was catching insects attracted by the flowers.

Juncos can easily be attracted to artificial feeding stations with all kinds of small seeds, cracked corn, coarse corn meal and grits. And they are also fond of fresh water in fountains big enough for baths, especially when the days get warmer in April. I found them very fond of bathing, even during the winter. They shook and fluttered in the falling rain, and visited springs in the thickets for regular flutter-baths. After bathing they perched on bushes a few feet above the ground and preened their feathers carefully. During the winter, Juncos are always in flocks composed of both sexes and immature birds, but I did not notice any tendency to break up into pairs until after the middle of February. Even then, it was only a *tendency*, for the majority still remained in flocks and apparently went north in mixed flocks.

BACHMAN'S SPARROW. Pl. 7, page 184

Peucæa æstivalis bachmani (Aud.). A. O. U. No. 575a

Field Identification. A shy, secretive, quick, darting sparrow of the broom-sedge corners, and smaller than an English Sparrow. The best field marks are the rufous color of the upperparts and the lack of streaks on the underparts.

Description. Upperparts rufous, the feathers more or less streaked with black and margined with gray; line over the eye buffy; breast and sides buffy without streaks; middle of the belly white; tail-feathers narrow, the outer ones much the shortest and grayish in color. Total length 6 inches.

Distribution. While they occur in the Sandhills all winter, these sparrows are more common in summer. In winter they are found as far south as Florida; in summer they live as far north as central Virginia, cross the Ohio River in a few places and even reach central Illinois at times.

Habits. In the Sandhills, Bachman's Sparrows remain unseen on the ground until one almost treads on them. Then they dart up and away a few feet above the ground, fly perhaps a hundred feet, and then they are swallowed up again by the grass and low bushes (Figs. 13 and 14). They begin to sing about March first and have the reputation of being the finest songsters among the sparrows. Their songs are comparatively loud, ringing, and very sweet, and in some respects resemble the songs of the Field Sparrows.

SONG SPARROW. Pls. 6 & 7, pages 168, 184

Melospiza melodia melodia (Wils.). A. O. U. No. 581

Field Identification. A dark brown bird, same size as the English Sparrow, that is partial to the thickets and hedges. The streaking of the breast that tends to form one large blotch is distinctive when supported by color markings given under Description. While Song Sparrows practically always show this breast blotch, there are a few other species that sometimes show a quite similar marking.

Description. Crown reddish, a gray strip through its center and another over each eye; upperparts brown, streaked with darker; tail reddish brown; black streaks on sides of throat; breast and sides marked with spots of blackish brown and usually a larger conspicuous splash in the center; belly white. Total length $6\frac{1}{3}$ inches.

Song Sparrows vary a great deal in color, in the Sandhills, and especially in markings. Some are so much darker than others that they appear like a different species. The markings on the breast vary in size, shape and distribution. On some birds the spots all seem to run together until the whole breast looks uniformly dark. On the other hand, some Song Sparrows have very little spotting on the breast except the "breastpin." In one very exceptional case the Song Sparrow had no distinct breastpin at all.

Distribution. Abundant in suitable places throughout the Sandhills during the entire winter. At this season, Song Sparrows are found as far south as the Gulf coast; but in summer they live just north of us in Virginia and north to Cape Breton Island, Quebec, Ontario, Keewatin, and the Great Slave Lake.

Habits. Song Sparrows are not dwellers of the forests, nor out in the open fields. They particularly favor those thickets that are over or near water (Figs. 14, 19, 22), but these thickets do not have to be either high or very wide, for the Song Sparrows are often content with a little patch of cane and weeds. They are also found in patches of weeds and blackberry briars out in a field or in a fence corner. They come to town and live in the cultivated shrubbery and are often in the weeds by the roadside. Still, the favorite haunts are the edges of weedy peach orchards, or cotton fields (Fig. 20), and especially low, damp, weedy cornfields bordered by cat-briar and wild grape tangles. Sometimes they are in the broom-sedge if not too far from thickets. Next to Swamp Sparrows and Savannah Sparrows, these are the sparrows that are most often seen near water, in gum tree swamps, and in the grasses of open flooded marshes. I have actually seen them standing in the shallow water of a brook when they did not seem to be bathing. Usually the Song Sparrows are on the ground or in low bushes less than five feet high, but they also perch on fence rails, in willows as much as twelve feet high, and in small pines as high as thirty feet above the ground.

On the ground Song Sparrows hop, but at times they are so rapid in their movements that a quick series of low hops make them appear as if "running along the ground like mice." No doubt they spend the nights in the thickets, for in the early morning as soon as the sun appears they can be seen edging out from the brush into the grassy fields a hop or two at a time. Unlike other sparrows, Song Sparrows stay close to the thickets and do not advance out into the fields far while feeding. At times they are nervous little fellows and keep twitching and hopping in the lower limbs of a bush, with their tails perked up as much as wrens would do. When Song Sparrows mount into the brush above their feeding ground, they hop up a limb or two at a time rather than make the whole distance in one flight. At times they are much less quiet than the White-throats and Field Sparrows. From these nervous movements as well as from the constant lookout they keep, it would seem that they are always ready to dive, at a moment's notice, into the safety of the thickets. As it is, Song Sparrows do not roam the fields in flocks as the Field Sparrows and White-throated Sparrows do, but stay in their own briar thickets, or nearby, one or two birds in a place. But they do not lack sociability, for there are generally a number of their fellows, either in other parts of the same thicket or hedge, or at least within such a short distance as to seem more or less like parts of a scattered community. Although they do not gather into large flocks or usually join the big mixed flocks of sparrows so common in spring, Song Sparrows are often seen near other small birds. Since these gatherings break up and reform easily it is probable that the presence of Song Sparrows with other birds is accidental or due to similar food or similar temporary haunts.

At the edge of one sandy field (Fig. 9) I found a gathering of Juncos, White-throated Sparrows, Field Sparrows and Song Sparrows feeding on grass and weed seeds. The Song Sparrows stayed in one place and scratched the ground with short backward kicks; the White-throated Sparrows often scratched the ground in the same manner, especially where there was a little pile of grasses or leaves; the Field Sparrows hopped across the ground and hunted for seeds as they went; but the Juncos were true rovers, either hopping out across the field or making short flights. Whenever an alarm occurred, all these sparrows darted at once to a thicket; but these alarms were usually short-lived and soon the birds would begin moving out into the field again. But the different methods of hunting caused the Juncos to move most rapidly and they went farthest out into the field, whereas the Song Sparrows stayed closest to the thicket.

The Song Sparrows' song is a trilling little tune generally given from a limb of a bush sticking above a tangled thicket, from a blackberry briar in a tangle of tall weeds, or from a low willow bush. They sing at intervals, mostly on warm days, throughout the winter, but they go north before their real song season begins. Song Sparrows are present in the Sandhills from October until the end of March, although they begin to decrease markedly in numbers after the first of March. Since they are typically northern birds, they are skillful at finding food during cold storms. But they like to perch in the warm sunshine and take sun baths. On warm, close mornings they often perch high among the limbs of leafless trees. In the early part of frosty mornings, they rest on stems protruding from cane and blackberry thickets for a few minutes before flying down for food. While warming up in this manner, Song Sparrows are motionless at first but their feathers are all puffed out and their breasts turned toward the morning sun. At other times they seek the shelter of the thickets against cold winds and feed under the sunny lee of the same protection.

During a snowstorm on January 10, 1927, I watched the Song Sparrows in a thicket at the edge of a low and grassy cornfield (Fig. 27), near Southern Pines. In addition to the birds in the thicket, others were safely tucked under the bases of tufts of grass bent over by the wet snow. Because the fallen snow showed no tracks, I judged the birds had gone under before the snow got much of a start and that they were letting it cover them with a blanket. Almost every grass tuft had a sparrow under it and some had two or three. Whenever I approached too near, the birds flew in alarm to the thicket, but they soon came back again to their snug little shelters. Not only were these birds protected from the storm but I found they were also feeding on the grass seed they found there. Later they began to work out from these shelters, scratching away the snow for seeds underneath. They also scratched beside sticks and logs where the fallen snow was thin, and close up near the bases of trees.

A great variety of grass and weed seeds are eaten by Song Sparrows in addition to seeds from crab grass, broom-sedge and dog fennel. Generally these seeds are picked up from the ground where they have been piled together by the wind or by running surface water. Song Sparrows also frequent the lake shores where they pick up the seed floated there by the water. In addition, they scratch the ground to uncover any seeds temporarily covered, and often fly up to pick the seeds from the weed stems themselves. The latter method is very useful when the snow covers the ground supply, for these weeds usually stick above the snow. Sometimes the taller stems spill their seeds down on the snow's surface and the Song Sparrows get them there. I have seen a Song Sparrow feeding under a privet, and once I saw one pick an insect from a stem of a blackberry, and I feel quite sure that insects are eaten during the winter whenever they are found during the seed hunts.

Song Sparrows are very easily attracted to our yards by opportunities to scratch under good thick shrubbery and thorny bushes. They will eat small seeds of all kinds, coarse corn meal and grits. But more attractive than artificial feeding is a bird fountain shallow enough and large enough for Song Sparrows to bathe in frequently. Since they are seen in twos all through the winter and the two sexes are too much alike to distinguish, it is very difficult to say just when they pair off for the mating season. Possibly the same pair remains together throughout the winter.

SWAMP SPARROW. Pls. 5 & 7, pages 148, 184

Melospiza georgiana (Lath.). A. O. U. No. 584

Field Identification. A reddish brown sparrow slightly smaller than an English Sparrow. It has a whitish throat less conspicuous than the White-throated Sparrow's, reddish wings without wing-bars, and an unstreaked breast.

Description. Top of the head streaked with black, *rufous-brown* and grayish; a grayish line over the eye; a blackish line behind the eye; back of the neck slaty-gray with a few black streaks; back reddish brown broadly streaked with black; "shoulders" rufous; tail rufous grayish brown; throat and middle of the belly white; breast and sides grayish washed with brown. In spring and summer the crown is chestnut; back of the neck more gray; forehead black; breast grayish and not washed with brownish. Total length 6 inches.

Distribution. This sparrow is rather scarce in the Sandhills, possibly because there are few localities suited to it, but it occurs throughout the winter. At this season Swamp Sparrows are found as far south as the Gulf coast; but in summer they live from New Jersey north to Newfoundland, Quebec, Keewatin, Mackenzie and Alberta.

Habits. These are birds of the open marshes, rather than the forested and flooded type of swamp, where they find a congenial home down in the water reeds and amid marsh plants. In the Sandhills, they are also found in the thickets over small streams, in the fields near such thickets, and in the heavy weeds and small bushes along the shores of ponds and small lakes.

On the ground they hop, but sometimes move so fast through the runways in the grass that they appear to be running. They are very quick and sprightly,—and nervous and tail-twitchy when under observation. They have a habit of carrying their tails comparatively high as they hop along the ground. Since these sparrows actually seem to prefer grassy areas flooded with water, they are restricted to comparatively few localities. In such places they are crowded together into communities, but I doubt very much whether they are actually together for companionship. When alarmed they appear to act each one for itself much more independently than organized flocks of sparrows should. Nor do they seem to gather with any other species, for Savannah Sparrows and Song Sparrows are the only ones near which I have seen Swamp Sparrows, even temporarily.

Swamp Sparrows remain hidden in the tall grasses until one almost steps on them. When they finally become alarmed, they hop quickly along a few feet, dart up with fast-moving wings, fly a hundred feet just above the tops of the grass with a jerky erratic flight, and dive once more down into the marsh. Usually they can not be found again, but sometimes a second glimpse can be obtained. On rare occasions one will alight on a bush or low tree.

Swamp Sparrows sing a pretty trill, generally from a cover of low brush and tall weeds, in March. It is not loud, and can not be heard far. The seeds of various water grasses and weeds are the favorite food, but they also eat berries from the sour gum, small flying insects, larger insects that they catch on the drier grounds, and worms and grubs that they dig from the soil.

FOX SPARROW. Pls. 7 & 10, pages 184, 262

Passerella iliaca iliaca (Merr.). A. O. U. No. 585

Field Identification. A big reddish sparrow larger than an English Sparrow and with heavy spotting of the underparts. But this spotting is variable, sometimes very heavy and sometimes almost absent.

Description. Upperparts rusty, streaked on the wings and back; tail bright rusty; underparts whitish, heavily streaked with rusty and reddish brown (sometimes these spots run together into a pronounced breastpin); belly white; lower half of the bill yellowish. Total length 7¼ inches.

Distribution. Fox Sparrows are common all winter in the Sandhills from November until March. At this season, they go as far south as Florida, the Gulf states, and central Texas; in summer they are all in Canada north of the United States, and breed as far north as the limit of trees at the edge of the Arctic barren grounds.

Habits. One of the greatest avian pleasures of the winter in the Sandhills is the presence of numerous colonies of these interesting sparrows, especially in Pine Bluff where they are really abundant

Figure 24. Holly Inn, Pinehurst, showing holly, long-leaf pines and shrubbery attractive to warblers and many other birds. Feb. 5, 1926.

under the thickest shrubbery in the dooryards (Figs. 17, 21, 25, 26). But these birds are also inhabitants of the thickets everywhere throughout the Sandhills, although their distribution is local and many places that seem suited to Fox Sparrows are without them. They are frequently on the edges of weedy fields (Fig. 20) and sometimes even out in the middle of small fields. They are not necessarily birds of the wet thickets for they are often found in high, dry localities, and are sometimes in the broom-sedge fields. They are often in shrub oak forests, at the edges of freshly burned-over ground, in open brush near springs, and in damp thickets under pines. Although they are ground-loving birds, they sometimes perch in arbors, on hedges and small trees, and even in trees forty feet above the ground.

On the ground, Fox Sparrows hop from one feeding ground to another. They even climb inclined limbs of trees by hopping up the limb. They are tolerant and will permit other birds to eat quite close to them. In the Sandhills, they show a decided social tendency and are usually seen in small groups. Liking the same food and the same kinds of haunts as several other species, they are often seen with, or near, them. While Fox Sparrows are often with Song Sparrows, Juncos, and White-throated Sparrows, there is no social inclination toward any, except possibly the White-throats.

In the Sandhills, Fox Sparrows are common in December, most abundant in January and early February, and then decrease in number throughout February. During this stay, they depend mostly on seeds of grasses and weeds for food, but they eat a good many insects also. Sometimes they find little piles of seed blown together by the wind, and again they pick up seeds washed up and deposited in rows at the edges of lakes, but their most characteristic method of securing food is to scratch for it. Other birds such as the Towhees, the White-throated Sparrows and the Song Sparrows scratch for seeds, but the Fox Sparrows are specialists at this method, and when they really try they make the leaves and dirt fly almost as lively as a barnyard fowl can. Fox Sparrows scratch with a series of three little scuffles forward and back with their feet spread apart a little, and then a quick jump backward with the feet flying out at each side at the same time. Sometimes they stop after each backward kick and pick up the food uncovered, and sometimes there are several series of scuffles and kicks before the active workers even pause. Often the Fox Sparrows are the only ones at work, and often the ground is too hard and icy for any birds lacking their expertness. They will sometimes begin to scratch the instant they alight. Indeed, I was going to say they start before their feet strike the ground for the action really seems to be more or less automatic. I remember one day seeing a Fox Sparrow eating small seeds and grains that had been artificially spread *on* the ground and yet that sparrow scratched, although all the food was on top of the hard ground. Scratching Fox Sparrows are so industrious and so efficient that they sometimes sink below the level of the ground in the holes they have dug. When they leave, the ground looks as if it had been gone over by domestic chickens instead of a bird not one-twentieth their size. Such work as this is of great value, for the ground is not only thoroughly turned over and cultivated, but it is fertilized with rich bird-guano at the same time. Many thousands of seeds must be effectually planted; and, since it is done on damp ground under thickets, it must mean a good deal in the preservation and maintainance of the shrub thickets.

Sometimes the Fox Sparrows eat the seeds contained in the dogwood berries, and sometimes they eat the pulp and reject the seeds. On January 19–22, 1927, I found Fox Sparrows eating the berries of a cedar. These were secured like the dogwood berries, either direct from the tree, or by scratching the ground under the tree. One bird was more original—it hopped up to a bunch of cedar berries which it picked one by one as it clung to the slender twigs, sometimes upside-down and doing climbing feats worthy of a Chickadee. Each berry was then carefully rolled round and round in the bill although I thought the bird finally ate both pulp and seed in each case. Another Fox Sparrow on the ground under the cedar, paid no attention to the cedar berries that its companions were eating all about, but gave its entire attention to scratching for seeds and insects. This last bird stayed in one place most of the time and only at long intervals did it hop to a fresh place.

Fox Sparrows also eat privet berries and can be attracted to dooryards by allowing the privet to grow untrimmed so that it can produce berries. They can also be attracted to ordinary feeding stations by small seeds and small grain.

TOWHEE. Pl. 10, page 262

Pipilo erythrophthalmus erythrophthalmus (Linn.)

A. O. U. No. 587

Field Identification. A strikingly colored black, brown and white bird a little larger than a sparrow. There is a sharp line of separation between the black (brown on the females) "bib" and the white belly, two white spots on end of tail, and red eyes. This is a brush-haunting bird that likes to be on the ground and among the fallen leaves under thickets, shrubbery, or piles of brush.

Description. The male has the upperparts black; throat and breast black and sharply separated from the white belly; sides rufous; tail black, the three outer feathers tipped with white, outer edge of the outer feather white; eye red. The female has the parts that are black on the male, grayish brown; eye not so markedly red. Total length 8½ inches.

Distribution. These birds are common throughout the Sand-hills during the winter. At this season other members of the species go as far south as southern Florida, the Gulf coast and Texas; in summer they go to the mountains of North Carolina or north as far as Maine, Ontario, Manitoba and southeastern Saskatchewan.

Habits. Towhees are primarily ground-dwelling birds in upland thickets, shrubbery of various kinds and brush piles. They are often found in gardens where they like best a tangle of luxuriant climbing roses allowed to run riot and form an impenetrable thicket. They are very fond of scratching under such a tangle, and also under thick-foliaged privet, hollies, cedars and magnolias (Figs. 21, 24, 25, 26). Out in the fields Towhees are found under the jungles growing over streams where blackberry briars, catbriars, sumach bushes, wild grape vines and growing brush make a safe retreat (Fig. 11). Here, these birds occasionally mount up into the thicket itself, or work a few feet out into broom-sedge corners (Fig. 19) or into old cornfields (Fig. 27) and cotton fields nearby. Thickets near ponds and lakes and over springs are well liked by Towhees, but upland thickets and even burned-over ground often harbor them. Although essentially ground-loving birds, they sometimes fly up into thick shrubbery and ever-

PLATE 8. EDGE OF CORNFIELD

1: Mourning Dove.	5: Crow. (Greatly reduced.)
2: Slate-colored Junco (female).	6: Slate-colored Junco (male).
3: Bluebird (male).	7: Cowbird (male).
4: Bluebird (female).	8: Cowbird (female).

(Figures 1–4 and 6–8, about ½ life size)

green trees, and even into bushes of their favorite jungles as high as fifteen feet above the ground. Rarely one is seen on the limbs of a dogwood, of a leafless oak, or in the foliage of a long-leaf pine as much as forty feet above the ground.

Towhees are quick and sprightly; and they can move across the ground by hopping quite rapidly, especially when they scuttle under a bush for protection. I have seen one fly from a flower bed to the trunk of a small oak about a foot above the ground and then climb up the ten feet of trunk, woodpecker fashion, with its tail braced against the trunk. It appeared quite adept at it, too, although it had to help itself along near the top by fluttering its wings a little.

Although as many as ten Towhees are sometimes seen together, they can hardly be called sociable, for the gatherings are of birds called together temporarily by ample food supplies easily secured. On the other hand, they are quite quarrelsome among themselves and there are frequent clashes and pursuits. And yet, it is noticeable that Towhees are a bit timid and ready to retire before Cardinals and smaller birds. With such a disposition, it is natural that they should avoid gathering with other birds. But because other birds such as Field Sparrows, Juncos, Song Sparrows, Fox Sparrows, White-throated Sparrows, Cardinals and Brown Thrashers eat similar food and live in similar places, they are often seen with Towhees.

Towhees stick so close to their beloved thickets, that they are seldom seen in flight. The most that one ordinarily sees is a flash of black, or brown, and white as they dart in alarm to the nearest brush. Sometimes they make short flights along the edge of a thicket; or, popping out of a bush, flying a few feet along its edge, and then popping in again. Rarely, they are seen climbing into a tree-top, limb by limb. Then from the top they may launch out across the fields to a distant hedge, flying in long sweeping curves with regular undulations up.

The songs of the Towhees are heard after the middle of February. As a rule they sing from bushes from five to twenty feet above the ground and sometimes higher. Sometimes they sing near streams and sometimes on higher ground, but always near a thicket. The song is pleasant, has many variations, is sounded before sunrise and is frequently kept going all day at intervals until three o'clock. They have a typical call heard very often from thick bushes and tangles when the birds themselves can not be seen. This note usually sounds like "jo-ree" several times repeated, but often the birds get impatient and call "j-reet, j-reet." Sometimes they even shorten it to "reed, reed." Occasionally, Towhees utter a distinct "che-wink, che-wink, che-wink."

Towhees are common in the Sandhills from October to April and then leave for their summer homes in the mountains, or farther north. In December, I found them abundant in the Carolina Inn grounds at Pinehurst, where they took genial sun baths while perched on bushes a few feet above the ground. On the other hand, they were the most active of all birds during showers although taking shelter under shrubbery in the hardest part of a rain.

Through a January snowstorm, I found the Towhees foraging under a little group of blackberry briars and weeds. The space there was about twelve feet in diameter, and yet the scratching birds had cleared all this ground of snow and turned over all the leaves. Later I found they had cleared a similar place under a dogwood tree where they ate the berries,—pulp, seeds and all.

Towhees secure practically all their food in winter from the ground, either as it lies naturally, or after they have scratched. This scratching is like that of Fox Sparrows. It is usually done under thick bushes, and under heavy evergreens like magnolias and hollies. Sometimes they scratch under privet for the privet berries and often they fly up into sumac bushes to eat their red berries. They also eat the seeds from alder catkins and crack up acorns with their bills to get the meats. Once I saw a Towhee leave its scratching, dart suddenly up from the ground and chase an erratic flying insect until it caught it.

Towhees come to dooryards naturally and it is easy to attract them by providing suitable shady places for them to scratch. They sometimes come to artificial feeding stations for small grains and seeds.

These birds are often in couples and small groups of both sexes throughout the winter, but it is very difficult to say whether they are actually paired. If they are, they show no very great affection toward each other and often separate for some little time.

CARDINAL. Pl. 10, page 262

Cardinalis cardinalis cardinalis (Linn.). A. O. U. No. 593

Field Identification. A flaming red, or reddish brown, bird smaller than a Robin. The best marks are the big red bills surrounded by black and the conspicuous red crests. This is the only bright red bird that winters in the Sandhills.

Description. The male has his chin and feathers surrounding his bill black; rest of plumage bright red; a noticeable crest; bill red. The female is similar, but her crest, wings and tail are dull red; upperparts brownish; underparts brownish gray, sometimes tinged with red on breast. Total length 8¼ inches.

I had been told that the bills of the females were lighter in color than those of the males. When the sexes were seen separately, the females' bills did *seem* lighter; but when I saw the two sexes together in the field I could not convince myself that there was any difference whatever. In winter the colors of the males' feathers varied from dull to quite brilliant. Of course there were more birds brilliantly colored in the spring after March first, but one or two were seen each month of the winter that were just as brilliant as any of the spring birds.

Distribution. The Cardinals are resident throughout most of their range, extending south to the Gulf states and north to South Dakota, Iowa, Indiana, Ontario, Pennsylvania and southern New York, and casually even north of this area.

Habits. Cardinals are generally distributed throughout the Sandhills except out in the largest fields and in the densest forests. They are in the oak-and-pine forests and in the gum tree lowlands, especially near their edges. Like many other birds their favorite haunt is the borderland between forest and open fields. They are sometimes in the broom-grass corners, but they particularly like thick briary jungles and hedges bordered by fields, especially weedy cornfields and cotton fields. They like wet lowlands and dry uplands both, and are found near springs, ponds and lakes. At times they are most numerous about farmhouses and in villages and towns, particularly where they find plenty of food and water and dense shrubbery for protection from enemies. While Cardinals are often on the sandy ground of old fields, and even on burned-over ground, or on freshly plowed fields, they prefer more weedy places. Because they collect seeds for food, they are often on the ground under thickets, or shrubbery. Since they like growing brush, it is not strange to find them about tree limbs cut and piled to await other disposition. Sometimes they perch on fences and telephone wires. On cold mornings they are quite apt to be near the brush over streams. Near human dwellings they seek out rose bushes for protection, and they like the heavy foliage of magnolias, cedars, hollies and privet, especially on cold days (Figs. 21, 24, 26).

Cardinals are often seen in oaks of all kinds, in cedars, mulberry trees, dogwoods, walnuts, sweet gums, sour gums and pines, as much as forty feet above the ground. Normally, they prefer the middle limbs of trees, at medium heights. Often on reaching a limb they jerk up their tails several times rather sharply and nervously, only to lower them again immediately, but more slowly. In one case where a female Cardinal chased another, the pursuing bird jerked up her tail, but the other one did not. Another nervous action that interested me was the raising and lowering of their crests. Both sexes have them and both keep them up most of the time, even when the birds are at rest. Occasionally a crest is lowered when there is no apparent reason for doing so. In spite of these nervous actions, the Cardinals appeared less subject to sudden panics than their companions of other species. All the others frequently dart off in alarm while the Cardinals stay behind quietly feeding, or at least are the last to fly. These birds also have the habit of perching motionless on a bush and resting there all puffed up, for as much as ten or fifteen minutes. Yet in the morning when birds first appear, it is the Cardinals that are wide awake first and immediately foraging for breakfast while the other species are still warming up in the early sunlight. Perched in the limbs, the males look very spruce and debonair and make a striking contrast when close to Blue Jays or male Bluebirds. When they fly they make flaming streaks across the yard, especially brilliant and striking when they fly across a background of heavy evergreen shrubbery. Often one streak follows another, for Cardinals chase each other quite frequently. They even fight amongst themselves, and steal tidbits from smaller birds, such as Towhees. Sometimes the Jays and the Cardinals are less pugnacious, but generally the two species are antagonistic.

It is very doubtful whether Cardinals have any special desire for each other's society, although I have seen as many as four or five together at the same time. While there is little sociability as such, there are some indications that Cardinals remain paired in winter. They do not gather with other birds except for foraging or some other physical reason.

In flight, Cardinals show most of the characteristics common to sparrows. Their wings being short and broad, the result is a quick-beat, rapid, direct flight. As a rule, these birds fly from tree to tree rather than for long distances. They are quick to dive into a thicket at a sudden alarm and skillful at flying among limbs and through foliage.

Cardinals are noted songsters, often singing all day long from early in the morning until late in the afternoon. So much do they sing in the latter part of the day that they might appear at times to prefer the afternoon, but on closer study this preference will probably be found due to some one eccentric individual bird. With the majority of Cardinals, mornings or afternoons appeal equally. As a rule they sing from rather low perches such as rose bushes and low trees like dogwoods and oaks. They also sing high up in gum trees and even on telephone wires. They sometimes sing for quite long periods and give quite a number of variations. Their songs are noted for clear whistles, cheeriness and persistency rather than for fine melody and musical tones. Like so many bird songs, it is difficult to express them in words. The common Cardinal song is a whistled "whit-whit-whit-whit, whit-tjeer, whit-tjeer;" but the next bird may sing "quit, quit, quit, quit, what-tjeer, what-tjeer;" and another may give "chee-ta-haa, chee-ta-haa, chee-ta-haa." I heard one Cardinal calling "tee-jeer, tee-jeer" answered each time by another male, "chip-chip-chip." One heard in Southern Pines had lengthened his "whit-whit-whit" into "whee-to, whee-to, whee-to, whee-to" quite suggestive of the Tufted Titmouse. These birds sing on warm days all through the winter, but rather softly until about the last of January. Then, the songs become full-voiced and ringing, but not given often until about the middle of March, when the real Cardinal song season begins. As with most species of birds, it is the males that do most of the singing, but at least one *female* Cardinal in Southern Pines sang just like a male bird in every way, on March 18, 1927. Naturally a bird with such powers of song has also numerous call-notes. The commonest one sounds like ''tsip, tsip, tsip'' and at other times like mere twittering. Cardinals often call to each other, either one sex to the other, or a bird of either sex to another bird of the same sex.

Since the Cardinals are resident in the Sandhills there are no regular seasonal movements. They are numerous enough so that from one to twenty can readily be seen each day. On cold days they retire to the protection of thickets and heavy shrubbery. On sunny days they like to take sun baths while perched on limbs and briars protruding from favorite thickets.

Throughout the winter, Cardinals depend largely on seeds and waste grain for food. The seeds are obtained by picking them direct from the weed stems, by foraging on the ground, and by scratching the ground in the same manner as Fox Sparrows and Towhees. While hunting on the ground, the Cardinals pick up and eat many small insects, beetles, grasshoppers and spiders, for all of these are more or less active in the Sandhills all winter. Some Cardinals visit old cornfields (Figs. 18, 20, 27), and secure occasional kernels from the waste ears. The only cultivated berries they favor in winter are those from the privet and the mulberry trees. But in December they eat wild grapes. In January, their tastes apparently become more diversified, for they then eat sumac berries, wild persimons, berries from the sweet elder, cedar berries and dogwood berries, collecting them both from the bush or tree, and from the ground beneath. Of the dogwood berries, the Cardinals eat the pulp generally, but once or twice they were seen to roll the seeds in their bills as if cracking and eating them. On January 25, 1927, a female Cardinal ate some cedar berries, rolling them about in her bill for some time and apparently picking out the seeds to eat. On three different occasions in January, Cardinals were seen fly-catching from the limbs of trees. In February, they sometimes flew to the tops of tall gums and tupelos to tear open the new buds.

As a rule, Cardinals like to be near human habitations and artificial feeding stations are so popular that they are usually the first to respond to offerings. While these birds come readily to elevated stations after they become accustomed to them, they prefer at first to pick up food scattered on the ground. To draw Cardinals, the feeding stations should be supplied with seeds, small grain, bread crumbs and cracked corn. These birds are also fond of fresh drinking and bathing water, and a good fountain will draw them in winter, but naturally still more in hot weather.

Cardinals are seen in couples throughout the winter and there are many indications that they actually remain paired. On January 6, 1927, a Cardinal male was seen to fly to the ground and then to a low bush, two feet high, fluttering his wings and uttering low calls. Soon two female Cardinals flew over him and then moved nervously about. When the male flew to a nearby tree, one of the females followed, uttering low calls. Then a second male Cardinal appeared and pursued the first as it jumped up limb by limb to the top of the tree. But when they reached the top they perched there for some time about two feet apart. Apparently this was an early and somewhat weak manifestation of the pairing season. On January 19, 1927, a male Cardinal was seen pursuing a female for a two- or three-minute chase in and out through the foliage. Then both flew over to a cedar together. By March 24, 1927, a pair near Jackson Springs had appropriated a section along the lake shore and were building a nest and driving off intruders.

PURPLE MARTIN

Progne subis subis (Linn.). *A. O. U. No. 611*

Field Identification. A blue-black swallow smaller than a Robin. This is the largest of the swallow family and the only one in the Sandhills as early as the middle of March, when they arrive from the south.

Description. The male is shining blue-black, with wings and tail duller. The female has the upperparts duller; wings and tail black; throat, breast and sides brownish gray touched with white; belly white. Total length 8 inches.

Distribution. In winter, Martins are found in Brazil; in summer they live from Jalisco, Vera Cruz, the Gulf states and Florida north as far as Nova Scotia, New Brunswick, Ontario, Manitoba, Saskatchewan and Alberta.

Habits. Martins are such useful insectivorous birds, destroying so many of the pests of mankind, that nesting houses and nesting gourds are placed everywhere in the Sandhills to attract colonies of them. In primitive days, they nested in hollow trees, but they have now abandoned such quarters since man provided better ones. They are highly gregarious birds and they prefer to live and nest in colonies. In the Sandhills, they are the only birds, except the unwelcome English Sparrows, that will occupy more than one room of a many roomed nesting house. In the autumn, Purple Martins sometimes gather in such immense numbers on their nightly roosts that their steady twittering is augmented into a distinct nuisance to their human neighbors.

CEDAR WAXWING. Pl. 4, page 114

Bombycilla cedrorum Vieill. A. O. U. No. 619

Field Identification. A trim bird of a rich grayish brown color and larger than a sparrow. It has a conspicuous crest and a yellow terminal tail band, and flies in close, compact, orderly flocks.

Description. Forehead, chin and line over eye black; crest brown and prominent; upperparts grayish brown; lower back, wings and tail gray; secondary feathers of the wing often, and tail-feathers more rarely, tipped with small, red, oval, sealing-wax-like tips; tail with yellow terminal band; breast brown, gradually changing to yellow on lower belly. Total length 7¼ inches.

Distribution. These birds are found in all parts of the Sandhills throughout the winter. During the winter, members of this species go as far south as Cuba, Mexico and Panama; in summer they are found in the mountains and northern parts of North Carolina north to Cape Breton Island, Quebec, Ontario, Keewatin, Alberta and British Columbia.

Habits. The movements of the Cedar-birds are very uncertain and depend largely upon a supply of food at all seasons. In December they are in the gum swamps after sour gum berries (*Nyssa silvatica*), and later they visit privet bushes and cedars, even in the largest towns and cities. Since these birds wander around a great deal from one feeding ground to another, they are often seen flying over all sections of the Sandhills. Where the privet bushes are allowed to grow untrimmed so that they bear berries, they prove very attractive to Cedar Waxwings. When flying from one feeding ground to another, they often stop to rest on any convenient tall trees—sycamores, oaks, gums, persimmon trees or pines. When they alight, they cluster in thick groups at the very tip of a tree if there be room, otherwise as near the top as they can. They are but seldom seen with other species, and then the gathering is due to seeking similar food. For this reason they are occasionally seen with Robins and more rarely with Purple Finches, Cardinals or Chickadees, but these groups are always temporary.

Waxwings fly in small groups of from ten to twenty birds, and their flight is very peculiar to the species. Their compact flocks fly very rapidly with slightly undulating flight, and maintain an almost military precision of movement. As they approach a resting place they suddenly wheel about, drop and sweep up in a whistling group. Sometimes as many as thirty of these smaller flocks will join into one big group, perhaps containing three or four hundred birds; but when they leave, they again split up into the smaller groups and fly to their next destination in quite a direct flight, in spite of the undulations and the occasional sharp turns and abrupt wheelings.

In the sour gum trees, they seldom take more than six berries at a time before moving to the next tree, so that they are then quite scattered and constantly in motion. Although feeding this way, one or two birds to a tree, it is astonishing how quickly an alarm causes them to gather in the air into a compact flock again. Indeed, orderliness and precision are always characteristic of Cedar Waxwings, no matter how excited they seem to get at a feast. At times I have seen them spring out from the foliage of long-leaf pines and catch flying insects in true flycatcher style. In January, 1927, I found the Cedar Waxwings true to their name and feeding eagerly on cedar berries a mile south of the Highland Pines Inn at Southern Pines. After feeding perhaps for ten minutes on these berries, the birds would fly down to a nearby spring for a drink, first one Waxwing and then another, and then still another, until all were closely gathered about the spring. After five minutes of excited chattering and drinking, they would all fly directly back to the cedars, and repeat again and again until fully satisfied.

Waxwings nest comparatively late in the season so that the following incidents can hardly be considered as connected with that activity, although they certainly do show the gentle, loving ways of these birds. On December 10, 1926, I was seated in a cornfield (Fig. 27) watching the Waxwings on the gum trees at the edge of the field. One couple in a liquidambar tree were not feeding. They hopped along a limb away from each other a few inches, but immediately hopped back again until they were close together and side by side. Then they hopped away and back again on the same small limb. When they came together, they pressed themselves close to each other and even appeared to lay their cheeks together. This movement was repeated again and again throughout several minutes with each bird looking very trim, well-groomed, slender and erect. Then they perched quietly side by side for five minutes, and finally flew away together to rejoin the other members of the flock that had left a minute or two earlier. Six days later I saw two other Waxwings doing the same thing.

LOGGERHEAD SHRIKE. Pl. 11, page 272

Lanius ludovicianus ludovicianus Linn. *A. O. U. No. 622*

Field Identification. A gray bird smaller than a Robin. Black and white tail and wings, with white markings showing conspicuously in flight; black bars through the eyes; heavy bill with hooked tip; steady and direct flight.

Description. Upperparts gray; wings and tail black; a white patch and a white wing-bar on each wing; outer, sometimes all tail-feathers tipped with white; black bar from bill through eyes to ears; underparts light gray. Total length 9 inches.

Distribution. Although not very common, Shrikes are generally distributed throughout the Sandhills in winter, and a few remain all summer and breed. Loggerhead Shrikes live from North Carolina south to Florida and west to Louisiana.

Habits. These birds are so generally seen perched on telephone poles or wires over open fields (Figs. 6, 9, 18, 20, 27), or peach orchards, that we come to believe they are always there. Still, Shrikes occasionally enter open shrub oak forests and even come to town at times. They like to hunt over weedy fields and orchards of all kinds, and over broom-sedge; in order to do so, the

Shrikes select a low but prominent perch from which they can see the slightest movement of mouse or insect within a comparatively wide territory. Freshly plowed fields are also favorite hunting grounds. In the course of their hunting, Loggerheads will often fly down to low convenient perches near where they have seen suspicious movements, even to the ground itself. Sometimes they alight on low bushes, stiff weeds or fences, sometimes on vines of a vineyard, and quite often on low trees. Usually the selected tree is a shrub oak, and on one occasion, near Aberdeen, a Shrike even selected an oak in preference to a nearby electric wire. These birds are also seen in mulberries and sycamores, but seldom, if ever, on a living pine.

It has been stated that Shrikes always fly up to the top of whatever observation post they select. This did not prove to be quite accurate so far as these Sandhills birds were concerned. If the telephone lines consisted of two or more layers of wires, they were usually on one of the lowest wires. This could easily be accounted for on the supposition that the birds wanted no wires to interfere with their view down, or with their swoop when they discovered prey, almost invariably below them. One Shrike was seen hunting along the edge of a shrub oak forest, where it alighted on seven different oaks. In every case this bird chose a limb below the top, but soon made its way, by hopping up a limb at a time, to the top. Once it perched on the lowest limb of an oak, less than half way to the top, and stayed there until it caught sight of an insect on the ground below it. Two or three days later, I found another one hunting in a peach orchard. This bird usually perched on the tips of the peach trees, but at times it alighted on the lower limbs and later hopped up to the top. Another was seen to perch on the lowest limb of a medium-sized oak in a not very prominent position and to stay there for several seconds. Usually, Shrikes perch at the *outer tip* of a limb whether it is on the lower portion of a tree or at the top. When perched on observation posts, they sit low and often in a distinctly crouching attitude, but they are actually alert and wide awake.

When Shrikes prefer hunting along a well-traveled road, they get extraordinarily indifferent to the traffic often passing within a few feet. They are solitary birds and are seldom seen more than one at a time except in the pairing and nesting seasons. They do not foregather with other birds and are not seen near them except by merest accident.

When Shrikes fly, they are apt to swoop down from their perch and fly along a few feet above the ground. As they near their next perch, they rise up to it in a sharp curve. Flight is about average in speed, but is very direct and the wings beat rapidly. Shrikes can leave the ground and rise almost perpendicularly to a perch overhead. Sometimes they stay as much as ten minutes on the same perch, and are then quite motionless except for turning their heads from side to side, or to glance down. They keep a keen lookout and usually turn their breasts toward the direction from which the wind is blowing. In the Sandhills, the food of the Shrikes seems to be insects and worms throughout the winter. They may catch mice once in a while, but I did not see one attempt to catch any small birds or molest them in any way. When Shrikes catch sight of grasshoppers, they dive quickly down to catch them and then carry them in their bills either back to the perches just left, or to more distant ones. One Shrike that I watched on February 12, 1927, made frequent swoops. Soon it caught a worm an inch long and also a big grub that it ate on the ground where caught. Then it flew a short distance and perched again, but immediately left this perch and flew thirty feet for another grub. Apparently it had caught sight of this prey instantly on alighting more than thirty feet away. Another Shrike was seen just south of Aberdeen that left its telephone wire and flew out over a grassy field hunting for insects. When well out on the field, it watched carefully all around. When an insect showed for an instant, it was promptly pounced upon and devoured on the spot. Then this bird fed on small insects, catching five in twenty minutes. After each catch it usually flew on up the field and against the wind to the next favorable weed stem. Another Shrike was also seen to swoop down and catch insects that attempted to fly past its perch. Still another hunting method was used on the golf links where a Shrike moved across the short grass feeding on the insects that flew up before it, and later dug for fat white grubs under the grass roots. In other places, Shrikes impale some of their prey on thorns, and the barbs of wire fences, and leave it there until wanted. But I saw none of this in the Sandhills al-

Figure 25. Highland Pines Inn, Southern Pines, in the long-leaf Pine forest, attracted many Mockingbirds.   Feb. 12, 1926.

though I looked carefully for evidences. The impression I finally arrived at was that the hunting was too poor to ever provide a surplus, during the winter at any rate.

Loggerhead Shrikes are solitary all winter, but early in February they pair and are then frequently seen together. On March 10, 1927, I saw one busily pulling at some cotton caught in the bottom of a bush. After tugging for a time, it pulled out a mass of cotton as big as its own body and flew off with it in its bill to a thick magnolia, where it was building a nest in a crotch twenty feet above the ground.

MOUNTAIN SOLITARY VIREO

Lanivireo solitarius alticola (Brewst). A. O. U. No. 629c

Field Identification. A white-breasted, bluish gray bird smaller than a sparrow; it can be identified by its white eye-ring, white underparts and two white wing-bars. It is not possible to tell this bird from the closely related Blue-headed Vireo that occurs elsewhere.

Description. Top and sides of the head bluish gray; eye-ring white; upperparts brown, sometimes tinged with bluish; two distinct wing-bars; underparts white; sides tinged with yellow. Total length 5¼ inches.

Distribution. This bird is rare in the Sandhills, for its usual winter home is in the sea-coast lowlands from South Carolina to Florida; and in summer it is in the mountains of North Carolina, Tennessee and Virginia.

Habits. These vireos deserve their name, for they are comparatively common in the mountains during the summer. In the Sandhills, they were seen on March 15, 1927, in the margins of thickets and in wild cherry bushes at the edges of an old cornfield (Fig. 22). Even for vireos, these birds were remarkably quiet and prone to go about their business in a way that made it difficult to watch them. My usual experience was to catch only occasional glimpses; one moment I saw them, the next moment they were gone without my knowing just where or how they went. They could not be called either shy or wild, but more appropriately "unobtrusive." They were partial to low growth where they gleaned their insect food from the bark and twigs of bushes and small trees.

WHITE-EYED VIREO

Vireo griseus griseus (Bodd.). *A. O. U. No. 631*

Field Identification. A grayish green bird smaller than a sparrow and having white eyes, yellow eye-rings, and two yellowish white wing-bars on each wing.

Description. Upperparts bright olive-green, more or less washed with grayish; two distinct yellowish white wing-bars; eye-ring yellow; throat whitish; belly white; breast and sides washed with greenish yellow; eye white in adult but hazel color in the young. Total length 5¼ inches.

Distribution. This species has not yet been noted in this section in winter, but it is known to occur such a short distance south of the Sandhills that it may be added to the list at any time. The earliest birds of this species noted were seen on March 22, 1927. In winter this vireo is in South Carolina, Georgia, Florida and Texas south through the eastern part of Mexico to Yucatan and Guatemala. In summer it ranges from central Texas and central Florida north to southeastern Nebraska, Wisconsin, New York and Massachusetts.

Habits. Usually the White-eyed Vireos are seen in the thickets along the streams and near swampy places and flooded forests (Fig. 11). Sometimes, at least in spring, they wander out into the drier shrub oak forest, although they never stay there long. They are rather nervous little birds flitting here and there among the smaller limbs. They are sociable, at least with Myrtle Warblers, although when the warblers leave the thickets, the vireos return to the thickets again.

Like so many of their nearest relatives, these vireos depend largely on a variety of insects caught by searching the small twigs and leaves of trees and bushes. Making use of their acrobatic ability, they examine the under side of leaves as well as the upper, so that they are as often seen inverted as they are upright.

PARULA WARBLER

Compsothlypis americana americana (Linn.). *A. O. U. No. 648*

Field Identification. A grayish blue warbler smaller than an English Sparrow and having a yellow throat, two white patches on the tail, two white wing-bars on each wing, and a greenish yellow spot on the back. It is an inhabitant of the damp lowland woods. If it is seen at all in the higher oak and pine forests, it is out of its usual haunt for some extraordinary reason.

Description. On the male, the upperparts are grayish blue; a greenish yellow patch in the middle of the back; two distinct white wing-bars; outer tail-feathers with a white patch; throat and breast yellow, an indistinct black or rufous band across the breast; belly white. The female has the throat and breast clearer yellow and the breast-band still more indistinct. Total length 4¾ inches.

Distribution. Properly speaking, these are not winter birds in the Sandhills, but arrive during the latter part of March, especially in favorable seasons. They spend their winters in southern Florida or the West Indies; in summer they live from Florida and Alabama north to the District of Columbia. North of the Potomac River there is a similar bird in summer known as the "Northern Parula Warbler."

Habits. These are probably the earliest of the migrant warblers to reach the Sandhills, and when their sweet song is heard, it is a sign that spring has begun again. Farther south their presence and comparative abundance depends on the presence of the long Spanish moss (*Tillandsia usneoides*), of which they make their nests. Here in North Carolina, the Parula Warblers use the Spanish moss where they can get it, but in other places they use the *Usnia* moss, according to Pearson and Brimley.

MYRTLE WARBLER. Pl. 4, page 114

Dendroica coronata (Linn.). A. O. U. No. 655

Field Identification. A lively black, white and yellow bird a little smaller than a sparrow. It is identified by two whitish spots on the tail and a yellow spot on the lower back. These show in flight, but the yellow may be hidden by the wings at times, and it is sometimes whitish instead of clear yellow.

Description. A yellow crown-patch sometimes hidden by brownish; upperparts brown, streaked with darker; two gray wing-bars; lower back yellow; outer tail-feathers with white spots near their tips; underparts soiled white, sometimes streaked. In spring and summer, the male has the crown, lower back and sides yellow; upperparts bluish, streaked with black; breast streaked with black. The female then has less black below than the male and her upperparts are browner and with less yellow. Total length a little over 5½ inches.

Myrtle Warblers, during the winter, show all gradations between the spring male plumage and the dull female and winter plumages. The majority begin to brighten and show new feathers in March, but the process of changing is irregular. In March some Myrtle Warblers are in brilliant plumage; some show a yellow tint on their crowns; some show a very bright rump; but even as late as April some birds are molting and still acquiring spring plumage.

Distribution. Myrtle Warblers are abundant in all parts of the Sandhills throughout the winter from October to May. At this season, other individuals go as far south as the Greater Antilles and Panama; in summer they live as far north as the limit of trees in northwestern Alaska, northern Mackenzie, Keewatin and Ungava.

Habits. Myrtle Warblers frequent all kinds of neighborhoods except the largest open fields. They live in all kinds of woods from the most open to the densest and gloomiest kind, but in the latter case they are apt to be in the foliage of the highest limbs. In addition to low ground, they frequent higher and drier lands such as plowed ground, old fields and oak-and-pine forests. Since they often catch their food on, or near, the ground, Myrtle Warblers are often there, and sometimes on burned-over ground. Still, they like low brush and shrub oaks better, and, at all seasons from November to April.

Like so many other small birds, these warblers like the hedges and thickets over small streams, especially when those thickets are bordered by low grassy cornfields or grassy cotton fields. They like best the borderland between the forests and the open fields. In addition, they come into the cities and are found in dooryard shrubbery of all kinds.

The movements of Myrtle Warblers are quick and lively. They hunt through the oak foliage, even picking insects from the under side of the unfolding leaves of spring, clinging and clambering with an expertness more expected of Chickadees. They can climb up and down rough tree trunks somewhat like nuthatches. On violently swaying twigs they can maintain their positions no matter how far or fast the motion. On the ground, Myrtle Warblers hop here and there erratically.

Although these warblers are rather ragged-looking at molting time, they are ordinarily trim and neat in appearance. Often their sudden movements will disclose a yellow tinting on their crowns that is not otherwise noticeable. Occasionally one is seen at rest or preening, but generally they are nervously dashing here and there, or darting after flying insects. They have more than the usual curiosity of small birds and usually take an interest in whatever other small birds are doing, and in passing bird-lovers too.

During the winter, Myrtle Warblers are in small groups, but in March they appear in large but very loosely organized flocks. Probably, they like to be in small groups of their fellows, but are not as gregarious as a good many birds, such as Juncos and black-birds. They do not seek the companionship of other birds, but are often seen temporarily with Pine Warblers, Field Sparrows, Juncos, Song Sparrows, Bluebirds, Mockingbirds, Robins, Blue-gray Gnatcatchers, Titmice and kinglets.

Myrtle Warblers fly straight or somewhat undulating, but from tree to tree rather than by long single flights. Usually, they are hunting insects, exercising all the sudden stops, twistings, turnings, dartings and erratic movements for which their short wings and long tails are so well adapted. At this style of flight, these birds are singularly expert, although perhaps not more so than most warblers.

Myrtle Warblers begin singing in the Sandhills as early as the middle of January, although theirs is not a song that would attract special attention from any one but a confirmed bird-lover. As a rule, they prefer to sing in a thicket, or on a perch hidden by evergreen foliage, rather than right out in the open as most song-sters do. They do not sing much in winter, however, and their true song season does not begin until after they leave on migration. Myrtle Warblers are seen throughout the winter, and it is hard to say just when they do begin moving north. Probably the first motion is a gentle moving on, with birds coming up from the south taking the place of those that leave so unobtrusively. But early in March the movement becomes conspicuous, and great numbers of these warblers are then seen constantly moving through the forests and across the fields in steady streams, flitting about a few minutes, and then passing on to the northeast. These movements are near the ground, or among the tree trunks, but at other times the birds are above the tallest trees. The general direction is from the southwest to the northeast, with fifty to a hundred warblers passing over a field each hour of every day for at least two weeks.

Insects are depended upon for food, and even during the coldest winter weather, these warblers can find some of the many kinds they like. They pick these insects up from the ground in forest and field, and from the furrows of freshly plowed fields. They hunt through the lowest brush, flit through the shrub oaks, and even search the limbs and foliage at the tops of loblolly pines and the tallest long-leaf pines. In the swamps and flooded woods, they search every twig and floating chip for insects emerging from the water and for any that may have alighted there for a moment. They pick up insects from the surface of the water, or if one happens to jump or fly, they dart out after it, no matter how far the insect flies. In addition to insects, Myrtle Warblers eat the berries of privet, sumach, and cedar, and probably many other small wild fruits. In the cedar trees, they balance on the ends of twigs and pick the berries; they hover before each cluster and twitch off one berry at a time; and they pick up berries that have fallen to the ground. Usually, they eat from four to ten berries at a meal, and then either fly away for a short time, take a rest, or preen their feathers before returning for another meal. Each berry is held in the bill and rolled about for some time, although both pulp and seeds are eventually swallowed. Apparently the cedar berries contain some material that adheres to the birds' bills, for they vigorously wipe them on twigs and small limbs. After eating, Myrtle Warblers customarily preen their feathers.

YELLOW-THROATED WARBLER

Dendroica dominica dominica (Linn.). *A. O. U. No. 663*

Field Identification. Smaller than a sparrow and distinguished by its black and white markings, yellow throat and breast, two white wing-bars on each wing, and two white spots on end of tail.

Description. Cheeks and sides of the throat black; a white spot on the side of the neck; a yellow spot in front of the eye and a white line over eye; upperparts gray; two white wing-bars; outer tail-feathers with white patches near their tips; middle of the throat and the breast yellow; belly white. Total length 5¼ inches.

Distribution. The Yellow-throated Warbler was not seen during the winter, but arrived as early as March at least. They are known to winter such a short distance south of the Sandhills that they may be found some day actually wintering here. They spend the winter in South Carolina, Florida, the Bahama Islands and the Greater Antilles. In summer they live between Florida on the south and southern Maryland and Delaware on the north.

Habits. Although the Yellow-throated Warblers are the most distinctive of the summer warblers of the Sandhills, they are not very common in either March or April. During the early spring at least, they are found in both the damper lowlands in the hardwoods, and in the limbs and foliage of the pines on the drier uplands. Sometimes they come into the shrubbery of dooryards. In the trees, their movements are quick, nervous and active, and they are very neat and trim in appearance for they spend much time in preening.

Yellow-throated Warblers are gentle and friendly, but are not really socially inclined, either toward other members of their own kind or toward other species. They sing a pretty, ringing song almost as soon as they arrive from the south, usually from the low limb of a pine or other tree.

As usual with warblers, these little birds are skillful insect catchers, and eat house flies, mosquitoes, ants, crickets, beetles and many other varieties of the smaller insects. Once I saw one on an artificial feeding station eating bread crumbs.

These warblers seem even fonder of bathing than most other warblers. They go regularly and often to their baths, and after bathing they spend several minutes carefully preening and arranging their feathers.

PINE WARBLER. Pl. 12, page 290

Dendroica vigorsi vigorsi (Aud.).   A. O. U. No. 671

Field Identification. This warbler, smaller than an English Sparrow, is difficult to identify, but fortunately it is the only olive-green and yellow bird at all common in the Sandhills in winter.

The size and shape of the bill and the two white spots on the tail show that it is a warbler.

Description. The male has olive-green upperparts, sometimes dulled with grayish; two whitish wing-bars; outer tail-feathers with white patches near their tips; underparts yellow, sometimes tinged with ashy. The female has more brownish on the upperparts; soiled whitish underparts; breast tinged with yellow. Total length 5½ inches.

Distribution. This warbler is not common in the sense that the Myrtle Warbler is, but it is found throughout the Sandhills at all seasons of the year. In the winter, Pine Warblers go as far south as Florida, the Gulf coast and Texas; in the summer they live as far north as Manitoba, Michigan, Ontario, Quebec and New Brunswick.

Habits. During the winter I found Pine Warblers usually in the scrub-oak-and-pine woods (Figs. 1, 2, 5), near, or on, the ground; and occasionally in thickets (Fig. 22) and hardwoods over damp spots and small streams. At times they were in low brush two feet above the ground, in low trees, or in persimmon trees, but once I saw them in a long-leaf pine at least forty feet high. On the ground, they forage amid the fallen leaves and hop nimbly along, for their movements are quick and as spirited as usual with warblers. They are more quiet than the Myrtle Warblers. They were seen to perch on, and cling to, the upright wires of woven-wire fences. I found the Pine Warblers very tame and also seemingly very curious as to why I was sitting so quietly in their haunts!

During the winter, these warblers are found in little groups of from two to six individuals. Sometimes a single bird is seen, but when that is the case it is almost always with other birds such as Myrtle Warblers, Juncos, Hermit Thrushes, Bluebirds or White-throated Sparrows.

Like the Myrtle Warblers, these birds are expert at catching insects that twist and dart here and there while in flight, but they also laboriously search the bases of shrub oaks and the ground nearby. Pine Warblers sometimes fly up and down the trunk of an oak as if picking insects from the rough bark. Their song is not a conspicuous one, but it is given on warm days in winter, although the real song season does not begin in the Sandhills until about the first of March. During the winter, Pine Warblers come and go, often becoming very numerous, as if their number had been augmented by additional birds driven down from farther north. These movements seem more or less local and temporary, for these birds are able to withstand the cold weather if they can secure sufficient food.

The winter food of Pine Warblers consists almost wholly of insects that they secure in a variety of ways. The normal method is to search the limbs and foliage, darting quickly out after any insect they start; but they also perch quietly on a limb and wait for prey to attempt to fly by, and then chase it. On January 15, 1927, several were seen foraging amid the fallen leaves and pine straw at the edge of a shrub oak forest. Here they tore old oak leaves apart and devoured the eggs and young of gall insects. On February 5, 1927, a Pine Warbler flew out into an open field with some Juncos and there hunted insects through the grass. When a frightened insect flew up, the warbler sprang up after it. As spring drew near, they hunted higher and higher in the foliage, even to the tops of long-leaf pines. No doubt they took vegetable food at times, particularly wild fruits and berries. And once I saw one take several sips from the fruit of a wild persimmon, on January 11, 1927.

Pine Warblers are fond of bathing even in the middle of winter. One was seen bathing in a ditch beneath a thicket, and then it flew up into the foliage of a pine to shake itself, although too hurried to preen just then.

PRAIRIE WARBLER

Dendroica discolor (Vieill.).   A. O. U. No. 673

Field Identification. A yellowish green warbler much smaller than an English Sparrow, with black streaks on the sides, no marks on the yellow breast and belly, rufous spots on the backs of the males and of some females, and the warbler's two white spots on the tail.

Description. The male has olive upperparts with reddish spots on his back; wing-bars yellowish and rather indistinct; outer tail-feathers with white patches at their tips; a yellow line over eye and black markings below eye; underparts yellow; sides streaked with black. The adult female has few, if any, reddish markings: the young female has gray-green, unspotted upperparts. Total length 4¾ inches.

Distribution. This is another warbler that does not winter in the Sandhills but arrives in spring early in April, or in late March in favorable years. In winter, Prairie Warblers are found in Florida, the Bahama Islands and the West Indies; in summer they spread out over the eastern United States from the Gulf states north to New Jersey, Pennsylvania, Ohio, eastern Kansas and south-eastern Nebraska.

Habits. Although these warblers are not exclusively grassland birds as one might infer from their common name, they are not inhabitants of the heavy forests, either. Their preferred home in the Sandhills is the old fields grown up to broom-sedge (Figs. 13 and 14), low brush and small saplings; and they also like the open oak-and-pine forests where the larger trees have all been cut down. These warblers, then, are perhaps more characteristic of the hot, dry fields than any other warblers are.

LOUISIANA WATER-THRUSH

Seiurus motacilla (Vieill). *A. O. U. No. 676*

Field Identification. A grayish brown bird the same size as a large sparrow. It is always seen near water and can be identified by its wagging tail and a white line over the eye.

Description. Upperparts grayish brown; a white line over eye; underparts white, sometimes tinged with buff; streaked with blackish on the sides. Total length 6¼ inches.

Distribution. This is another warbler that does not winter in the Sandhills but arrives in spring before the end of March. In winter, these birds go to Mexico, the West Indies and Colombia; in summer they live from Texas, Georgia and South Carolina north to Minnesota, Michigan, Ontario, New York and New England.

Habits. Water-thrushes are excessively shy and retiring. Not only are they difficult to find because of the impenetrable nature of their haunts, in the immediate vicinity of forest streams, but they are also very wild and quick to take alarm. But they can be found by persistence. The song of the Louisiana Water-thrushes is unique and not to be compared with that of any other bird; it is loud and ringing and voices in itself the very essence of the wilderness.

AMERICAN PIPIT. Pl. 11, page 272

Anthus rubescens (Tunstall). A. O. U. No. 697

Field Identification. A brown, sparrow-like bird a trifle larger than an English Sparrow. It can be recognized by its walking gait and the white tail-feathers noticeable in flight but also showing slightly as the birds walk.

Description. Upperparts grayish brown; an indistinct buffy line over eye; buffy wing-bar; outer edges of tail white; underparts buffy, streaked with dusky on breast and sides. Total length a little over 6¼ inches.

Distribution. These birds are present in the Sandhills only during the winter from November to late March. At this season other individuals are found as far south as Guatemala; in summer they are all north of us as far as Alaska, Great Slave Lake, Keewatin, northern Quebec and Newfoundland.

Habits. Pipits are not found in forests or wooded areas, but are seen only in the largest hay fields, winter-wheat fields, old cornfields where the stalks are all down, and in old cowpea fields. Although I looked for Pipits there, I did not find them on plowed fields, even on those plowed fields that were near other fields on which they ranged daily. A flock of one or two hundred stayed more or less continuously on the fields near the Pinehurst Dairy.

On the ground, Pipits are noted as *walking* birds quite given to roaming and walking across the fields. When it is necessary, they can run quite rapidly after insects, and even appear to prefer running short distances to flying from place to place on the field. While running, they hold their heads steady and do not move their tails up and down. As most of our bird literature speaks of the constant "wagging," of the Pipits' tails while the birds are on the ground, I watched for this sign, but to my great surprise I found tail-wagging was not a constant habit in the Sandhills in winter. As these birds walked, their heads nodded forward and back at every step, and their bodies and tails swung from side to side in time with each step. In every case this sidewise movement of the tail was an accompaniment of the body movement, and I did not see a single Pipit move its tail *sidewise* independently of the body. But I found there was another movement of the tail, *up and down*, that was sometimes made. Of one hundred and forty birds watched on January 28, 1927, some *tipped their tails up and down* rapidly while walking and while resting on the ground but many of them did not. Ten days later, I noted that only a few of these Pipits moved their tails up and down, and that even these movements were noticeable only when the birds alighted after flight, and then there was only two to five movements. On March 1, 1927, I observed that when these birds *stopped walking* they moved their tails more or less regularly, but the motion was not noticeable *while* they walked, and disappeared altogether when they ran. Late in the winter, the Pipits all moved their tails up and down, during momentary pauses from their insect hunting. One bird walked up a four-inch flat timber to the top of a fence; and a second one alighted on the fence wire. Even while perched two or three minutes on this wire, this bird only tipped at times, and not more so than many other species would do in a similar position, and certainly not so much as a Sparrow Hawk usually does. From these various observations, I came to the conclusion that movement of Pipits' tails from side to side while walking, was an accompaniment of the swinging body just as it is with many other species of walking birds; that the movement of the tail up and down two to six times was usual just after a flying bird alighted, but at other times the movement had to be carefully watched for to be detected; but that these movements increased in frequency as the season advanced toward spring. Arthur T. Wayne (1910, page 178) seems to say that non-wagging is a mark of the western *Sprague Pipit*. But since Pearson and Brimley do not list *Spragueii* in North Carolina, I could hardly assume that all these Pipits were of this form.

Occasionally Pipits occur one or two at a time, but generally they are in flocks of from twenty to two hundred birds, and seem to thoroughly enjoy each other's society. Pipits do not gather with other birds, although I once saw a flock of Red-winged Blackbirds and Cowbirds fly out to an old pea field and alight near some feeding Pipits. No doubt this was purely accidental, but it was the only time that I saw other birds even near a flock of Pipits.

The flight of Pipits is light, airy and gently undulating, and usually twenty to sixty feet above the surface of the fields. Their flocks are not at all compact, but are apt to be loose and straggling and with a wide front, although the birds often string out into a long line with the birds in the rear following the general direction of those in front. They often fly singly from point to point in the same field, but when they are alarmed, or when ready to leave, they all fly up at the same time. As they spring up, each bird utters a soft, low "dee, dee." After flying a few hundred yards as if actually leaving, they may swing around in a big circle and fly back to alight again near where they started. This nervousness is more marked in windy and rainy weather. In windy weather, Pipits generally fly against the wind and also alight facing the wind. On February 5, 1927, I observed a flock rise in flight until well above all scattered trees, then fly a half-mile away, gradually rising higher and higher, and then swinging around in a big circle only to come back and dive down near the spot from which they started a few minutes earlier. Later, on the same day, they again flew high, but when nearly over the field they were going to, they swooped quickly down in a long string of descending birds. Three days later, they circled round and round the same field, gradually getting lower and lower until just above the ground surface.

Pipits eat insects and the seeds of various grasses and weeds, throughout the winter. They are often found in old cowpea fields, but feed there only on seeds and insects picked up as they roam across under the stalks above them. Sometimes they run down an escaping insect or jump up for a flying one. When insects get more abundant late in the winter, the Pipits feed on them more and neglect the seeds. During the snowstorm of early March, 1927, they foraged on the ground trampled down by the pigs at the stock-yards. During cold rains, the Pipits paid little attention beyond shaking themselves once in a while, but when a hard shower came, they quickly sought partial shelter under the lee of tufts of grass and behind fence posts. Ordinarily these birds rather like rain and often stop their steady search for food to take a shower bath, later shaking themselves vigorously and then preening.

MOCKINGBIRD. Pl. 10, page 262

Mimus polyglottos polyglottos (Linn.). *A. O. U. No. 703*

Field Identification. A gray bird that appears more slender than a Robin, but is actually the same length. It has a white patch

PLATE 9. BRUSH AND JUNGLE BIRDS

1: Catbird.
2: Turkey Vulture.
3: Black Vulture.
4: Red-tailed Hawk.

5: Screech Owl (reddish phase).
6: Screech Owl (gray phase).
7: Tufted Titmouse.
8: Hermit Thrush.

(Figures 1, 5–8, about ⅓ life size; Figures 2–4, about ⅕ life size)

on each wing that flashes out broadly in flight, white tail-feathers, yellow eyes, and a slender decurved upper bill.

Description. Upperparts gray, with wings and tail much darker than the back; each wing has a white patch; two white wing-bars; three outer tail-feathers on each side mostly white; underparts grayish white; eye, light yellow in mature birds. Total length 10½ inches.

Distribution. Mockingbirds are not migratory at any season of the year, but are abundant in favorable localities throughout central and eastern North Carolina. Beyond this state they range north occasionally to Massachusetts, New York, and southern Ontario and usually to Ohio, Indiana and Illinois; west usually to southern Iowa, eastern Nebraska, Oklahoma and Texas; and south to the Gulf states and the Rio Grande River.

Habits. Mockingbirds are so generally seen near human habitations that it is often assumed that they are essentially dooryard birds. But I doubt if this is so because of any particular liking of these birds for man. Probably they live in dooryards because enemies (other than domestic cats) are fewer, and because cultivated shrubbery (Figs. 17, 21, 24, 25, 26) provides good nesting sites. In addition to these dooryard Mockingbirds there are many more that live far away from houses, and these are usually in, or near, thickets, especially where a stream or a bit of water encourages a more luxuriant thicket, and a growth of blackberries, wild grapes and other berries eaten by them. Other individuals are found out on the pine barrens at times. Mockingbirds live largely on the ground in winter. They seem to like garden walks and driveways, especially if they have been freshly raked or scratched. Mockingbirds also like soil that has just been spaded, and they are often out on plowed fields, on old weedy cornfields, or cotton fields. They are often observed on golf links, and sometimes hunt through rather tall grass. Underbrush, shrubbery or rose bushes are favorite haunts; but the tops of these bushes are still more favored. These birds are even seen perched on stumps, fences and prostrate logs. Next to bushes, low trees are chosen perches and at times the higher limbs of quite tall trees are utilized, even as high as sixty feet above the ground in gums and ten feet higher on tall oaks. At times, Mockingbirds are to be found in shrub oaks, turkey oaks, white oaks, persimmons, peach trees and other cultivated fruit trees. But evergreen and thick-foliaged trees like magnolias, hollies and pines are sought for protection from weather or enemies. The heavy shrubbery and the untrimmed privet bushes at Pinehurst are so very attractive that at least fifty pairs of Mockingbirds live there constantly. Since these birds live about houses, we often find them perched on our buildings, on our porch railings, on the porch chairs and even on the window sills. Occasionally, they perch on electric wires, but not often, although one was seen singing from such a perch.

While I would not call their flight swift, it is quick enough for short distances. On the ground, they can run quite rapidly, and move with the greatest ease under, or through, thick shrubbery. In slipping through cat-briars and thorny growth, only the Catbirds and Brown Thrashers can equal them in silence and dexterity. Mockingbirds on the ground have a great many of the ways of Robins; they run like Robins, feed like Robins, and hold themselves erect and look around as Robins do. But Mockingbirds also hop on the ground at times. They move about at all hours of the day and even feed when it is almost dark, but it is not known just how much they may move about when they are singing at night, probably not very much. Mockingbirds in evergreens have a typical way of running along limbs and in and out among the leaves.

Mockingbirds are neat, trim, well-groomed birds, always alert and active when necessary, but often quietly perching on some observation point where they can survey their domains. For each bird claims a certain territory as its own, driving away all rivals with extraordinary dash and courage. From their nesting areas, they will not only drive off all rival Mockingbirds, but also all other of the larger birds that they can master or intimidate, and they will even attack any cat or dog that may stray too near. When winter comes, they still claim their own territories, although they may not be the same as in summer, and any other Mockingbirds that alight on, or even approach, the wild berry bushes, wild grape vines, and wild small-fruit trees within the limits are quickly driven off. I have even been attacked, myself, when I ventured to gather a few wild grapes from a Mockingbird's winter supply. In winter, these birds are more tolerant of other species, permitting them in the same bush or tree, and even on the same limb without

Figure 26.   Thick shrubbery very attractive to birds, Pinehurst, Feb. 1, 1926.

protest; but apparently they do not permit another Mockingbird within sight at any time. On January 27, 1927, a mile south of the Highland Pines Inn, I found a Mockingbird trying to keep five Robins out of a cedar. Whenever the Robins perched outside the cedar the Mockingbird seemed content, but the instant a Robin flew to the cedar the Mockingbird pounced upon it. Naturally, when two or more Robins flew to different parts of the same cedar, the guardian was exceedingly busy; and when all five Robins decided they wanted berries, the best the Mockingbird could do was to chase each one in succession while the other four ate all they could. Another day I found a single Mockingbird near the Southern Pines Country Club attempting to drive off a flock of fifteen Rusty Blackbirds that were eating berries from the Mockingbird's dogwood tree. In this case, the guardian did actually drive off each blackbird it attacked, but it could only attend to one at a time. Meanwhile, the other fourteen ate merrily on, and even the blackbird just chased returned as soon as the Mockingbird turned its attention to another.

Mockingbirds are very curious, so when I appeared one morning near one's home by Holly Inn at Pinehurst, it flew to a tree over my head to see what I was, and what I was doing. There it indulged its lively curiosity until another Mockingbird flew over and chased it away. Then this second bird perched over me, looked me over, and even flew several times about me. This was hardly a case of "the hunter hunted" but it was decidedly one of "the student studied." Indeed, I found later that one of the surest ways of finding these birds was to go and sit in any unusual place until they found me. They never failed, unless I was well hidden, and they usually scolded me well.

The monopolizing and guarding traits of Mockingbirds are extended over man's domesticated fruit and berries as well. I remember once in May, an old negro told me that "strawberries would be ripe in a week." "How do you know, Gregg?" "Boss, this very mornin' I seed that ol' mocker a-walkin' up and down between the strawberry rows, wift he hands in he pockets lik he done planted and hoed the whole she-bang!'"

Since Mockingbirds are about human habitations (Fig. 25) so much, it is but natural that they should be tame at times. They are often seen in front of large windows tilting at their own reflections in the glass. When our gardener was at work, he often had two or three attendant Mockingbirds, especially when he spaded or raked the ground.

Mockingbirds are solitary throughout the winter, not even as many as two together, or even in the same neighborhood, before the annual pairing season in late February. It appears doubtful if they ever actually associate with other birds; on the contrary, they drive other birds away. Such irascible and pugnacious birds have many enemies, or at least they chase, or fight with, many other birds as well as with members of their own species. Since they are of a somewhat similar disposition and habit, it is natural that Mockingbirds and Blue Jays should often clash. This rivalry continues with varying fortunes; sometimes the Jays have the better of it, and sometimes the Mockingbirds are more successful. Next to Jays, the Brown Thrashers are their most persistent antagonists, with first the Mockingbirds and then the Thrashers triumphant. I used to think the Mockingbirds did not bother the smaller birds, but I afterward found they did, although to a lesser extent. Evidently, it is the large size and assuredness of the Mockingbirds that seem more threatening to a smaller bird. Among themselves, the Mockingbirds often have pitched battles, both actual fighting and the mimic warfare of the mating season. With all this audacity, it is but natural that Mockingbirds should show no alarm when Turkey Buzzards dash over their heads.

Ordinarily, the Mockingbirds fly low and from tree to tree; but they sometimes fly over high up in the air and from pine top to pine top. In pursuit of insect food, they make flycatcher-like sallies from the tree-tops, and are able to catch flying insects by chasing them, twisting and turning skillfully when needful.

Mockingbirds are resident in the Sandhills. Not only can the species be found at all seasons, but the individuals seen in winter will be found somewhere near during the following summer. They appear to like warm weather even when it gets quite hot, but they can also endure quite severe cold without seeming to suffer. They are active even during cold rain storms, and care little for them, in spite of the fact that their feathers are rather fluffy and poor at shedding rain. On the other hand, they are fond of taking sun baths.

In spring and summer, when insects are numerous, Mockingbirds devour large quantities of ground-inhabiting species, and also catch many of the higher flying insects on the wing. But great as the number of injurious insects destroyed by the adults is, that quantity is small before those caught to fill the ever-hungry nestlings! All in all, a family of Mockingbirds on the premises is one of the best protective agencies of North Carolinian gardens. And even at the edges of peach orchards, cornfields, pea fields and other crops, they give effective aid to the farmer; and, most telling of all, they destroy some of the worst enemies of cultivated cotton. Not only are these birds expert at catching flying insects, but they hunt through the grass and herbage as well. Once, I found a Mockingbird that eagerly devoured the big white grubs that fell out of logs at the chopping block. Even in winter, these industrious and active birds catch many insects and grubs; but their principal winter foods are berries of the dogwood, cedar, privet, holly, sour gum and sumach, as well as wild cherries, frost grapes, persimmons, and practically every other fruit and berry then obtainable. In the spring, they sometimes have an overfondness for garden strawberries; but their taste lasts only a few days, or until other food becomes more plentiful. Such damage as they cause, is trifling, and the gardener seldom holds a grudge for them. On the contrary, house owners usually try to attract these birds to their dooryards. Mockingbirds will come to artificial feeding stations for bread crumbs or suet, but the most attractive offerings are raisins and dried currants. Often a dish of clean, fresh water will attract them when nothing else will. If a regular fountain big enough to bathe in, is provided, still more will come, for they are fond of bathing, getting more thoroughly wet than most birds do, and then preening in a tree nearby. Naturally, they bathe more in hot weather; but also use baths freely in winter.

Since I noted a pair of Mockingbirds as early as January 27, 1927, it may be that at least some pairs remain together throughout the winter. On January 30, 1926, a pair were seen ''dancing'' on the ground, a mating ceremony peculiar to these birds. Occasionally, a Mockingbird will dance alone, but usually a pair take part together, and they may dance either in the morning or in the afternoon; or the same pair may dance in both the morning and the afternoon, even of the same day. This dancing is very light and airy, partly actual dancing and partly mimic battle. As the two birds face each other within a few inches, they spring lightly up and down, with quivering wings and dangling legs. Suddenly, one or the other leaps a foot or two lightly to one side, and then comes back again in a series of dainty little jumps scarcely an inch high. Then a sudden hop a foot or two high into the air, the dancer slowly falling back on trembling wings, only to repeat again and again, but sometimes introducing the sidewise leaps between the vertical hops. Whenever the bird is on the ground between either the leaps or the hops, it keeps up its rhythmical little jumps. Usually, the two birds leap and hop together, but sometimes one follows the other, or they alternate. At times, the dancing birds will rise together, striking at each other with outstretched feet in pretended battle. All through these very graceful and very dainty movements, the birds keep their tails in constant motion, first down as far as they will go and then immediately up again. The tails do not quite touch the ground—for the dance is performed on the ground, or on a boulder, or on a grassy lawn—but are never quite still.

It is because of their skill at mimicry that these birds have received their common names of "Mockingbirds." No doubt they are the most famous bird mimics in the world, but different individuals differ very much indeed, some being good mimics, and some lacking the ability. All varieties of birds are imitated, especially those that nest in their neighborhood. Among the birds most frequently "mocked" in the Sandhills are the Cardinals, and very often the imitations are so perfect that they can not be told from the originals. Frequently, the Mockingbirds give the "peto" of a Tufted Titmouse. I mention only these two, not because they are most frequent, but because they are the most easily recognized of the Sandhills birds. Mockingbirds imitate so many other birds that a good many people lose sight of the fact that these birds have numerous notes and a song of their own. Scolding notes, or rather notes that sound like scolding notes to us, are the most numerous and are often used when the birds are chasing each other. Under somewhat similar conditions, they may utter high-pitched screeching notes or a series of "clucks." Once, I heard a Mockingbird give a loud, harsh, grating call as another Mockingbird flew over high above it.

In spite of their intensely interesting ways, their mannerisms and their audacious courage, it is mainly as songsters that Mockingbirds are so widely known throughout America, and captive birds have carried their fame around the world. Their song is very fine, rich and varied. As a rule, it is sung from near the ground, but the height of the singing perch varies, and even the same bird either has several perches from which to sing, or it selects a new perch for each song, and, in addition, it sings while actually flying. A large number of the songs are delivered from perches in, or near, dooryards, but they are also heard in the wild thickets, in the shrub oaks, and even out on the pine barrens. I have no records of birds actually singing on the ground, but I have seen them sing from low stumps and prostrate logs about two feet above the ground. They sing from a growth of low bushes and from single bushes and trees out in the open, at an average height of fifteen feet above the ground although the height varies from two to forty feet. They sing more in slightly cloudy weather and clear weather, but they also sing even during quite hard showers. They are very apt to sing just after a rain has ceased. Mockingbirds begin singing early in the morning and keep on singing at intervals all day, although most other species are quiet during the heat of midday. Indeed, these birds seem to sing regardless of heat, but they do not indulge in much night singing until the warm nights of early summer commence.

In the Sandhills, Mockingbirds are heard singing at intervals all through the winter, but the early songs are very soft and only a mere shadow of what they become later. They are the ''whisper songs'' and can be heard only a few feet away. Soon after the first of January, they begin singing fragmentary parts of their songs at full tone and loudness. These fragments increase gradually in length and completeness until the middle of February, and the real season of full, powerful song commences shortly after the first of March. During March, 1927, I heard as many as five different Mockingbirds singing several times each day in Southern Pines, but the very best of the songs were heard in April.

During the warm nights of June and July, Mockingbirds sing after dark and sometimes keep up their wonderful music all night. The song is often given and is of so surprising and masterful a quality that the singers well earn their reputation as being among America's best avian songsters, with few equals so far as variety and power of utterance are concerned, and none equaling them in power of mimicry. Individual Mockingbirds vary a great deal; but when one of the better musicians is singing in the soft, scent-laden, moonlight air of an old romantic southern garden, he gives a melody so ethereal and so very lovely that it will haunt the hearer's memory, and make it seem impossible that any other bird could ever equal it.

CATBIRD. Pl. 9, page 236

Dumetella carolinensis (Linn.). *A. O. U. No. 704*

Field Identification. A dark-slate, almost black, bird larger than a sparrow, having a black crown, and a chestnut spot under the tail.

Description. Most of the plumage dark slaty gray; crown and tail black; a chestnut spot just under the tail. Total length 9 inches.

Distribution. These birds are rare in the Sandhills during the winter and may be entirely absent during some severe winters. They become more common in April and then remain throughout the summer. In winter, some Catbirds go as far south as Panama; in summer, they live as far north as Nova Scotia, Quebec, Ontario, Saskatchewan, Alberta and British Columbia.

Habits. Although Catbirds sometimes come into the dooryard shrubbery in winter, they seem to be more frequent at that season in the tangles of cat-briars, wild grapes and brush over the small streams that flow through the Sandhills. When they are found in the dooryard, they become very friendly, indeed, much more so than the Mockingbirds do. Catbirds are lovers of our gardens and often follow a gardener about as he rakes and plants.

In most of their interesting ways and quaint mannerisms, the Catbirds outdo the Mockingbirds. In fact, no other of the Sand-hills birds has such droll ways. When Catbirds mount on top of the shrubbery to sing (and they are less likely to do so than either Mockingbirds or Brown Thrashers), they drop their tails straight down. But on the ground, they carry them high above their backs or allow them to flop waggishly over to one side or the other.

Their food habits in winter are wholly beneficial from the stand-point of their human friends, as they live on insects, sumach berries, wild grapes and other small swamp fruits.

BROWN THRASHER. Pl. 10, page 262

Toxostoma rufum (Linn.)   A. O. U. No. 705

Field Identification. A reddish brown bird longer and more slender than a Robin, and having yellow eyes, a long tail, and two whitish wing-bars. The underparts are heavily streaked. Brown Thrashers get their food on the ground and seek protection under low bushes and shrubs, so they essentially are ground-loving and ground-dwelling birds.

Description. Upperparts reddish brown; two whitish wing-bars; underparts whitish (buffy in autumn and early winter) and heavily streaked, except on the clear white throat and middle of belly. Bill curved. Total length 11½ inches.

Distribution. These birds are present in the Sandhills at all seasons of the year. In winter, some individuals go as far south as southern Florida, the Gulf coast and Texas; in summer, they live as far north as Alberta, Manitoba, northern Michigan, Ontario, Quebec and Maine.

Habits. Like some other ground dwellers, Brown Thrashers often mount rather high into the trees, especially to sing. So they may be seen at almost any elevation, but are broom-sedge-corner, thicket and open forest birds, and not found in either open fields or thick forests. They prefer the borderland between the woods and the open fields, and are often found on the edges of weedy corn-fields, and in the tangles of briars, vines and brush growing over a stream (Figs. 13, 14, 17, 19, 22, 27). They may be found either in open spots or under low bushes or low-growing shrubbery. This liking for the ground extends throughout the year, and does not seem more marked at any one season. Even in nesting time when their nests are actually in low bushes or shrubbery, the birds them-selves are more often on the ground than elsewhere. Sometimes Thrashers are in the long grass under the pine saplings (Fig. 1), and they like to be near piles of limbs trimmed from oak trees. Occasionally, they perch on a fence.

In the Sandhills, Brown Thrashers are as much dooryard birds as they are dwellers in the wilds, and are found in shrubbery and under the roses. Sometimes they nest in the rose bushes. These birds are seen in oak trees so often that it actually seems as if they prefer oaks to all others, naturally haunting the lower limbs most. Although usually in leafless trees in winter, they also frequent such evergreens as hollies, magnolias, and cedars (Figs. 24, 25, 26), but for some unknown reason they are seldom seen in pines.

Thrashers walk as a rule, and hop at times when they want to go faster, but they can run rapidly when seeking shelter and chasing insects. In their movements, they are quick and active, and very skillful at slipping through briars and heavy brush. Brown Thrashers are essentially such solitary birds that it becomes noticeable when they pair off, and they are never seen in groups with the exception of family parties. They have some of the monopolistic traits of Mockingbirds. Once I saw a Thrasher occupying a feeding station to the exclusion of all other birds, although not itself eating.

Brown Thrashers do not actually associate with birds of any other species, but they are such active birds they are frequently seen with other birds because of similar habits or similar food. In the rivalries and animosities of the bird life of the thickets, the Brown Thrashers take some part. They have frequent contests with the Blue Jays and Mockingbirds with varying success, but with other species Thrashers clash only occasionally.

The flight of these birds is marked by long, gentle undulations, but they are expert enough to make flycatcher-like sallies into the air and to chase lively, erratic insects through the grass. Sometimes they miscalculate and dash headlong against closed windows.

The song of the Brown Thrashers is very fine and in many ways superior to that of the Mockingbirds, being louder, richer, and having a greater range. This song is almost always delivered from the top of a fair sized tree, and usually from thirty to forty feet above the ground. Most of the singing perches I have seen, were at the tips of leafless oaks. These birds sing at all hours during the mornings and late afternoons, and sometimes at noon on cold days. One cold morning a Thrasher sang from 7:15 A. M. continuously until after 9 A. M., when the thermometer was at 23° F., although there was no wind. At other times, I have heard one sing continuously for more than two hours. I have heard the same bird sing in the morning and again in the afternoon, and another one singing both before and after sunset.

During the latter part of March, 1927, I was so fortunate as to find a Brown Thrasher singing on some oaks over a thicket, at the edge of a pine forest facing several open fields, on Weymouth Heights, at the edge of Southern Pines. He afforded me an interesting study, because he sang there many days in succession on one or the other of the leafless trees along the thicket; and, still better, a nearby Mockingbird often sang in rivalry, perhaps unconsciously. Sometimes one bird sang while the other was quiet; sometimes they both sang at the same time; and often they sang in the same tree and within a few feet of each other. Usually, they sang in oaks about twenty to thirty feet above the ground, the Mocker generally a few feet below the top of the tree while the Thrasher was higher up as a rule, and on the very tip of the tree every time except once when he was five feet below the tip—although still thirty feet above the ground. To my great surprise, neither bird offered any objection to the presence or singing of the other.

It is the custom in the south to credit the Mockingbird with the finest song, and many who hear an unseen Brown Thrasher will believe it to be a Mockingbird. Among those who know, the Mockingbird is conceded to be a wonderful musician, but the Brown Thrasher also has its champions. A characteristic of a singing Brown Thrasher is that he will generally repeat his theme twice. But the Trasher of this "competition" often repeated three or four times, which improved the effect, if anything. He exhibited more volume and tone and perhaps more range; but the Mockingbird's song was more varied and the variations were finer. On the other hand, the Mockingbird's song was injured by many stops to interpolate notes and calls, and was not so rich as the Thrasher's song. These two birds sang at all hours during daylight and usually did a little better during a light rain. As a result of a careful study and comparison of these songs for ten days, I concluded that both were very fine musicians and their songs so wonderful it was impossible to tell which was the better, or even to decide which one I liked the better!

In the Sandhills the earliest song heard from any Brown Thrasher was on February 4, 1927, when a few notes were given; but the real song season did not commence until three weeks later, and was then interrupted for ten days by the extraordinary snowstorm of early March.

Brown Thrashers have some ability as mimics but they do not exercise it as often as the Mockingbirds. Although the Thrashers are not generally as good mimics, some are better than many of the Mockingbirds.

While Thrashers are seen practically every day in the same places and in the same numbers, it is impossible to say whether the individuals present in winter also stay all summer. Perhaps the Brown Thrashers that winter in the Sandhills go north in spring, and their places are filled by others coming up from the south. But the Thrashers that winter in the Sandhills are actually affected by the severer cold spells and storms, though perhaps not so much as some other birds. On March 3, 1927, after a two days' snow, a Brown Thrasher was so cold and apparently discouraged by the unusual conditions that it allowed me to almost step on it before flying. It then alighted on a shrub oak where it looked very bedraggled and puffed up with the cold. But it might have been suffering more from lack of food than because of low temperature.

Brown Thrashers seek their food largely on the ground, using a number of methods. The most characteristic one is to throw leaves and surface dirt aside with quick, wiping side-thrusts of the bill and head, done so vigorously and effectively that the leaves and dirt are thrown to a considerable distance. The food so uncovered is then eaten much as Towhees and Fox Sparrows do. But Thrashers are seldom seen scratching with their feet. Some combine several methods. One was seen that picked the ground for a time and then alternated its picking strokes with some sidewise scoops of its bill. Later it ran swiftly along for six feet and caught an insect that was flying low. Another Thrasher was seen making flycatcher-like sallies from the ground, and later from well up in an oak. They sometimes chase lively, erratic insects through the grass, and at other times adopt the Flicker method of digging down a good inch and a half into the sandy soil, probably for grubs. Brown Thrashers sometimes pick up acorns and carry them away in their bills, and later open them as the Jays do. But they are ground birds, unlike the Jays, and when they try to split the shell from an acorn by pile-driver blows, they often drive the acorn down into the soft ground. In spite of this difficulty, they persevere and the shell eventually flies off. I have seen one eat a shelled acorn in a few bites. Apparently, acorns are an essential part of their winter food.

Although the food of the Brown Thrasher consists largely of insects, they also devour seeds of various kinds. It is hard to say just how many seeds they pick up from the ground, but they occasionally fly up on the weed stalks and pluck the seeds direct. In addition to seeds, they eat other vegetable food such as the pulp and seeds of wild grapes. On December 14, 1926, a Thrasher was seen perched on a grape vine, and might have fooled me into thinking it was eating grapes. But this grape vine really hung just above a fine bunch of sumach berries, and later the bird moved into the sumach itself, and continued its feast on another bunch. It ate for some minutes, quite stripping one head of all fruit; then rested a few minutes before eating another score of the berries. Later, I found that sumach berries were a favorite food, at least during December. Most other birds consume only a few berries at a time, but the Thrashers are apt to eat them continuously for several minutes. They sometimes eat persimmons, smilax berries or other small wild fruits.

Brown Thrashers are perhaps less easy to attract to artificial feeding stations, but they will come at times to feed on bread crumbs, nut meats or suet. As a rule, they like water better and a pan of fresh water, or a bathing fountain, is sure to attract them. They are very fond of bathing, especially when the weather gets warm in spring. In earthenware saucers, they will bathe when it is as cold as 55° F., and when it is warmer they bathe regularly twice a day. But they do not stop taking shower-baths just because artificial baths are available. They are even out in steady rains, thoroughly shaking themselves as the heavy raindrops soak their plumage.

As early as February 18, 1927, two Brown Thrashers were seen together and they gave every indication that they were paired. Soon after that, they began collecting nest material. As early as the middle of April they build their nests, and the female lays her first eggs usually before the end of that month.

CAROLINA WREN. Pl. 10, page 262

Thryothorus ludovicianus ludovicianus (Lath.). *A. O. U. No. 718*

Field Identification. A bright, lively, reddish brown bird smaller than a sparrow. The small size, lively motions and perked-up tail show this bird to be a wren; the color, the whitish line over the eye, and the large size (for a wren), distinguish it from other wrens.

Description. Upperparts reddish brown, finely barred on wings and tail but not barred elsewhere; a long white line over the eye; underparts lighter; throat whitish. In summer, the worn breeding plumage is faded and dull. Total length 5½ inches.

Distribution. Carolina Wrens are found in the Sandhills at all seasons of the year. They go as far south as northern Florida, the Gulf states and Texas; and in summer they live as far north as Nebraska, Iowa, Ohio, Pennsylvania and extreme southern New York.

Habits. These little birds like the weed and briar thickets (Figs. 14, 22) that are usually as common over streams of all kinds. They like to be near water, and are sometimes found in gum swamps and on dry hillsides near ponds and lakes. Occasionally, these wrens are seen on the ground. In the Sandhills, they are dwellers in the dooryards and about houses, more even than in wilder haunts. Almost all kinds of shrubbery attract them, but they like the thickest, thorny kind the best. While they are generally in the bushes and lower growth, they sometimes go higher into trees, even as much as thirty feet above the ground in large oaks.

Wrens hop quickly here and there. Their movements are always quick and dodging, and they usually carry their tails cocked up at an extravagant angle, but not always. Perhaps the Carolina Wren may be more nervous and more continually in motion when conscious of being observed, but I have found them acting in the same way when they could not have known I was near. So constantly in motion are these wrens that it is rather a relief to find one quietly perching, as they sometimes do.

Carolina Wrens are almost always alone, or at most but two birds together, but they are sometimes seen with other small birds such as Juncos and Chickadees. Once, a wren was seen with some Song Sparrows, but the sparrows soon moved on and left the wren behind. During short flights, a wren's movements are erratic and darting, but when one flies out across a field, its flight is straight and direct, although the beat of the wings is very rapid indeed.

The song of the Carolina Wren is loud and vigorously given, but so continuously repeated for such long periods that we grow tired of the simple refrain. Otherwise, it is quite pleasing, espeeially in winter and early spring when so many other birds are quiet. The refrain is usually repeated three times, then a short wait before repeating again. Sometimes it has a distinct "wheeudel" or "tea-kettle" sound, but individual songsters differ very much. Sometimes two wrens appear to have a real duet, for one will sing and then remain quiet while the other sings. Usually, these little birds sing from a bush, or heavy shrubbery, where they can not be seen, but occasionally they fly up into leafless trees, and sometimes sing there as high as thirty feet above the ground. In the Sandhills, the Carolina Wrens begin to sing as early as the twentieth of January, and can generally be heard every day after that, but wren songs still increase in power and frequency even after the first of March.

These wrens are common throughout the Sandhills during the winter, but perhaps not as common as they become after the first of March. In cold weather, they seek shelter in the brush over streams, and during rains I find them under thick shrubbery. Their food is largely made up of insects, both of ground beetles and of flying insects caught while in flight. They can be drawn to dooryards by providing crumbs, suet and fresh drinking water. Some Carolina Wrens appear to stay in pairs all winter. On January 21, 1927, I saw one out evidently "house-hunting." First, it flew all about the foundation and under the timbers of an old house. Then to the tops of the corner posts of the house, to the eaves, and examined all old crevices and crannies, even clinging to the ancient weather-boarding to look into every wide crack. Then it flew successively to the trunk of a mulberry, a cedar, and a walnut, where it critically inspected every hole, fork, crevice and rotten limb. I do not know whether it made a selection or not, for I had no chance to go back later. But these wrens in the Sandhills build nests in all kinds of places.

BEWICK'S WREN

Thryomanes bewicki bewicki (Aud.). A. O. U. No. 719

Field Identification. A cinnamon-brown wren smaller than a sparrow or a Carolina Wren with a long black fan-shaped tail.

Description. Plain brown upperparts, with perhaps a few black bars on longest wing-feathers and central tail-feathers; whit-

Figure 27. Winter in the cornfields, a fine place for birds. View about a mile south of Highland Pines Inn, Southern Pines, Feb. 20, 1926.

ish line over the eye; outer tail feathers black, each tipped with white; underparts grayish. Total length 5 inches.

Distribution. An occasional visitor to the Sandhills in winter. At that time, these wrens are found as far south as the Gulf coast and Florida, and north almost as far as in summer; in summer, they live from the mountains of Mississippi, Alabama, North Carolina and Arkansas north to Nebraska, Illinois, southern Michigan and Pennsylvania.

Habits. In the Sandhills, these wrens frequent the dooryards, especially about the cottages at Pinehurst (Fig. 26). They are rather uncommon and not nearly so often seen and heard as the more numerous Carolina Wrens. Perhaps the Bewick's Wrens are a little less nervous than the former; still, they have most of their characteristic ways. The song of the Bewick's Wrens is described by Ridgway as a fine, clear, bold song, uttered as the singer perches with his head thrown back and tail pendant—a song that may be heard a quarter of a mile or more.

WINTER WREN

Nannus hiemalis hiemalis (Vieill.). *A. O. U. No. 722*

Field Identification. A dark, brownish wren much smaller than a sparrow, and distinguished by its dark color, small size, short tail held vertically over the back, a light line over eye, and the absence of whitish on the underparts.

Description. Upperparts warm dark brown, barred on wings and tail, and indistinctly on the back; buffy line over eye; underparts lighter and heavily barred near the very short tail. Total length just over 4 inches.

Distribution. Winter Wrens are rather scarce in the Sandhills, but occur throughout the winter. During this season, they are found as far south as northern Florida, the Gulf states and Texas; in summer, they live in the North Carolina mountains and as far north as Alberta, Manitoba, Ontario, Quebec and Newfoundland.

Habits. These tiny wrens live in the thickets over streams and along the shores of brushy ponds, and sometimes in the shrub oaks on the hillsides above the streams. Occasionally, they are observed in dooryards, even in the edge of towns, but they are very shy and are not often seen anywhere. Since they do not sing often, if at all, during the winter, they can not be so easily located as the Carolina Wrens. They are alert little fellows and their short, stumpy tails stick up at right angles to their backs. Winter Wrens look very much like mice as they hop along the ground, or dart under a pile of brush. As usual with wrens, these birds are closely observing and examine everything as they go along, particularly hollows in trees and stumps. They do not nest in the Sandhills, but a ready knowledge of every warm nook and cranny must be serviceable to them in cold, stormy weather.

BROWN CREEPER

Certhia familiaris americana Bonap. A. O. U. No. 726

Field Identification. A brown and white streaked bird smaller than a sparrow, and seen only on tree trunks or flying. Identified by its mottled back, its comparatively long decurved bill, and by its habit of creeping *up* a tree trunk with its tail pressed against it for support.

Description. Upperparts streaked white, dark brown and buff; lower back reddish; tail grayish, the feathers stiffened and sharply pointed; underparts white; bill curved downward. Total length just over $5\frac{1}{2}$ inches.

Distribution. Creepers are not common birds in the Sandhills, but an occasional one may be found at all times between November and the last of March. In winter they range as far south as northern Florida, the Gulf states and Texas; and in summer they live as far north as Manitoba, Ontario, Quebec and Newfoundland.

Habits. Usually, Creepers are to be found on trunks of gums and water-loving trees, but they also frequent oaks, loblolly pines and long-leaf pines. Because oaks are so common in the Sandhills, their trunks are where creepers are most often seen.

Only once in all my experience have I seen a Brown Creeper pause and even appear to move backward, or downward. But this one instance may have been due to a bit of bark giving way. If it did, the Creeper quickly secured another grip an inch below, and went on up the tree as if nothing had happened. While their general direction is always upward, they sometimes spiral the trunk or limb, and sometimes work along the under side of a horizontal limb. Their movement is by short or long hops, but these hops are so close to the bark that the movement well merits the description of "creeping," and the Creeper the name of "tree mouse."

Creepers are always industrious and hard-working. Generally, they are alone in winter, not foregathering with others of their own kind, or with birds of other species. Once only, I found some Ruby-crowned Kinglets close enough to say the Creepers and the Kinglets were associated.

Their flight is usually short, and from tree to tree. When Creepers make a long flight, their course is slightly undulating, while the speed is fast for such a small bird. They do not catch any insects in flight, but appear to depend altogether on such insects, insect eggs and cocoons as they find in the crevices in the bark. To find a sufficient supply of these, the Creepers work constantly and fast.

WHITE-BREASTED NUTHATCH. Pl. 12, page 290

Sitta carolinensis carolinensis Lath. A. O. U. No. 727

Field Identification. A bluish gray bird smaller than an English Sparrow and identified by its white cheeks, absence of black line through the eye, its long and slender bill, and its white underparts. This is another frequenter of the tree trunks, but it climbs down as well as up, and it does *not* press its tail against its support. These birds are noted for the peculiar attitudes they assume, especially the way they hang on the bark head downward and then bend their heads back and twist them around.

Description. On the male the top of the head is black; sides of the head white; rest of upperparts bluish gray; indistinct whitish wing-bar; outer tail-feathers black, tipped with white; underparts white, tinged on lower belly with reddish. Females have top of heads tinged with bluish. Total length 6 inches.

Distribution. These are not common birds in the Sandhills, but they may be found at any season of the year. They live as far south as the Gulf states and as far north as Minnesota, Ontario, Quebec and Newfoundland. They do not appear to be migratory in any part of their range.

Habits. While I have seen one of these nuthatches actually on the ground, their proper place is in the trees, usually on the trunks and larger limbs, but sometimes perched on small twigs. They are to be found on the oaks, pines, sycamores and walnut trees, generally in the middle parts, but sometimes at the bases and sometimes at the very tips of even rather tall trees.

Nuthatches go down tree trunks head first, and I have yet to see one back down as woodpeckers do. Their skillfulness as climbers, and their sure-footedness are all the more remarkable in view of the fact that they do not steady themselves with their tails. As they move up a tree, they prefer a series of low hops with their bodies turned a little sidewise, but they can go straight up if they wish to do so.

These nuthatches are solitary except when in pairs, or in family parties, and seldom with other species. Once, I found a White-breasted Nuthatch near two Tufted Titmice drawn by the same food. The food of the nuthatches is largely the same as the Creepers'; namely, insects, insect eggs and cocoons picked out of the cracks and crevices in the bark. If we wish to attract these birds to our gardens and about our homes, it is easy to do so by hanging up bones with a little meat still attached, or by tying suet to the trunks and limbs of the garden trees.

RED-BREASTED NUTHATCH. Pl. 12, page 290

Sitta canadensis Linn. A. O. U. No. 728

Field Identification. A bluish gray bird smaller than a sparrow. Like all the nuthatches this one goes down as well as up and does not use its tail as a support. It is smaller than the others and has a rusty-colored breast.

Description. Male has top of head and a broad stripe extending back through his eye black; white line over eye; upperparts bluish gray; outer tail-feathers black, tipped with white; cheeks and chin white; rest of underparts rusty brown. The females have bluish gray replacing the black of the males. Total length a little over $4\frac{1}{2}$ inches.

Distribution. This nuthatch is an irregular visitor to the Sandhills in winter; sometimes present, and sometimes not. While some individuals winter as far south as the Gulf states, they are peculiarly northern birds, breeding in our northern states and Canada as far north as Alaska, northern Canada and Newfoundland.

Habits. These little birds are found on the trunks of oaks and pines on the drier lands, and on the gum trees of the swamps. When they appear in dooryards, they may be on magnolias and most other cultivated trees. At the Mid Pines Club, I found three on some gum trees growing out in the lake. They are curious and fond of investigating everything unusual in their path; in addition, they go in and out of every crevice, natural or otherwise, on the tree where they are working. They eat insects and insect eggs that they extract from the bark of trees. They can be attracted about Sandhills homes by tying pieces of suet to trunks or limbs of trees.

BROWN-HEADED NUTHATCH. Pl. 12, page 290

Sitta pusilla Lath.　*A. O. U. No. 729*

Field Identification. A bluish gray brown-headed bird much smaller than a sparrow. Like other nuthatches, this one can be identified by its ability to go both up and down vertical tree trunks without using its tail as a support.

Description. Top and back of the head brown; a white spot on the back of neck; rest of upperparts bluish gray; outer tail-feathers black and gray tipped; underparts grayish. Total length 4½ inches.

Distribution. These birds are occasional in all parts of the Sandhills. They live as far south as southern Florida, the Gulf states and Texas; and as far north as Missouri, the Ohio River and Delaware. In all parts of their range, these birds are resident and non-migratory.

Habits. Brown-headed Nuthatches are occasionally on bushes, but generally on the trunks of loblolly pines, long-leaf pines, shrub oaks, gums and hardwood trees of various kinds. Several times I have seen them on fence posts, where they often make their nests. They may be found about the bases of trees, on the trunks, or high up among the limbs. In addition to hunting the bark of trunks and limbs, they often search the foliage of pines, especially about the bases of the bunches of needles, for their food. They even visit the tops of long-leaf pines as much as forty feet above the ground. Brown-headed Nuthatches often come to the trees in the largest towns and cities of the Sandhills. Sometimes these dainty little birds are on dead trees, but not nearly so often as on living ones.

Like all the nuthatches, the Brown-heads are expert creepers and climbers, able to go up or down, spiral a vertical trunk, or even creep along the under side of a horizontal limb. In all this climbing, they move by short hops, generally with their bodies turned a little to one side or the other, and they may turn after going a few feet with their bodies turned one way, so that the other side is then uppermost. Occasionally, they perch crosswise on a twig and may rest motionless for some time in such a position.

These little birds are very tame and friendly. When in pairs, they are devoted to each other. I have seen a Brown-headed Nuthatch near two Ruby-crowned Kinglets and a Downy Woodpecker, but I doubted very much if they were really associating together. This is the only time I have noted even temporary grouping of this Nuthatch with other species. Generally, they fly from tree to tree with a gently undulating flight, but with strong and rapid wing-beats.

Perhaps these nuthatches do not "talk" as much as some others. Yet, I have heard them utter a sweet little "pri-u, de-u, de-u," quite like a song, in the mating season. They also have a number of chirps and kissing notes, and a "dee-dee-dee" comparable to a Chickadee's note. A lively twitter is the call of one Brown-headed Nuthatch for its mate.

Brown-headed Nuthatches are not only found in the Sandhills throughout the year, but there is no variation in numbers during the winter or the migration seasons of other birds. They eat small insects that they pick out of crevices in the bark and from the spaces about the bases of needles on both the loblolly and long-leaf pines.

If they do not actually remain paired throughout the winter, as I think they do, they pair off either late in the winter or very early in the spring. I have seen two that seemed to be a mated pair as early as March 11, 1927. Five days later, I found a pair industriously digging in the dead stub of a small gum tree standing on the shore of a small lake. This stub was twelve feet high and eight inches in diameter, and the birds were at work eight feet above the ground. The digging bird (and only one worked at any one time) worked in all positions, but really preferred to hang head downward from the trunk above the hole; even when working in this position, it did not touch its tail to the bark, except accidentally. This Nuthatch gave its strokes like a woodpecker, but slower and at a rate of about fifty strokes a minute for at least thirty minutes. Then its mate came and relieved it. Although these birds were small, their digging strokes were powerful and could be heard quite a distance, perhaps as much as two hundred yards, and had a rhythmical beat. Several holes were started on the southeast and south sides of the same gum stub, which did not seem at all rotted, or even weakened. Later, I found that while four holes had been dug to a depth of an inch or more, all had been abandoned and the nest located elsewhere. I did not find the nest of this particular pair, but Brown-headed Nuthatches are known to nest and lay eggs as early as the last week in March in the Sandhills.

TUFTED TITMOUSE. Pl. 9, page 236

Bæolophus bicolor (Linn.). *A. O. U. No. 731*

Field Identification. A crested, grayish brown bird smaller than a sparrow, and identified by its rufous sides and its loud whistled "peto" note. Its big black eyes show a strong contrast to its trim gray plumage.

When seen against the sky, where its color can not be discerned, this bird looks very much like a small jay. When the crest lies back on the crown, its long feathers stick out behind so that it is noticeable then as well as when erect.

Description. Forehead black; upperparts gray, tinged with brown on the back; underparts white; sides tinged with reddish brown. Total length 6 inches.

Distribution. These birds are found throughout the Sandhills, in suitable localities, at all times of the year. In fact, Tufted Titmice are resident and non-migratory wherever found. They live as far south as Florida, the Gulf coast and Texas, and as far north as Nebraska, Iowa, Illinois, Indiana, Ohio, Pennsylvania and New Jersey.

Habits. Tufted Titmice are birds of the open forests of oaks and pines (Figs. 1, 2, 5, 16) so common in North Carolina. They are also found in the thickets at the edges of fields (Figs. 14 and 19) and in small groves of trees, and even in single trees, if not too far from the nearest woods. They are often seen in the shrubbery of dooryards and in shade trees. They are sometimes to be seen on the limbs of small bushes, and even in the tall reeds of marshes where the only trees are small willows. But this might be explained by these birds' evident fondness for water.

Titmice are quick and spirited little birds, often seen darting into, or under, brush and thick trees. They are not usually seen on the ground, except for the moment it takes to pick up an acorn. They perform acrobatic feats on slender stems and twigs of trees, and sometimes they fly to a small branch and alight upside down on its under surface. While they may associate with their fellows in small groups, they do not travel in flocks larger than a half dozen birds, as a rule. Sometimes these Titmice actually seem to join with Chickadees, Juncos or White-throated Sparrows. With Fox Sparrows, Field Sparrows, Blue Jays, Cardinals and Myrtle Warblers, their association is probably only accidental and very temporary.

Since these birds like acorns and some other kinds of food that the Blue Jays eat, they are subjected to some persecution on the part of those big blue rascals. But Titmice can hold their own, or fly away, if they prefer. Like the Blue Jays, Titmice are great talkers, but they haven't the large variety of notes and calls in which the Jays delight. The whistled call of the "peto" bird is uttered all through the winter, but becomes more and more noticeable and insistent after the first of February. This "peto" note endlessly repeated over and over again is the song of the Titmice. These birds are like the Carolina Wrens in having many pleasing, liquid notes that would be highly appreciated if it were not for the endless repetition and monotonous beat that makes them almost annoying when heard over long periods of time. At times the song is given in a whisper with the bill closed; then, it can not be heard more than twenty or thirty feet away, when it is particularly sweet and pleasing. Sometimes the "peto" note is shortened, or varied, until it almost loses its identity, and occasionally a Titmouse will sing "dee-dee-dee" very much like a Chickadee. Often Titmice sing from the middle of a thicket, but at times they sing from the limbs of shrub oaks and small pines.

Tufted Titmice are resident birds well able to stand any degree of cold or stormy weather that is likely to visit the Sandhills. On cold mornings I often found them all fluffed up and under the protection of the jungles and thickets over streams.

During the winter at least, the favorite food of Titmice is the acorns supplied by the innumerable shrub oaks, post oaks and turkey oaks. From January to March, I found them hunting acorns, occasionally on the ground, but generally in the trees themselves. Quite often they knocked the acorn from its twig and then flew down to the ground after it. Titmice do not open their bills wide enough to admit the whole acorn, but they sometimes pick it up by its stem, or more often, they simply spear the nut with their sharp, closed bill and fly up to a limb with it that way. Once on a suitable limb, the acorn is firmly held between the bird's two feet and strong downward blows are rained upon it. This hammering is rapid and very effective, so that it does not take long to scale off the shell, and then the soft interior meat is eaten in small pieces. Titmice spend much time hunting over the twigs and smaller limbs, and especially over butts where branches have broken, and on upper and lower surfaces of dead limbs, looking for hidden insects. At such work, they hunt very much like Kinglets. Sometimes they search the lowest limbs, but soon after that they may be on the twigs as high as fifty feet above the ground. Very often Titmice sing as they hunt. At times they spring out after insects flying by them, and sometimes they tear the tent nests of caterpillars to pieces. On February 11, 1927, near the Mid Pines Club, a Titmouse picked up an oak apple an inch or more in diameter, carried it in its bill to the crotch of a tree and there dug through its half inch of tough material to feed on the hundred or so small white grubs in its center. Occasionally, Titmice eat a few dogwood berries. Pieces of suet tied to the limbs of trees will usually soon receive a call from Titmice if there be any in the neighborhood. They also will eat bread and doughnut crumbs. Saucers of clean, fresh water are still more attractive to them.

Tufted Titmice pair off and mate early in March, and begin nesting soon after that time.

CAROLINA CHICKADEE.. Pl. 12, page 290

Penthestes carolinensis carolinensis (Aud.). *A. O. U. No. 736*

Field Identification. A spirited, black and white bird much smaller than a sparrow and readily identified by its black crown,

PLATE 10. BRUSH AND BACKYARD BIRDS

1, 2: Towhee.
3: Brown Thrasher.
4, 5: Cardinal (female, male).
6: Mockingbird.

7: Purple Finch (male).
8: Purple Finch (female).
9: Carolina Wren.
10: Fox Sparrow.

(All figures about ⅕ life size)

its black throat, its white cheeks, and its "chick-a-dee" note frequently repeated.

Description. Top and back of head, and throat, black; cheeks and sides of head white; upperparts gray; breast white; belly and sides touched with light buff. Total length 4½ inches.

Distribution. Not common, but may be found in ones and twos throughout the Sandhills at all times. Wherever they are found, these birds are resident and non-migratory. They live from Florida, the Gulf coast and Texas north as far as Nebraska, Iowa, Illinois, Indiana, Ohio, Pennsylvania and New Jersey.

Habits. These interesting little fellows are always seen near trees of some kind: on the gums in the lowland swamps (Figs. 3 and 11), on the shrub oak and pines in the drier forests (Figs. 10 and 15), and on all kinds of shade trees in the villages and towns. They may be found on the trunks near the ground, in the lower limbs, or high up on the very tops of quite tall trees. I have even seen a Chickadee in a peach orchard, although it did not stay there very long.

Chickadees are so given to doing gymnastic feats on the ends of twigs, or in evergreen foliage, that we hardly know what to make of them when they act more sedately. They forage up and down a slender, swaying twig, or turn upside down under it, and still maintain their balance and their poise perfectly. Usually, I found only one or two Chickadees together, but sometimes they were with Tufted Titmice, kinglets, Carolina Wrens or nuthatches. Chickadees are so lively and bob around so unexpectedly it is rather difficult to describe their flight. Only when they start to fly across a field, do they show their hesitating and slightly undulating flight.

Usually one hears the Chickadees' call note before the little callers, themselves, are seen. Sometimes they are silent, but generally they announce themselves promptly. Besides the "chick-a-dee" notes, they have several other pleasing ones, but none so characteristic.

In the woods and thickets, Chickadees keep up a steady hunt along the limbs and twigs of trees, advancing constantly from tree to tree. Their food consists of small insects, larvæ and tiny insect eggs that they find on the bark. They are easily attracted to door-yards and about our homes by hanging up bones with bits of meat and gristle attached, to a tree or bush. They will also eat cheese and suet, and pick up bread and doughnut crumbs.

GOLDEN-CROWNED KINGLET

Regulus satrapa satrapa Licht.   A. O. U. 748

Field Identification. A greenish gray bird much smaller than a sparrow, with a very short bill. Both our Kinglets give a peculiar momentary lift of the wings as they hunt along the limbs and through the foliage. This species has a yellow crown quite easy to see, and a white line over each eye.

Description. Upperparts gray, but showing a greenish tinge in good light; center of crown (in male) orange bordered by yellow and black; a white line over the eye; underparts dull whitish. The female has no orange on her crown. Total length 4 inches.

Distribution. The Golden-crowned Kinglet occurs in all suitable localities throughout the Sandhills from November to March. In winter, these little birds are found as far south as Florida, the Gulf states and Mexico; in summer, they live as far north as Alberta, Keewatin, Ungava and Cape Breton Island.

Habits. These Kinglets are always seen about trees, or dooryard shrubbery, and not out in the open fields. They are found on oaks, loblolly pines, long-leaf pines, gum trees, persimmon trees, and other deciduous trees. Some days they are on the hardwoods more than they are on the pines; usually they are on the lower parts of the trees.

The Golden-crowned Kinglets are very fond of climbing around, under cover, the limbs and twigs of bushes and trees, and engage in all sorts of climbing activities. Apparently, they are very nervous. The peculiar, momentary lift of their wings seems almost automatic and without any intention on the part of the birds. Usually I found them one or two at a time, but sometimes they were in small groups of as many as seven individuals. They are often seen with Ruby-crowned Kinglets, or at least so near each other as to appear to be associated, but I did not see them with any other birds, strange to say.

At times during the winter, I heard these kinglets give short kissing notes, later becoming distinctly "tsee-tsee." Finally, a kinglet repeated these "tseeing" notes so many times, and with so

Figure 28.   Dr. Achorn's Residence at Pine Bluff, showing trees and shrubbery about the house.

many variations, that the performance could be called a song. This song was given several times from a thicket, and then from the limb of a loblolly pine protruding above the ticket. Generally the singer was about twenty feet above the ground, but kept moving constantly from place to place although singing most of the time.

While these kinglets depend mostly on picking insects from limbs and twigs, or on those that fly up before them, they dart out at intervals after flying insects. Sometimes they hunt the opening blossoms of trees and shrubs to prey on the small insects attracted by the flowers, and quite often they look over the bases of the bunches of loblolly and long-leaf needles for the tiny insects that hide there. In spite of their almost universal insect hunt in winter, I noticed one Golden-crowned Kinglet fly over and take two bites from each one of two persimmon fruits on January 1, 1927.

RUBY-CROWNED KINGLET. Pl. 12, page 290
Regulus calendula calendula (Linn.). A. O. U. No. 749

Field Identification. A greenish gray bird much smaller than a sparrow, and having a white eye-ring, two whitish wing-bars, but no white line over the eye. If the red *crest* flashes up, it of course identifies the bird as a male Ruby-crown, but the crest is so seldom seen that it is useless to look for it.

In contrast with the Golden-crowned Kinglets that are generous in showing their pretty *crown patches*, the Ruby-crowned Kinglets are very chary about showing their *crests*. Of a hundred Ruby-crowns seen in the Sandhills during the winter, only five individuals showed any sign of a crest. On one bird, a streak of color could be seen when the intensity and direction of the light was just right. Another one showed a ruby patch about six times the size of an ordinary pin head. The third kinglet showed some color about half the time, but at no time did it show plainly. Finally, I found three kinglets foraging among the needles of some pine saplings, but for several minutes I could see no color, nor any crest at all. Suddenly, one of these birds shot up its flaming crest several times in succession. It was a pretty thing to see, but apparently too pretty to show often for I saw it only a dozen times that day. A week later, a fifth kinglet showed its crest just as the fourth one had done.

Description. Upperparts gray, tinged with olive-green; crown with a generally concealed crest of bright red; wings and tail darker gray, but the feathers edged with olive-green; two whitish wing-bars; underparts dull white tinged with buffy. The female lacks the red crest. Total length 4½ inches.

Distribution. The Ruby-crowned Kinglets are present in all parts of the Sandhills from October to the last of April, and seem to be about as common at one time as at another. They are undoubtedly more common in this territory than the preceding species. In the winter, they go as far south as Guatemala; in summer, they live as far north as Alaska, Ungava, New Brunswick and Nova Scotia.

Habits. Ruby-crowned Kinglets are birds of the forests, of the borderland between forest and open fields, and of dooryard shrubbery, but not frequenters of open fields of any kind. They like the thickets over streams and the brush along the shores of ponds, but are often in the shrub oaks and pines on the drier upland (Figs. 10 and 15). They are often in low bushes, but perhaps more in loblolly pines and long-leaf pines, while they are seen so many times in the foliage of the short-leaf pines (*Pinus taeda*) that they must search out the rather scattered individuals of that tree. Although they are never very far from pines, the Ruby-crowns are fully as often on deciduous trees, such as oaks, maples, persimmons and liquidambars. While generally near the ground, these kinglets are sometimes seen in the liquidambars and short-leaf pines as high as thirty feet.

During the winter, the Ruby-crowned Kinglets are solitary most of the time, or with only one or two other Ruby-crowns. Once I noted four together. While the two species of kinglets were often near enough to each other to show that they were more or less going along together, they were so seldom actually in the same flock that it was questionable whether they were really associated. Ruby-crowned Kinglets were also seen with Myrtle Warblers, Blue-gray Gnatcatchers, Juncos and Cardinals, but probably all these gatherings were accidental and temporary, except possibly some Juncos and Ruby-crowned Kinglets seen on February 26, 1927. When they fly, these kinglets show a peculiar, jerky, undulating flight that is more or less characteristic of them.

During the winter, they depend largely on small insects for food. At times they are on the ground amid the fallen leaves, searching herbaceous plants less than a foot high, or on the twigs of low bushes or shrub oaks, but often on the three species of pines searching the trunks, limbs, twigs and the bunches of needles. When hunting the clusters of pine needles, the kinglets search carefully at the base of each needle and in the little pockets between the needles, frequently swinging back down below the clusters, and sometimes hovering in mid-air on fast-beating wings before the clusters. One kinglet that searched the tufts of needles appeared to catch an insect every five or six seconds as long as I watched it, and another one found something to eat on every four inches of pine limb that it searched. Sometimes the Ruby-crowned Kinglets hunt insects in the cedars, hollies, gums and dogwoods. In this limb and twig hunting, they depend chiefly on picking insects from the bark, or on catching those that fly from the bark. But many of these birds perch on limbs and dart after insects that attempt to fly past them. Sometimes the Ruby-crowns collect dogwood berries from the ground and eat them, but reject the seeds probably, and occasionally they take a few sumac berries. More often they consume cedar berries, both pulp and seeds, and some of the pulp from wild persimmons. Apparently they do not care as much for persimmons as do some other birds, for the Ruby-crowns usually took only two or three sips at a time, and never more than five sips of the juicy pulp. I thought several birds seemed to treat the persimmons more as a drink than as a food.

Ruby-crowned Kinglets can be readily attracted to our gardens and dooryards by providing them with suet, bread crumbs or small bits of doughnuts on our artificial feeding stations. In fact, kinglets, nuthatches and Chickadees will all respond to the same three kinds of food in about the same way, and all of them like suet and bones tied to trees rather than laid on a flat surface.

BLUE-GRAY GNATCATCHER

Polioptila caerulea caerulea (Linn.).   *A. O. U. No. 751*

Field Identification. This is a nervous, bluish gray bird much smaller than a Sparrow. It is identified by a black tail bordered on each side by white that shows both while at rest and in motion, and by a conspicuous white eye-ring surrounding a small dark eye.

Description. A conspicuous white eye-ring surrounding a small dark eye; front of head black; upperparts bluish gray, a little whitish on wings; central tail-feathers black, graduating to white outer tail-feathers; underparts lighter gray than upperparts. The females lack the black on their heads. Total length 4½ inches.

Distribution. This species has not yet been noted in the Sandhills in winter, but it is known to winter such a short distance to the south that we may add it to the winter list at any time. They arrive from the south in late March. In winter, these Gnatcatchers live in South Carolina (coast region), the Gulf states, southern Texas and as far south as the West Indies and Central America. In summer, they are found from southern Texas and central Florida north to Wisconsin, Michigan, Ontario, Pennsylvania, Maryland and New Jersey.

Habits. Gnatcatchers are beautiful little birds usually seen in the thickets along water courses and near swampy places at the heads of ponds. Sometimes they wander out on the drier lands where the shrub oaks grow in open pine forests, and there they may be seen hunting through the leafless limbs, or amid the new leaves just opening in late March, or amid the foliage of the longleaf and loblolly pines. They are rather nervous little chaps, flitting here and there and not staying long in any one spot. They work *up* a branch as a rule, and often climb to the very tip of a slender shoot that appears almost too slim to support their weight. But they are as acrobatic as the Chickadees and often do their "stunts" on the ends of twigs and on clusters of foliage. They are always extremely busy, but are also sociable, frequently gathering in early spring with Myrtle Warblers and Ruby-crowned Kinglets. They do not go far from the lowland vegetation, and when the Myrtle Warblers work out into more open country, the Gnatcatchers fly back to the thicker brush.

In the brushy areas, the Gnatcatchers show all the skill of warblers in chasing insects, but do not spend quite so much time on the wing as the Myrtle Warblers do. When they fly out across an open space, their flight is low, jerky and slightly undulating. These birds are more given to searching bushes and twigs, but perhaps not so much as the kinglets. The food of the Gnatcatchers is chiefly insects. Sometimes they fly up into the loblolly and longleaf pines and search the big bunches of needles like nuthatches.

The Winter Birds of the

270

HERMIT THRUSH. Pl. 9, page 236

Hylocichla guttata pallasi (Cab.). A. O. U. No. 759b

Field Identification. A brown bird larger than a sparrow, and having a reddish tail distinctly different in color from the back, and a spotted breast.

Description. Upperparts olive-brown; tail reddish; underparts white, or nearly so, spotted on throat with wedges of black gradually changing to round spots on the breast. Total length almost 7¼ inches.

Distribution. These thrushes are to be found throughout the Sandhills, but only during the winter. At this season, they are found as far south as Cuba, Florida, the Gulf states and Texas; in summer, they live as far north as a line drawn from southern Yukon across Canada to northern Quebec.

Habits. Hermit Thrushes are birds of semi-open forests, thickets, swamps, and the shrubbery of dooryards of both country places and the towns and cities of the Sandhills. They are not found in the open fields, nor very often in the densest heavy forests. While they are seen most frequently in damp places near streams and ponds, and occasionally on the damp ground under gum trees in semi-swampy locations, they are by no means restricted to such places and are sometimes found in the dry oak-and-pine forests. Though they are ground-loving birds, they often fly up on the bushes of a thicket or alight on piles of brush. I saw one pair of Hermit Thrushes first on the ground, then on a brush pile, and an instant later they flew up to the top of a gum tree for a few minutes, and then down to the ground again. They are often seen on the lower limbs of cedars, shrub oaks, and gums, but they also perch in the higher limbs of all four, and even in a walnut fully sixty feet above the ground. Very often they will perch high in a leafless tree before making a flight out across an open field. Once I found one on an isolated fruit tree in an old cornfield.

Hermit Thrushes sometimes walk and rarely hop, but generally they run, often quite rapidly. They have the Robin-like habits of running across the ground, stopping often and stretching up straight, and at times get their food in the Robin's way of stopping and "listening." In trees, Hermit Thrushes are apt to alight on the lower limbs, and if they care to go higher, they jump up limb by limb. They are very light and airy in their motions and rather more graceful than most birds. While tame enough to permit approach to within a few feet, they are not bold or obtrusive, but rather seek to avoid observation. At times, they perch quietly and without movement for from ten to thirty minutes at a time. In spite of this ability to remain quiet at times, they have a characteristic habit of moving their tails up and down both while on the ground and while perching higher. Sometimes the tails move slowly up and down, but when the birds are nervous, excited or alarmed, the tails are dropped below the line of the bird's backs and then raised sharply until at right angles with the backs; then they are dropped again slowly, and raised once more after a short interval. This action is much quicker and more frequent after a flight. Often when thrushes perch after unalarming flights, the tails are not raised and lowered, or at most only two or three times. While perching quietly and resting, their tails do not move; and when the birds are busily running across the ground hunting, the tails move up and down occasionally at long intervals.

These thrushes are very pugnacious, and whenever two or three are seen together, they are sure to be chasing each other about. Throughout the winter Hermit Thrushes are generally solitary, and even found alone in heavy hardwood forests far from any openings where other birds might be expected. Then, they are "hermits" indeed. Only on a very few occasions did I find two or three consorting peaceably together; they are distinctly not social, either with other members of their own kind or with other species. Such times as I found them near Purple Finches, Cardinals, White-throated Sparrows, Juncos, Song Sparrows, or Robins, the gathering was evidently accidental and very temporary.

Usually Hermit Thrushes make short flights from tree to tree rather than long ones. Their flight is easy, direct and very much like that of Robins. The beats of the wings are rapid, and although the birds are nervous and easily excited, they are nearly, or quite, silent. I did not hear a single note before they left for their northern homes!

Hermit Thrushes are common in the Sandhills from November to April. Their shy, retiring ways probably cause them to be thought less common than they really are. When it is cold, they fluff out their feathers or droop their wings. In bright, sunny weather, they fly up on the bushes and soak in the warm sunshine; in stormy weather, they seek cover under thicket tangles and under heavy evergreens, and are then very disinclined to move.

Most of their food is picked up from the ground. On December 30, 1926, I found a Hermit catching small insects in a gum swamp, some of them actually from the edge of a shallow pool. And one was seen darting here and there on some open ground where it caught ten insects in a minute, then ate three cedar berries; next it ran nimbly a few feet and dug out a two-inch earthworm, then ate cedar berries again. During at least the latter part of the winter, Hermit Thrushes often resort to the cedar trees for berries. Many of these berries are gleaned from the ground where they have fallen, and some are picked direct from the twig where they grew. A favorite method is to perch on a limb a foot or so below a cluster of cedar berries, then jump up to the cluster, pick a berry while hovering before it, and then drop back to the perch below. By this method, a thrush will secure and eat as many as five berries in a minute, swallowing both pulp and seeds. Eating cedar berries never lasts very long, both because the Hermit Thrushes seem to think a half dozen berries enough for one meal, and because the Mockingbirds that claim the cedar berries for their own, think a half dozen are just six berries too many for the thrushes! At times, Mockingbirds chase the Hermits vigorously in and out the limbs of the cedars, and round and round the dense foliage. On a cold morning after a snowstorm, a Hermit Thrush ran over the ground under a dogwood and ate some pulp from the dogwood berries, but seemed far more interested in catching some insects that appeared as the ground warmed up under the direct rays of the sun. Early in the winter and before the berries were all gone, I found a pair on a bush in a gum swamp. After remaining quiet for two or three minutes, they flew up into a sour gum tree and each ate three or four of its black berries.

Although I found two Hermit Thrushes together at times throughout the winter, I could not be sure that they were actually paired. The fact that a third Hermit was promptly chased away whenever one appeared, argued for it, but on the other hand I found no additional indications of pairing.

PLATE 11. GOLF AND POLO GROUND BIRDS

1: Robin.
2: Horned Lark (male).
3: Horned Lark (female).
4: Killdeer Plover.

5: Logger-headed Shrike.
6: American Pipit.
7: Meadowlark.

(All figures about ⅛ life size)

ROBIN. Pl. II, page 272

Planesticus migratorius migratorius (Linn.). A. O. U. No. 761

Field Identification. A gray-backed, red-breasted bird larger than a sparrow, with a black head and two faint white spots on its tail. This northern form spends only the winter in the Sandhills; in spring the Southern Robin comes up from farther south and replaces the northern birds that have gone north to nest and raise their young. The two forms cannot be differentiated in the field.

Description. Top and sides of the head black with a white dot above and another below the eye; upperparts grayish slate color; tail black with a white spot at its tip on each side; throat white, streaked with black; rest of underparts rufous; bill yellow. Total length 10 inches.

Distribution. Common in certain localities in the Sandhills, and is found as far south in winter as Florida and the Gulf coast; in summer, they live as far north as the limit of trees extending from northern Alaska to Ungava and Newfoundland.

Habits. In winter, the Robins (that is—the northern form) live largely in swamps and dense woods and are seldom seen in dooryards, or on lawns or fields. They are never very far away, however, and all through the winter may be seen flying high over all sorts of forests and fields, and also over the villages, towns and cities. At times throughout the winter, they are found in the oak-and-pine woods and in the thickets over streams at the edges of fields, and occasionally they are in broom-sedge-corners and peach orchards. A goodly share of the time they spend on the ground but they are not there so much in winter as in summer. They are seen more in trees, and at times on the very tops of persimmons, sycamores, and tall gums and long-leaf pines.

Evidently, the staying of the Robins in the swamps, and their absence from dooryards and gardens, varies a good deal in different years, and is perhaps controlled by the quantity and quality of the wilderness food, as well as by weather conditions and the time of arrival of the southern Robins. In the latter part of January, 1926, I found several on the golf links at both Pinehurst and Southern Pines and noted later that they gradually increased there after the first of February. During that same winter, Robins did not appear to any extent in dooryards until after the first of February, when a few single birds appeared at widely scattered points in Pine-hurst, Southern Pines, Aberdeen and Pine Bluff. After that date, they increased steadily in numbers at all points. During the winter of 1926–1927, a total of only seven Robins were seen on all the golf links and dooryards visited, although I probably visited more points than during the preceding winter; but they were to be found in the swamps and heavy forests at all times. During the latter part of February, 1927, they showed a tendency to leave the swamps for the civilized areas, but a severe snowstorm on the first of March in-terfered with the movement, so that it was March 8 before the first Robin (probably of the southern form) was seen on a golf links, and two days later in a dooryard. After these dates, the southern Robins kept on arriving and occupying dooryards and lawns as well as the fairways on the golf links.

During the winter the Robins stay in flocks, usually small flocks of two to twenty in a group, although these groups often unite in great straggling aggregations up to as many as 400 individuals. When the birds are in flocks, the smaller groups, as well as the larger aggregations, are loosely knit, and often each Robin is sepa-rated by quite a space from the nearest member of the flock. When they alight on the tree tops, the flocks are similarly scattered, a dozen birds occupying from two to eight trees. With their loose organization, these flocks show a marked contrast to the compact Waxwing flocks that often fly near them. These Robins are very uneasy and nervous, darting here and there in all directions.

On the night of January 19, 1927, the Robins stayed in a big swamp, about three miles southeast of Southern Pines, but in the morning they left it and flew in small flocks to a group of cedar trees to feed on the berries. As they approached these cedars they became very cautious, flying high and stopping on several tall trees in succession to look around before proceding farther. One of them must have seen me, for it started a two-syllable alarm cry and kept it up until all the other Robins had joined it, and all flew away. The next day, they were even wilder and more suspicious, uttering alarm notes at the slightest provocation, and constantly leaving their feast and flying up to high observation points to look. One Robin flew down to a spring, but on seeing me seated in the brush more than a hundred feet away, flew off again without its drink. After eating cedar berries for an hour or two, they returned to the big swamp.

Although evidently liking the companionship of birds of their own kind, the Robins did not gather with birds of other kinds except accidentally and temporarily. Even the number of times I saw Robins and Waxwings together, was due to both species being fond of sour gum berries.

Robins sing on warm days throughout the winter a good, full-throated "cheerily, cheerily, cheer-up." But about the first of March, the real song season commences with the arrival of the southern Robins. Much of this singing is given from the tops of tall pines, but sometimes a song is sounded from a thicket, or even in the depth of a swamp.

Although the time varies somewhat with the severity of the season, most of the migrating Robins pass south through the Sandhills early in December. Then, they often gather into immense flocks, especially where attracted by favorite foods such as dogwood, sour gum, or cedar berries. On December 10, 1926, I found great straggling flocks about a mile south of the Highland Pines Inn, where they were over small fields separated from each other by a series of thickets and hedges (Fig. 20 and 27). First a loose flock of 300 Robins flew by, followed in a short time by three other flocks, or rather waves, of 400 Robins each. Soon after passing me, these large flocks broke up into a number of smaller ones, and then groups of from 2 to 15 birds continually passed over me going in all directions. With 1,500 Robins passing and repassing continuously over those few fields and groves of trees, the air seemed literally filled with birds going to, or returning from, the sour gum and dogwood trees. Although this count was only of birds in my immediate vicinity, I could see more Robins in flight in all directions as far as my powerful binocular could reach.

With the beginning of March these Robins leave for more northern homes, and the southern Robins begin to appear. It is very evident from the changed disposition of the Robins that these are different birds from the winter ones. The southern Robins are tame and come familiarly about the gardens and lawns, and soon commence to sing more and to pair off and look for nesting sites.

Throughout the winter, the northern Robins depend upon insects, wild fruits and berries for food. Insects are eaten all winter, being picked up from the ground as the Robins run here and there, and no doubt many more are caught in the trees. Some Robins adopt the Thrasher plan and throw the leaves about with their bills and side thrusts of their heads. After a cold, snowy day, one was seen working like a Thrasher, the procedure varied by catching the leaves in the bill, bracing back and pulling. Then, as the leaves gave way, the Robin darted forward to search the ground so uncovered. It was not until the tenth of March, 1927, that I noticed any of the familiar digging and searching for earthworms.

In gathering wild fruits and berries, the Robins appear to select one kind and eat them as long as they last, and then change off to the next kind. In early December, they throng to the dogwood trees to pick and devour the pretty red berries. They also pick them up from the ground, beneath, but never eat more than three to six at a time before flying off to another tree. After the middle of December, Robins flock to the sour gum trees where they eat the black berries as they did the dogwood. During December and early January, they eat the pulp of wild persimmon fruit. Later, they eat cedar berries much as they did the dogwood berries except that they pick most of the cedar fruit direct from the tree, and less from the ground. The first cedar berry eating to amount to anything was on January 10, 1927, and the last just fifteen days later. On January 17, 1927, I saw Robins eating mistletoe berries. Early in February, 1926, I found them eating the little black berries from privet bushes. Of course I do not mean to say that they eat only the food mentioned between the dates given, and nothing else. As a matter of fact, they eat insects at times, and mix their fruit and berry diet a little. But the great bulk of the different kinds of food is eaten as indicated. I should judge they eat dogwood berries until the most easily procured supplies are gone, then turn their attention to sour gum berries as long as they last, and finally take persimmons and cedar berries because the more desirable fruits are gone.

BLUEBIRD. Pl. 8, page 210

Sialia sialis (Linn.). *A. O. U. No. 766*

Field Identification. A dainty little blue, or bluish, bird, larger than an English Sparrow, and having cinnamon or reddish brown underparts.

Description. The male has his upperparts blue, sometimes so tinged with rusty in winter that the blue is quite dull; throat, breast and sides dull cinnamon-rufous; belly white. The female's upperparts have a grayish tinge and her underparts are paler than the male's. Total length 7 inches.

Distribution. Common at all times throughout the Sandhills. In winter, Bluebirds go as far south as southern Florida, the Gulf coast and southern Texas; in summer they range as far north as Manitoba, Ontario, Quebec and Newfoundland. They are found as far west as the eastern part of the Rocky Mountain states; and west of that they are replaced by other forms of Bluebirds that do not occur in the east.

Habits. Bluebirds are present throughout the Sandhills in both cultivated places and in the wilderness. They are seldom seen in very dense, heavy forests, but they occur in open pine and shrub oak woods (Figs. 5 and 16), and among the hardwoods over streams and along the shores of ponds and lakes (Figs. 3, 10, 15). In spite of being so often in forests, and in the thickets at the borderland between the forests and the open fields, I should say that old cornfields and cotton fields (Figs. 6, 9, 18, 20, 27) are the preferred haunts, but there must be elevated perches of some kind near, for Bluebirds do not like to alight on the ground. Like many other birds, they prefer old weedy fields to bare ground, although they are often seen hunting over *freshly* ploughed fields, and they haunt the broom-sedge-corners (Fig. 19). Bluebirds are noticeable in the peach orchards (Fig. 7) for they are about the only birds that are at all frequent there. But their presence in the peach orchards is wholly beneficial, for they are invariably catching more or less injurious insects. I have also seen them over dewberry fields for the same purposes. Bluebirds stay around farmhouses, and along the edges of golf links, and frequently come to the shade trees and shrubbery of towns and cities. In fact, they are one of the birds that are no wilder in winter than they are in summer, and that do not change their ways and dispositions as the northern Robins do when they migrate to a southern climate. Bluebirds perch on all kinds of bushes and trees. While the great majority of these perches are at medium heights of from ten to thirty feet above the ground, some Bluebirds will perch at the very tips of the tallest long-leaf pines, sometimes a hundred feet above the ground. Of course, birds fond of perching on telephone wires are conspicuous objects, and are much more apt to be seen there than elsewhere—so much so, that fully one third of all Bluebirds seen are on telephone wires.

That Bluebirds can fly up and alight sidewise on the trunk of a pine or gum, shows a certain amount of agility and clinging power. They have a good deal of practice at this sidewise perching; for it is a favorite method used at the entrance to their nesting holes in trees, and I have seen one do it in December, when it flew over and curiously inspected a hole in a dead stub of a tree. Bluebirds are possessed of a fair amount of curiosity, not only in such cases as this, but they often watch other birds to see what they are doing. At times, these birds profit by finding a new source of food that the other birds have discovered. All through the winter, Bluebirds are in singles and couples and small flocks of usually less than eight birds, but sometimes as many as twenty or thirty birds together. While these larger gatherings are temporary and soon split up into smaller groups, they show that the Bluebirds like to be with their fellows to that extent. Since I noted Bluebirds with Juncos eighteen times, it is possible this was because of sociability; and I saw Bluebirds with Myrtle Warblers and Pine Warblers often enough to assume a liking between these birds. But association with other birds appeared only accidental and temporary. Probably because of both species perching so much on telephone wires and hunting in similar places, Bluebirds were seen near Shrikes twice.

On March 12, 1927, I found a Bluebird on a telephone wire singing an enticing warble with its bill closed most of the time. Five days later, another bird did the same thing while perched on an oak and about six feet above the ground. At intervals all through the winter, they sang good, full songs in addition to the whisper songs just mentioned. On January 20, 1927, one was heard singing a fine sweet warble for fifteen minutes from the tip of a forty-foot tree rising out of a tangle of wild grapes, briars and sumac (Fig. 6). This tangle was at the edge of a cotton field not far from the Highland Pines Inn. For a time he sang on this tree and then flew out across the cotton field to a black walnut. During his flight over the cotton, he kept right on singing with undiminished power and sweetness. On the black walnut, he sang from the very tip fully fifty feet above the ground for five minutes more

Figure 29. Jungle of trees and shrubs in rear of Dr. Achorn's lot. A favorite haunt for winter birds.

before he finally flew away over the fields and forests, still "bub-
bling o'er with liquid notes."

Although Bluebirds are common at all times of the year in the
Sandhills, it is very doubtful if the same individuals that are
present in winter remain and breed during the summer. Probably
the birds that winter here, leave and go north in spring and
their places are taken by other Bluebirds from the south. This
seems all the more probable because during cold spells I found
Bluebirds gathered in large flocks of as many as seventy birds in
most unusual places. They did not seem to be familiar with the
country and its supplies of food and water. But with warmer
weather these large flocks of strangers disappeared and the familiar
birds were found again in the usual small groups. It seemed as if
these stranger flocks were birds driven down from the north by the
temporary cold, and the movement bore testimony to their easy
and ready mobility. About the middle of March, I found Bluebirds again in larger flocks and showing all the restlessness of
migrating birds. A few days later, I found a few with the big
flocks of Myrtle Warblers then passing through the Sandhills on
their way north.

Insects are their staple food throughout the winter. All through
December, January and the first half of February, Bluebirds perch
on various observation posts to watch for insects, some being as
high as telephone wires twenty feet above the ground, and others
are as low as cornstalks and only a couple of feet high. From
these perches the birds watch until they see insects and then
swoop after them. In some cases this hunting is very much
like that of Shrikes, and again it resembles that of the Phoebes.
In only one instance did I see a Bluebird fly out and hover over a
field. This bird did not swoop, but soon returned to its post. All
during the winter, Bluebirds catch their prey down near the ground,
but after the middle of February, they pursue and catch higher-
flying insects. But they still use the same kind of observation posts,
although they now fly out after passing insects in true flycatcher
style. On February 5, 1927, I found some more original Bluebirds that flew down on the polo field and hunted along the ground,
through the low grass, for their insects.

At times during the winter, possibly when the insect hunt
becomes too strenuous, Bluebirds eat berries from the sour gum,

wild cherries, sumac and dogwood berries, and some kind of bright red berries growing on low marsh bushes. In spite of this juicy food, bluebirds are fond of water. On December 7, 1926, I found twenty-four Bluebirds of both sexes gathered closely about the butt of a long-leaf pine in a forest of shrub oaks. Here, they were drinking the water caught in the bottom of an old turpentine boxing.

At intervals along the edge of the golf links at the Southern Pines Country Club, barrels of water were sunk into the ground for the convenience of the golfers. But the birds, too, found this water. One morning there were sixty-eight Bluebirds clustered about the top of one of these barrels. The water was too low to be easily reached, so the birds had to hang head downward from the rim to get any. At one time, there were seventeen hanging from the rim drinking at the same time, but when a Flicker came, they vacated half the barrel edge to it; and when a Mockingbird came, all the Bluebirds flew away.

During the early part of the winter, both sexes of Bluebirds are seen together in the different flocks, but about the first of February they begin to pair off, and are then seen commonly in pairs, although small flocks continue until late in March. It is thus evident that some pairing is done before the birds travel north. About the middle of March, the plumage becomes markedly brighter although as early as January 4, 1927, a male Bluebird was noted with colors as bright as any in the breeding season. I did not see any actual mating until March 12, 1927, but by eleven days later I had noted this pair so frequently near a house south of Aberdeen that it appeared likely they had settled for the summer and were perhaps even then building a nest.

For additional information on life histories and descriptions of birds, especially in summer, see:

Pearson, T. Gilbert, C. S. Brimley and H. H. Brimley. *Birds of North Carolina.* North Carolina Geological and Economic Survey, Raleigh, N. C. 1919. Pp. 1–380.

Chapman, Frank M. *Handbook of Birds of Eastern North America.* D. Appleton & Co., New York and London. Revised, 1926. Pp. 1–530. Price, $4.00.

BAILEY, FLORENCE MERRIAM. *Handbook of Birds of the West-*
ern United States. Houghton Mifflin Co., Boston and New York.
1917. Pp. 1–574. Price, $6.00.

REED, CHESTER A. *Land Birds East of the Rockies.* Doubleday Page & Co., Garden City, New York. Price, cloth $1.25, imita-
tion leather $1.50.

REED, CHESTER A. *Water and Game Birds.* Doubleday Page
& Co., Garden City, New York. Price, cloth $1.25, imitation
leather $1.50.

HOFFMAN, RALPH. *A Guide to the Birds of New England and
Eastern New York.* Houghton Mifflin Co., Boston and New York.
1923. Pp. 1–357. Price, $3.00.

BAILEY, HAROLD H. *The Birds of Virginia.* J. P. Bell Co.,
Inc., Lynchburg, Va. 1913. Pp. 1–362. Price, $5.00.

WAYNE, ARTHUR TREZEVANT. *Birds of South Carolina* (no
bird descriptions). Contributions from the Charleston Museum,
Charleston, S. C. 1910. Pp. 1–254. Price, $4.00.

COUES, ELLIOTT. *Key to North American Birds.* Estes and
Lauriat, Boston, Mass. 1903. Vol. 1, 1–535; Vol. 2, 536–1152.

Dr. John Warren Achorn.

A WOODSER

A "Woodser" is one who loves the Big Woods.
He does not go there to hunt and fish,
　Beyond the physical needs of each passing day.
The trees are his brothers—
　The oak, the birch, the pine, the fir tree.
Their presence is soothing and restful,
　Never irritating nor enervating. They restore him.
A tree is the most human thing that grows out of the ground.

He recognizes the Earth as the First Mother.
He feels that the same Great Force that runs
　The trees, the flowers in their beauty,
And the waterfall whose voice never marks time,
　Runs him. There comes to him in the wilderness
A sense of possession, not found elsewhere;
　Never his among the towering bricks and mortar
Of the great metropolis with its streets of stone.

He feels that he is an integral part of the world
In which he lives, and not a trespasser.
　The "little river" is his and it's the other fellow's.
It is not posted. If either fellow catches a trout,
　The other broils it, and when supper is over
And the pipes are lit,—
　Both gather inspiration from the same picture,
On the sunset side of the mountain.

Both gather boughs from the same fir tree for beds at night.
Here they can pray to the God of Nature and obey nature's law.
　Here they can cultivate faith in the spiritual and find it.
A man may hunt the woods for game,
　He may hunt the marts of trade for a dollar;
But all the time and everywhere,
　Man is on a "still hunt" to find himself.

JOHN WARREN ACHORN,—*Woodser*

NEEDED:

POCKET BIRD GUIDE OF LAND BIRDS IN WINTER IN THE SOUTH

By Dr. John Warren Achorn

There are hundreds of northern tourists, south in winter, who would keep up their amateur bird studies and their everyday interest in birds, if they were as completely provided with colored identification plates, of birds that winter in the south, as they have been provided with plates covering the spring migrations, and the appearance of birds at that season, in our northern tier of states. This question of interest in birds in the south in winter is largely one of identification. These northern bird tourists with tuneful ears—ear and eye students we will call them—have been "raised" on the colorful appearance of our birds during the spring migrations, and on listening in at their mating songs; and upon these two factors, and "call notes" their skill in identification rests to a considerable degree.

In the south, from November until March, birds are not in song. Many of them are in their traveling suits instead of their wedding clothes, their characteristic markings in many cases are wanting or different, the classic pictures of males in our popular bird books, based on northern coloring, are of little help for purposes of identification, while the descriptions of females that end with the discourteous phrase "paler and duller" are often well matched by the poor illustrations that go with them. Bird students, native to the south, see birds wintering in the vicinity of their homes, whose dress and colors do not tally with any pictures in the bird books in their possession. Ear and eye students from the north become of necessity sight students in the south. For many bird students, the perceptive faculties are the best faculties they possess. Natives and tourists alike when on a "hunt" exclaim in dismay, "Oh that's a sparrow" if they flush one or more in the fields they are crossing and they often do. To them all sparrows look alike. They turn to their pocket guides for help, but the illustrations in them are too poor to be of much use, to students of limited experience.

286

Mighty few amateurs can identify difficult birds in the field from written descriptions in our standard bird books. The thing is too difficult, too FUSCOUS (fuss-cuss). Practically all amateur bird students south in the winter are up against it. With the aid of accurate plates where identification is difficult and with the help of descriptions that are as characteristic as possible, this feature of bird study in the field, now so discouraging to many, would be met and overcome. The identification once made by never so limited an observer, is seldom lost, because *all sparrows are so different.* Breaks in the final identification of birds seen almost daily are disconcerting. Some students because of this, lose zest for certain groups of birds, while others lose confidence in their powers of observation. May this not be a fundamental reason why bird study in the south has progressed so slowly? The exact opposite should be the case. The trees are not in leaf, our winter birds are not so numerous as to discourage beginners, out of door conditions are favorable and the going is good. With our winter birds known, as a background, amateurs are equal to the spring migration. They are not as likely to lose their heads, as they otherwise would be, when thirty varieties of warblers and half as many birds of other kinds come trooping along with their ladies at their heels.

Bird study that began in New England years ago has gradually spread over the country. But northern pictures and descriptions do not always square with southern needs and conditions in many vital particulars. We should have those particulars because we need them. We need a Pocket Bird Guide done in colors of a certain percentage of the birds that winter inland in the south; a book that young and old will enjoy to look at and study, and one that everybody can afford to buy. Then we will see bird clubs multiply. Then eye and ear students from the north will become diligent sight students in the south, and our native students will not "give it up" but "get busy" and finally challenge all comers for honors in this field of endeavor.

BIRDS OF THE SANDHILLS

By Dr. John Warren Achorn

The Sandhills constitute an exceptionally good region in which to study birds and winter is the best time to do it, especially for beginners. The trees are not in leaf, the seeing is good, and the birds are not so numerous as to discourage an amateur; still there are enough of them to keep one busy and guessing all winter. The climatic conditions are favorable for out-of-door sports, and the walking is usually above criticism. One travels dry-shod everywhere in these Sandhills. Hunting birds for identification along our wooded roadways and silent paths is ideal sport, not alone because of the birds, but for the beauty of the surroundings and the kind of exercises afforded.

The study of wild birds in the "open" tests one's eyesight, one's memory, one's idea of colors and one's hunting skill. The hunting instinct is a great asset in this sort of work. It can be acquired. For hunting grounds we have the "wild lands"—open woods of oak and long-leaf pine; we have weed-grown fields and high meadows where seed-bearing weeds grow taller in one season than a man's head. The poorer the soil the taller the weeds. We have marshy places, bordering some of our streams. We have evergreen cover on both sides of these streams, usually in narrow strips, enabling one to hunt either side successfully, without penetrating the tangled undergrowth. Here there is water for our birds to drink and bathe in; and here the small birds flock for shelter from winds and storm and cold. It is for this kind of cover that small birds rush when they see us coming, especially if we are not hunting but are doing something else. The shrubbery about many houses with gardens is a standing invitation for birds that are socially inclined to put in the winter months with us and take life easy. The ornamental shrubbery of these gardens is full of feed for birds, and the garden soil rich in things they love to scratch and search for.

Many birds are attracted about our houses because they are fed regularly. It is a common thing to see flocks of birds made up of a dozen different kinds, in the back yards of some of our

288

good neighbors on frosty mornings, waiting for a call to breakfast. Even the Hermit Thrush, so elusive in the northern woods, where it sets up housekeeping, is quite friendly with us. It often rests on the ground or sits in some low bush and looks us over, so near at hand that one can see its markings and colors without the aid of a bird glass.

The Hermit Thrush is the "Jenny Lind" of the Bird World. Birds and flowers have personalities—as much so as people. The Robin belongs to the Gentry—there is nothing aristocratic about a Robin. Its Colonial red vest and slate colored coat, cut half way between a swallow tail and a cutaway, points to its station in bird society. The Esquire of Colonial days dressed just as the Robin does. The character of his vest and the cut of his coat made it possible for him to greet people with becoming dignity in his parlor, and when their backs were turned, without making any change, slip quietly out of the room, through the kitchen into his back yard, and swap horses with a stranger.

The English Sparrow is an Irishman with an English name. This Irishman wears a pepper and salt suit that won't show dirt, and for the best reasons. He is always ready for a scrap in a dusty road over what may have been dropped there.

Pansies are "get-rich-quick" people—they are not to the manor born. They can afford to hire good milliners, and they do, who dress them prettily; they are clever enough to see the need of that. Tulips belong to the aristocracy of the flower world. Dahlias are blockheads.

Birds are not in song in winter. The only bird that sings regularly about our Southern homes, out of season, is the Carolina Wren. Sometimes the Mockingbird gets the "marrying fever," and sings for awhile, but he soon gets over it. The White-throated Sparrow has been known to sing here at times, during our "six weeks of winter."

Bird study with us, then, is a matter of identification by sight. We believe that identification by sight is the better way to learn birds. A song in the bush is not a bird in the hand.

If three different sparrows fly from cover, where a recognized song was heard, which one of the three did the singing? Tuneful ears may locate birds by their "call notes," but when flushed, the question that instantly arises is: "What bird is that?" One good way to hunt birds is to sit down on a camp stool in a favorable location and keep still.

With our winter birds known, as a background, amateurs are equal to the spring migration. They are not likely to lose their heads, as they might otherwise do when many varieties of warblers and quite as many birds of other kinds come trooping along in the springtime with their ladies at their heels. "We have with us," in the winter, 85 birds—60 males and 25 females that we distinguish from their mates. And still there are quite a few birds left, mostly sparrows, that none of us so far have been able to make out. The total number of birds resident in the Sandhills in the winter has never been summed up for us by a recognized ornithologist. Here is an easy chance, then, for one who is skilled in the science of birds, to make us all happy. We believe we saw Redpolls in January; and last fall, one year ago, Starlings were sighted on the Pine Bluff Bird Reservation by competent observers. The birds have never been recorded in North Carolina before.

With the advent of spring, 43 other varieties, so far known, migrate over these hills. Amateurs have learned to recognize 50 birds here in two months' time. The better way to hunt is in groups of two and three, and never in large groups if one is really in earnest about this thing. A leader who may know 50 birds by sight should act as a Bird Scout for the other two. Birds always shy at sight of a crowd. Birds are wild things, they fly on motion. Their eyesight is sixteen times as strong as man's. They do not wait to have their pictures taken. A Bird Scout who allows those in his charge to plunge about, wave their arms, point eagerly, or hustle from excitement, who does not keep his command bunched, never gets ahead much. Neutral colors should be worn.

Birds are recognized by their conspicuous field markings—flight, size, actions, mate, etc. All these factors may be needed to settle the question of identification if it is in doubt. Hunting birds with a bird glass, instead of a gun, appeals even to the big game hunter, for he finds in it real sport that tests his skill. Good bird glasses are an essential. When a bird is sighted, a glass that will bring it down, colors and all, is necessary to one's peace of mind and the proper use of the English language.

(Reprinted from *The Magazine of Southern Pines*, March, 1924.)

PLATE 12. SECOND GROWTH FOREST OF LONG-LEAF PINE

1: White-breasted Nuthatch (male).
2: White-breasted Nuthatch (female).
3: Red-breasted Nuthatch (male).
4: Red-breasted Nuthatch (female).
5: Brown-headed Nuthatch.

6: Pine Warbler.
7, 8: Carolina Chickadee.
9: Ruby-crowned Kinglet (male).
10: Ruby-crowned Kinglet (female).

(All figures about ½ life size)

BIRD GOLF

By Dr. John Warren Achorn

Most people, young and old, like to play games.

There is all the difference in the world between playing a sporty game with birds instead of golf balls for pawns—a set of three persons following certain rules—and the old fashioned way of going on a "hunt" of identification, as is still the practice, with a "gang" at one's heels all talking at once. In the one case there is real sport ahead, for good players; in the other, except for the leaders perhaps, nothing but lazy exercise. Birds shy at sight of a crowd.

To stimulate bird study in the south the game of Bird Golf was invented. It originated with the Sand Hills Bird Club, Pine Bluff, N. C., next door to Pinehurst, the great golf center.

"We have with us" in winter, 85 birds—60 males and 25 females—that we distinguish from their mates. We play a "sight" game as the birds are not in song from November until March. A bird scout and two players constitute a set. A bird scout of the first class knows 75 birds by sight.

We "hunt" and play Bird Golf on certain days each week at an agreed upon hour. Beginners hunt, experts play, the game. All who wish to hunt or play are given an even chance under competent scouts. No beginner is expected to play in a game who does not know by snapshot sight, in the field, at least 25 birds. Otherwise the game would drag. Two weeks' study of an hour a day and four "hunts" will usually qualify a beginner for the game. Most people know 25 birds, in their mind's eye. It costs nothing for them to say so, but it costs a little study and effort to prove it in the field.

When sets are made up of a scout of the first class and two players who know 50 birds each, and a game is started with half a dozen sets in the field, there is something doing in the way of excitement and real sport. A scout acts as timekeeper for his set, and one of his players writes down the birds scored. A score card that folds for use in the field is carried in the left hand. Nine links of 10 or 15 minutes, duration each, constitute a game. Male birds

291

count one and female birds count three. Birds[1] identified count but once in a game.

The hunting instinct is a great factor in winning any game. For instance, scouts equally well qualified as to the number of birds they know, take out sets. They play the short game or 9-hole course of one hour and thirty minutes. The final score for three sets is, 24, 22 and 12. Knowing where to hunt, how to hunt and hunter's luck are all expressed in these figures.

A bird scout who allows his players to wave their arms, scream or shout, to dance or hustle from excitement, who does not keep his players bunched—since only birds seen by two players in any set count—never wins a game. A good way to hunt birds or bears is to sit down on a moss-cushioned stump and keep still. Wear neutral colors.

The game of Bird Golf can be played anywhere and at any season of the year. Good bird glasses are necessary to the sport.

The Sand Hills Bird Club of Pinebluff, and the Savannah Audubon Society are the only two bird clubs in this part of the South, and strange to say both clubs are under the management of Maine men. H. B. Skele of Oxford County, Maine, is president of the Savannah Audubon Society, while I hold a similar position with the Sand Hills Bird Club. By vote of the commissioners this town within its corporate limits was made a bird reservation Nov. 6, 1922. The town is a mile and a half east and west, and a mile on its north and south line. It is well watered by constant streams, and there are two artificial lakes within the town limits, the larger lake being nearly a mile long. There is plenty of cover for the birds in Winter along these streams or branches; evergreen cover. We have built 150 bird-houses and bird-boxes this year and have set them up for purple martins, bluebirds, wrens, tree swallows and the like. We plan for 500 bird-houses and boxes. The town itself has only 120 houses and camp cottages in it, but it boasts electricity and running water so we can and do live like other folks.

Here, under the auspices of the Sand Hills Bird Club, we train our bird scouts to know by sight 50, 75 or 100 birds. One student coming here from Pennsylvania between Feb. 24 and April 23 has

[1] See rules for playing the game.

learned to recognize in the field 100 birds. She has been decorated a master scout. There are at least six other students who will pass the 100 mark this season. Students have come from as far away as Ohio.

When a Bird Club starts here in the South our plan is to send to that club one of our bird scouts—who shall teach half a dozen "grown ups" to recognize and know at least 50 birds in the field. In this way the foundation for field work is laid, and once started right it will grow steadily. In no other way can everyday bird clubs of limited resources in the South be advanced, according to our view. Mrs. E. C. Ritchie, of Camden, S. C., started a Junior Civic League last fall, listing 60 members at the initial meeting. There were beautiful presents for the best imitation bird costume, for the best imitation bird call, for the best bird poem or story, etc., with introductory talks and stories by older people and refreshments beyond compare, but no out-of-door work of any kind. Last week she wrote us that the very boys who took prizes at the opening session were out on the streets with slingshots firing away at every bird they saw, with intent to kill. The parents of these children buy their sling-shots for them.

The way to save situations like this is to teach the children to hunt birds for identification with a bird glass instead of with a slingshot, and this is what, with the bird scouts we develop, we shall hope to start new bird clubs doing. In the North there are always older members in any club who are equal to teaching the younger members and beginners of uncertain age, to know and recognize birds in the field. In the South we have no such background upon which to found a club, and so we are trying to devise a plan that will work.

We must have the National Association of Audubon Societies behind us, and a pocket bird guide that will picture the land birds in winter around us as they actually appear, with characteristic descriptions that will help in the identification. Then we will succeed and the bird clubs in the South will multiply. It was to help this idea along that Bird Golf was developed. It is a sporty game when played with fair skill, but, like any other game, drags when there are unskilled players in any set.

(Reprinted from *Portland Evening Express,* May 4, 1923.)

The Winter Birds of the

BIRD GOLF
SCORE CARD

TIME OF "GET AWAY" *9:00 A.M.*   TIME OF "SHOW DOWN" *11:00 A.M.*

BIRD SCOUT *John Achorn*

PLAYERS *Chas. C. Adams*

Alvin G. Whitney

PLACE *Pine Bluff, N. C.*

DATE *Dec. 7, 1925*

LINKS

1 TIME _____

2 TIME _____ SCORE _____

3 TIME _____

4 TIME _____

5 TIME _____

6 TIME _____ SCORE _____

7 TIME _____

8 TIME _____

9 TIME _____

Birds seen that should have been identified but were not made out,—No. _____

HANDICAP _____

TOTAL _____

RULES FOR PLAYING THE GAME

Time of short game, 1 hour and 30 minutes. Time of each link, 10 minutes. Return, 2 hours.

Time of long game, 2 hours and 15 minutes. Time of each link, 15 minutes. Return, 2 hours and 45 minutes.

Time within which all players shall return to meeting place, 2 hours 45 minutes. Preferably, two players, with Bird Scout, constitute a "Set." Each set decides for itself when and where to start to play. Play begins with the first bird seen, if counted. Over-time play on any link must be deducted from the next link. Only birds recognized by two or more in any set count. Birds must be recognized by their conspicuous field markings, colors, flight, size, actions, mate, etc. Birds known only by their song or call notes, do not count. Birds of a species or either bird of a pair recognized, but sex not determined, count as a male bird. Birds identified count but once in a game. Male birds count 1, female birds count 3.

Birds seen long enough for identification but not made out,——1   2   3
4   5   6   7   8   9   10.

Official Score Card, Sand Hills Bird Club, Pine Bluff, North Carolina

N. B. This score card is intended for the use of amateur bird students. It is a game which is easily developed and in the playing affords pleasure as well as healthy exercise. It also satisfies the true hunting instinct, quickens the perceptions and noticeably strengthens the memory. It appeals both to the old hunter and the Scout, whether boy or girl. A member of any Club who knows by sight, 25, 50 or 75 birds, is entitled to qualify as a 1st, 2nd, or 3rd class Scout, and wear a badge indicating his rank. He must be decorated by the President of the club to which he belongs. Any boy or girl Scout is entitled to "Caddie" for visitors playing under the auspices of the Club.

Score cards 8 x 10 inches, to the bottom of which this slip attaches, fold to pocket size for use in the field. These can be stuck on to any kind of paper for use.

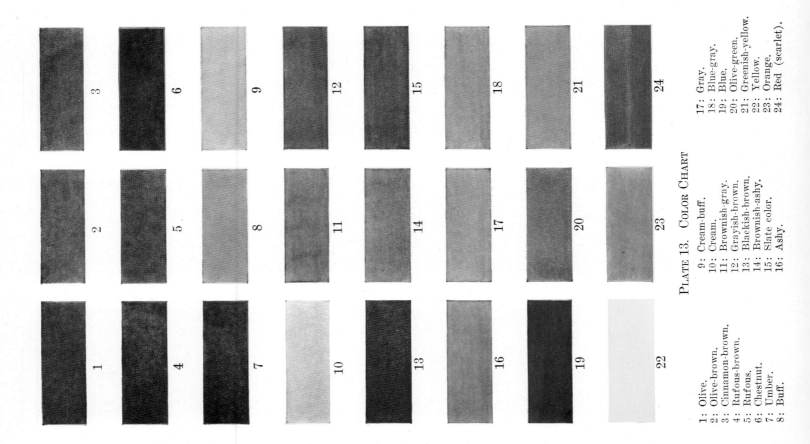

PLATE 13. COLOR CHART

1: Olive.
2: Olive-brown.
3: Cinnamon-brown.
4: Rufous-brown.
5: Rufous.
6: Chestnut.
7: Umber.
8: Buff.

9: Cream-buff.
10: Cream.
11: Brownish-gray.
12: Grayish-brown.
13: Blackish-brown.
14: Brownish-ashy.
15: Slate color.
16: Ashy.

17: Gray.
18: Blue-gray.
19: Blue.
20: Olive-green.
21: Greenish-yellow.
22: Yellow.
23: Orange.
24: Red (scarlet).

INDEX